The AGE of PARADISE

Christendom from Pentecost
to the First Millennium

John Strickland

PARADISE AND UTOPIA

The Rise and Fall of What the West Once Was

VOLUME I

ANCIENT FAITH PUBLISHING ✚ CHESTERTON, INDIANA

The Age of Paradise: Christendom from Pentecost to the First Millennium
Copyright © 2019 John Strickland

Published by:
  Ancient Faith Publishing
  A Division of Ancient Faith Ministries
  P.O. Box 748
  Chesterton, IN 46304

Unless otherwise specified, Scripture quotations are from the New King James Version of the Bible, © 1982 by Thomas Nelson, Inc., and are used by permission.

ISBN: 978-1-944967-56-7

Printed in the United States of America

Contents

O precious paradise, unsurpassed in beauty, tabernacle built by God, unending gladness and delight, glory of the righteous, joy of the prophets, and dwelling of the saints, with the sound of thy leaves pray to the Maker of all: may He open unto me the gates which I closed by my transgression, and may He count me worthy to partake of the Tree of Life and of the joy which was mine when I dwelt in thee before.

Orthodox Hymn for Forgiveness Sunday
before the beginning of Great Lent

Introduction

BEFORE THERE WAS A WEST, there was Christendom. This book tells the story of how both came to be. It is the first part of a longer history that commands our attention and respect, even though we are increasingly a people without memory of it.

Today we Westerners live in an advanced state of cultural oblivion. We are almost totally rootless. We know there is a crisis of values going on around us and that it is becoming harder and harder for our culture to sustain itself. Suicide rates, addiction rates, divorce rates, abortion rates—all indicate a dark age more self-destructive and, therefore, more ominous than any before.

Strangely, however, as we descend ever more deeply into this darkness, our economy feeds and entertains and liberates us as never before. The world marches progressively forward, yet we are progressively paralyzed by its rootless passions. Seeking more and getting more, we realize that we are in fact becoming less and less—incomparably less than our ancestors. To live authentically as they lived and to hold to values that have been handed down in a hallowed tradition stretching back into the mists of antiquity—this no longer seems possible.

But we are aware, some of us, that the West was once a civilization very different than it is now. We are aware that Christianity was once the core of that civilization, even if it coexisted with and made use of the riches of classical humanism. We are aware, finally, that if we want to reestablish strong and nourishing roots for our culture, we will need to take the Christian past seriously, for Christendom is what the West once was.

This book is the first of four volumes on the history of Christendom, a civilization with a supporting culture that directs its members toward the heavenly transformation of the world. It appears at a time when the Christian roots of the West appear desiccated and nearly lifeless. In fact, as we look on, these roots are systematically being ripped out of the soil. In their place, secular and not-so-subtly antichristian ones are being laid in their place.

In the rural corner of America where I happen to live, for instance, recent newspaper articles document how a high school has fired its head coach for praying publicly at a football game; how a school district has intentionally recruited as its head psychologist (that is, the official responsible for the mental health of hundreds of teenagers) a man who has undergone "gender reassignment" and dresses on campus like a woman; and how a city council has broadened the criteria by which it allows community members to open meetings, encouraging public invocations of atheistic values and neo-pagan deities. Innumerable examples from other parts of the United States and beyond are documented almost daily by the mainstream media, which for some reason still regards as newsworthy the cultural eradication of Christendom.

But no one is really surprised by this anymore. What used to provoke indignation in social conservatives has become simply normative. A generation ago, James Davison Hunter popularized the term "culture war" to describe the conflict between defenders of traditional social values and their progressive opponents in America.[1] Hunter wrote in the wake of the Reagan era, when conservative political forces such as the "moral majority" appeared to offer effective resistance to the advance of the sexual revolution, especially to its landmark *Roe v. Wade* Supreme Court victory legalizing abortion nationwide.

That political momentum faltered in the 1990s during the Clinton administration, and the Obama administration, coming after an eight-year Bush interlude, seemed to advance the progressive cause even further. At the height of the progressive advance, the Supreme Court, in its 2015 *Obergefell v. Hodges* ruling, redefined marriage to include same-sex relationships. In the aftermath of this momentous but unsurprising event, President Obama ordered that the White House be flooded with rainbow colors to signify his administration's support of the cause.

The victory of Donald Trump in 2016 suggested a coming revival of the conservative cultural agenda, yet its long-term impact is uncertain. The possibility of defending Christendom through political measures has become highly questionable.

Recently, four books have earned widespread attention for acknowledging this. Rod Dreher's *The Benedict Option* speaks the most emphatically about the new circumstances of the twenty-first century. "The culture war that began with the Sexual Revolution in the 1960s," the book's introduction states as a matter of fact, "has now ended in defeat for Christian conservatives."[2] Another work, Anthony Esolen's *Out of the Ashes,* concludes with similar words. "The world around us is not Christian," it observes, adding that "it is not even sanely pagan."[3]

Obergefell v. Hodges "confirmed in a uniquely forceful way," writes Charles Chaput in *Strangers in a Strange Land,* "that we live in a country very different from the past. The special voice that biblical belief once had in our public square is now absent." The result is that the West has become a hostile civilization for traditional Christians. "People who hold a classic understanding of sexuality, marriage, and family have gone in just twenty years from pillars of mainstream conviction to the media equivalent of racists and bigots."[4] In the terse words of R. R. Reno, author of *Resurrecting the Idea of a Christian Society,* "Christendom is no more."[5]

BUT IS CHRISTENDOM really dead? We might pause here and ask what the noble but rather ambiguous word *Christendom* really means, or rather ought to mean. Its origins are in the Old English used at the ninth-century court of King Alfred of England. Linguistically, it relates to *corpus christianum,* a Latin term meaning "Christian body" that was coined in the West and, after the Great Schism, came to denote territories subject to the pope of Rome. This meaning is itself distantly related to *respublica christiana* ("Christian commonwealth"), another, more explicitly political, Latin term which can be traced as a concept as far back as the time of Emperor Justinian. These ecclesiastical and political connotations are what Warren Carroll had in mind when, about a generation ago, he wrote a massive six-volume *History of Christendom.*

However, such a use of the word is unnecessarily restrictive. It suggests as a precondition that a civilization worthy of the name Christendom would include a significant level of political support for Christianity. This excludes the centuries before Constantine, and it excludes much of the West's recent history. Furthermore, this definition finds its fullest expression in a very limited historical context, namely the Roman Catholicism of Western Europe between the eleventh and sixteenth centuries.

I will use the term Christendom more inclusively. It will denote an entire civilization that sprang from traditional Christianity at the very beginning of the Church's history. This is not a study of church history as such, however, though the Church will surely play an important role in it. It is a history more in the mold of what Christopher Dawson long ago pursued—what can be called a cultural history of Christian civilization. For as that illustrious Roman Catholic scholar noted, Christianity is a "culturally creative" force that extends well beyond ecclesiastical life conventionally understood.[6] In particular, its doctrine of the Incarnation inevitably impels the Church toward a comprehensive engagement with the world or *cosmos* around her.

Indeed, this and subsequent volumes will show how very cosmological the culture of Christendom is. Some people think of Christianity and its concern for the kingdom of heaven as inherently otherworldly. This can be very misleading. When God became man, the world was transformed from the distant creation of an utterly transcendent deity to the sacramental means through which the eternal kingdom of heaven was made immanent. In fact, it was a heresy to believe, as did the early gnostics and docetists, that Christ's assimilation of the world to Himself was of limited importance or somehow unreal.

And since traditional Christianity's cosmology was grounded in the dogma of the Incarnation, so too was its anthropology. Man (*anthropos* in

Greek), as part of the creation, was directly transformed by the Incarnation of Christ and the indwelling of the Holy Spirit. He becomes the *microcosmos,* the "little world" that most directly experiences heavenly immanence.

This experience is not passive. From its inception, Christendom contained what can be called a "transformational imperative," an evangelical mandate to participate in the renewal of the cosmos by bringing it into alignment with the kingdom of heaven. No other religion has done or ever could do this. That is why Christendom became the civilization that most changed the course of world history. Inspired and sometimes driven by this imperative, its children have spent two thousand years seeking more from the world than it could possibly offer in its natural state.

But there were two fundamentally different ways of acting on the transformational imperative. The first was rooted in the Christian virtue of humility. It was penitential in character and guided Christendom during its first fifteen centuries. Following Christ's commandment to repent, traditional Christianity directed attention within, calling for the spiritual transformation of one's own life. Its most elaborate expression was the cultural ritual of a season of fasting that occurred every year before the celebration of Christ's Resurrection. Because it was basically optimistic about the capacity of man to enjoy communion with God—the Gospel's account of the prodigal son being the most powerful expression of such hope—early Christendom's transformational imperative fostered the experience of the kingdom of heaven, or paradise.

Another, very different response to the transformational imperative appeared at the time of the Renaissance. Wearied by unduly pessimistic accounts of the human condition that had been mounting in western Christendom for centuries (the Christian East was comparatively free of this development), intellectuals began to redirect the imperative, as it were, in an external direction, resulting in a mode of transformation rooted in the Christian virtue of zeal. While the gospel inspiration in this case may have been Christ's cleansing of the temple, the result was often a condescending indignation. Simply put, humanists and the nihilists that followed them ceased to see the world's misalignment with the kingdom of heaven as their own fault and instead blamed it on others.

A spirit of indignation motivated humanists, beginning with Petrarch (who himself, it should be said, was thoroughly capable of repentance), and only grew in the centuries that followed. Increasingly detached from the virtue of humility and the practice of repentance, modern Western intellectuals and those influenced by them were ultimately carried by indignation to a rejection of traditional Christianity itself. The secular Enlightenment, the age of romanticism, and, most starkly, the revolutionary transformations of Jacobin France and Communist Russia all reveal this.

If the public ritual of Lent characterized the culture of early Christendom, then the public ritual of electoral debate has come to characterize that of modern Christendom. Both are profoundly optimistic and promise worldly transformation, but on very different terms. The first is directed toward paradise. The second follows a path toward *utopia*.

This Greek word literally means "nowhere." It was coined during the Renaissance by a Christian humanist named Thomas More, whose zeal for the kingdom of heaven expressed itself as indignation that nowhere in the Western Christendom of his time could that kingdom be fully experienced. It is possible to say, therefore, that the history of the West either leads to paradise or it leads nowhere.

In the volumes that follow this one, I will show how a fundamentally penitential and internalized experience of worldly transformation shifted during the Renaissance to an indignant and externalized one. The transition was a fateful moment in the history of Christendom. The rise of pessimism about man and the world that preceded and actually provoked it was an existential threat to Western culture. It was a cultural crisis, not unlike the one the West is living through today. And like ours, it demanded a response.

Only two roads forward were open at the time to the men and women of Christendom. The one finally chosen was the one not yet traveled, one that redirected the West from the kingdom of heaven to the opportunities and pleasures of the natural world. The other option would have been the West's rediscovery of Eastern Christendom, where the trusted path to paradise was well traveled and familiar. This would have made for a very different rebirth of ancient culture during the Renaissance. Fatefully, that was a road not taken.

ONE HUNDRED YEARS AGO, an obscure German philosopher named Oswald Spengler published the first volume of a work entitled *The Decline of the West*. If the year 2018 seemed a bad one for our civilization, 1918 was incomparably worse. Christianity was in shambles, an object of scorn for the educated, and for its part humanism had been exposed as an illusion by the blood-soaked battlefields of the First World War. Europeans and Americans—the core population of the West—were wearied of a civilization that appeared to offer only misery and false promises of progress.

Spengler's declension narrative, his account of the imminent fall of everything that Westerners considered elemental about their civilization and culture, proved compelling. The book became a bestseller. Then came the Great Depression, Stalinism, Nazism, and the Second World War. Spengler appeared to have been a prophet.

But he was mistaken. The West did not collapse. It did not even begin to waver. It fought the most exhausting wars in history and emerged a global powerhouse. And in the century since Spengler's book appeared, the West has expanded immeasurably, becoming a beacon of economic prosperity, social justice, and political liberty throughout the world.

True, its totalitarian movements may have brought unprecedented devastation, leaving political elites instinctively suspicious of grand ideas. Its high culture may have collapsed, and the modernism that once mesmerized its artists has proven for many almost totally bankrupt. Nor has the Western Christianity that survived the corrosion of secularization done much to help, though prominent intellectuals and theologians from Karl Barth to T. S. Eliot to C. S. Lewis have been inspired by it.

Spengler's predictions were wrong, but they were wrong for the right reasons. His diagnosis of cultural disease was basically correct, even if the patient made an unexpected recovery.

On the centennial of his famous book's publication, Spengler offers a way of thinking about the West that distinguishes sharply between *culture* and *civilization*. For him, the first precedes and is substantially distinct from the second. An originating culture, he believed, forms itself and eventually, if it is effective, transforms the world around it by institutionalizing its beliefs and values. The result is a civilization that represents a kind of externalization of those beliefs and values, a formalized system of life that ultimately perpetuates itself regardless of the original culture's strength or health. Civilization, according to Spengler, is thus the "inevitable destiny of the Culture."[7] However, if the originating culture begins to falter, as surely the Christian culture of the West has done, the civilization it produced continues forward without it. Uprooted from its beliefs and values, it inevitably seeks new ones.

Such is Christendom. As a civilization, it arose from traditional Christian culture in the first century and continued to draw its strength from that culture for a millennium. This was an *age of paradise*, a period when the experience of the kingdom of heaven was universally manifested in worship, thought, and the arts. Christendom's cultural center of gravity was the East, where church fathers defined salvation as deification, as man's immediate sacramental participation in the life of God.

However, in the eighth century, a distinctly Western variant of Christendom began to appear under the influence of an historically contingent alliance between the Roman papacy and ideologues at the court of Charlemagne. By the eleventh century, this process of dissociation reached a critical point. With the permanent severing of sacramental communion between West and East in 1054, an *age of division* ensued.

In Byzantium and later Russia, the Orthodox Christian East tended to maintain its adherence to Christendom's originating culture. The West, on the other hand, embarked upon a series of doctrinal innovations such as papal supremacy and purgatorial punishment that substantially altered the character of its faith and culture. At the end of this age, Protestant reformers in the West would justify their division from the Roman Catholic Church by asserting that that church had itself departed from the early Church they indignantly sought to restore.

By now, however, Western Christendom was losing its original cultural moorings. The centuries that preceded the Reformation were marked by a quandary. Disengaged from the East, where the culture of paradise continued to flourish in practices such as iconography and asceticism, the West began to experience a creeping disquietude that eroded its confidence in man's capacity for communion with God. Intentionally discomforting images of the suffering Christ began to proliferate (as did the famous "dance of death"), and for millions of believers, an inestimably long period of purgatorial punishment loomed beyond the grave before they could hope to experience the joy of paradise. It was at this time that the kingdom of heaven was effectively banished from this world to another one.

Seen in this context, the Renaissance was less a rediscovery of classical humanism than a reaction against Western Christendom's growing cosmological and anthropological pessimism. Secular humanism filled the void created by the decline of traditional Christianity and would sustain the West for centuries to come, offering a radically different but no less compelling point of reference for the transformational imperative. During this *age of utopia*, Christendom would rise to new heights, but as a civilization no longer rooted in the culture that gave birth to it.

If civilization is the tragic "destiny of culture" that Spengler said it is—that is, if it perpetuates its various political, intellectual, economic, and social formations long after its cultural soul has withered—then the disasters of the twentieth century are the inevitable result of the West's fall from traditional Christianity. An *age of nihilism* was the only outcome possible for a civilization that had lived on the counterfeit culture of secular humanism for so many centuries. What is remarkable is that during those centuries this culture assumed so many monumental expressions, from Michelangelo to Marx.

But a reckoning was inevitable, as announced with characteristic indignation by the atheist Friedrich Nietzsche. His nihilism seemed to be confirmed by the experiences of totalitarianism and total war. These horrors were so unprecedented that they caused the West after the Second World War to descend into an abyss of self-doubt and pluralism, a phenomenon that has been carefully analyzed by George Weigel.[8]

At the dawn of the third millennium, post-Christian Christendom is saddled with an abortion death toll ranging in the millions, as birth rates, in Europe at least, indicate the onset of demographic suicide. It is a civilization unable to revive the faith necessary to restore its original Christian culture and too cynical about its erstwhile ersatz culture of secular humanism to sustain it on a grand scale any longer. We have truly become "hollow men," as T. S. Eliot put it in his poem of that title, forming "prayers to broken stone." We know not what—or whom—to honor anymore, yet we still bask somehow in a fading glory. We Westerners have ceased to be what our culture once made us.

BUT THE HISTORY OF THE WEST has not reached its end. In fact, there are real grounds for hope. After all, the Christian faith that gave rise to Christendom is nothing if not a source of hope—hope in the communion of God with His people, hope in the resurrection of His Son Jesus Christ. I have related the appearance recently of a group of four books about our current cultural crisis. If each of the four can be likened to a distinct instrument playing harmoniously with the others, then this quartet is certainly composed in a minor key. It is best played *adagio*, slowly. Yet what begins mournfully can, like Beethoven's famous *Fourteenth String Quartet*, end vigorously in a major, triumphant key. Though they lament the decline of Christian culture in the West, this countercultural Christian quartet, as the books might be called, is by no means defeated by it.

Archbishop Chaput in *Strangers in a Strange Land* opens his account of Western culture with an explicit reflection on hope. Christians, he reminds his readers, do not have "the luxury of despair."[9] The most somber of the four authors, Dreher (*The Benedict Option*), may not see much hope in a sudden cultural turnaround, but his call for a "strategic withdrawal" of Christians from mainstream society is made with the understanding that eventually a new day will dawn when the West will again appreciate the value of its Christian roots.[10]

Even more so, in *Resurrecting the Idea of a Christian Society*, Reno exposes the moral inconsistencies and deceptions of secularism, claiming that an explicitly Christian society will again be appealing once these have played themselves out.[11] And in like manner, Esolen in *Out of the Ashes* predicts a spiritual awakening of the Western world. Someday, he concludes hopefully, our society will shake itself from the tortured dream of secularism to ask why it once embraced gender ideologies, practiced mass abortion, and surrendered so shamelessly to the moral cant of self-worship. When such "stupidities, cruelties, and lies" are finally exposed for what they are, he predicts, the Christian vision of society will again resonate in our public square.[12]

One thing is certain. The road ahead requires a resolve on our part to understand how we got to where we are today. C. S. Lewis famously noted that to make progress, a civilization requires a goal. If the road it has chosen is leading it away from that goal, progress requires a retracing of its historical steps to the crossroads where it made the wrong turn.[13] The need to return to a more authentic, more traditional basis for our culture has become increasingly obvious in recent years, as our esteemed countercultural Christian quartet reminds us.

Answers to the questions these authors raise can be found in history, and many of the answers lie deep in the recesses of our most distant past. We only need to look and resolve to learn from what we find. This book will show that conventional accounts of the crisis are historically shortsighted. One of the failings of contemporary cultural conservatives is that, like many Americans, they lack a deep understanding of history. Their most distant horizon is in fact not all that distant. For some, the crisis of American culture is traced to Puritanism, and for others, to the even more recent framing of the Constitution. The sexual revolution of a mere generation ago is likewise presented in many cases as the most important point of reference. However, none of these events was primordial. Their unquestionable importance lies in the fact that they, and others with them, were set in motion by an event yet more causal and deeply rooted in the Western past.

That event is the Great Schism, the severing of sacramental communion between East and West that culminated during the eleventh century. Before it, there was no distinct "West," nor was there a necessarily antipodal "East." There was simply Christendom. The division of it set in motion a millennium of cultural decline that is finally being exposed by the nihilism of our times. The loss, for the West, of a cultural and spiritual linkage to the East—that great bearer of Christianity's most paradisiacal features—was a tragedy more epic than any in history. It was a tragedy, in the classical sense, because it resulted from a vigorous and high-minded effort to transform the world spiritually. It was epic because it resulted in a parade of worldly achievements that no other civilization has ever matched.

Yet history is, as the great Orthodox theologian Georges Florovsky once stated, a "creative tragedy."[14] We can learn from it, and we can grow spiritually through our contact with those who made it. It may break our hearts to think of what could have been. But the reality history reveals to us is worth more than all of our modern dreams and disappointments. Only by returning to the deep past can we hope to see what we have lost. Only by remembering, or more precisely by re-remembering—for this will require an act of remembering in a new way—the history of what the West once was can we ever hope to recover what it once again might be.

When the Night Was Far Spent

THE CONTRAST COULD NOT have been greater. Jesus was entering Jerusalem as the Savior of the world, but He was doing so while riding a donkey. Everyone thought He should have been riding in a chariot.

That, after all, had been the example of Julius Caesar. Decades earlier, Caesar had famously entered the city of Rome in a "triumph," the ceremonial return of a victorious general from foreign conquests. On that occasion Caesar came to his capital after conquering the known world, and the spectacle of his entrance became a fixture in the culture of pagan antiquity. He rode in a chariot, the ancient world's equivalent of a battle tank. Surrounded by his army, trailed by the enemies he had taken captive, he advanced into a throng of supporters carrying palm branches in their hands as an acknowledgment of his victory. It was a victory for which he alone took credit. As one of his banners on that occasion declared, "*Veni, vidi, vici*"—"I came, I saw, I conquered."

But military subjugation was not the way of Jesus. He, by contrast, came to the Jewish capital as the messianic Prince of Peace. This prophetic title used in the Book of Isaiah should have enabled the Jews who lined the streets to make sense of the incongruous donkey. After all, hadn't Zechariah prophesied that the Messiah would appear to His people as "lowly and riding on a donkey" (Zech. 9:9)? As the crowds shouted "Hosanna in the highest," however, they harbored a very different expectation of the Son of David; they expected Him to be as fearsome and implacable as the great Caesar. Little did they know that the palm branches they held in their hands to welcome their king linked them to a victory defined not by conquest but by meekness and sacrifice.

Jesus' entry into Jerusalem during the week of His Passion in AD 33 was a triumph of sorts, but not in the worldly sense. It was rather a manifestation of the kingdom of heaven. He had proclaimed this kingdom throughout His ministry, declaring that it is not of this world. It was a kingdom of love in which enemies were forgiven and the powerless were exalted. It was a kingdom offering a different kind of peace from the so-called peace of Rome, or *pax romana*, that Caesar had pursued through force of arms. This kingdom offered an everlasting peace to a world that, however settled and prosperous and even glorious it might become, could never escape sorrow and death. "In the world you will have tribulation," Jesus assured His disciples after departing the city that day, "but be of good cheer: I have overcome the world" (John 16:33).

The contrast could not have been greater. Jesus Christ and Julius Caesar were both victors, but their triumphs marked very different kinds of victories.

For the moment, it must have seemed to both Jews and Gentiles that final victory belonged to the way of Caesar. For in a matter of hours Jesus had departed Jerusalem to prepare for a confrontation with earthly authorities later in the week. Apart from a handful of disciples, few were prepared to stand by Him under the circumstances. The very people who had shouted hosanna now called for His crucifixion. Pontius Pilate, the Roman official who presided over the trial, had been appointed by a successor to Julius Caesar, Emperor Tiberius. And when the Jewish leaders themselves declared they recognized "no king but Caesar," Pilate was compelled to put Jesus to death.

In fact, the Rome of the caesars was by this time more prosperous and powerful than she had ever been. On the surface, her civilization and the culture that supported it consisted of brilliant things—brilliant philosophy, brilliant statecraft, brilliant art. These are the very things that have been celebrated in the West since the time of the Renaissance, and they indeed proved impressive and enduring. But there was much below the surface that even advocates of our post-Christian culture today would find disturbing.

A good example can be found at Villa Jovis, a palace towering over Italy's Bay of Naples on the Island of Capri. A lover of Roman antiquity will not find much to admire in its brooding ruins today, even if swarms of tourist boats compete for views from the sea below. But two millennia ago, at the time of Christ's crucifixion, it was a place full of majesty from which Tiberius Caesar ruled much of the known world. It was here, presumably, that the emperor received Pontius Pilate's report about the execution in Jerusalem of a subversive Jew named Jesus of Nazareth.

Tiberius was the most powerful man in the world, but he was never at peace. He had built Villa Jovis for fear that the fate of Julius Caesar—who had been brutally assassinated in Rome—might one day be his. It turned out he had reason to be afraid. Several years after the palace's completion, the head of the Praetorian Guard in Rome did in fact organize a conspiracy that was only halted by ruthless bloodletting and vengeance.

Thus saved, Tiberius entrenched himself even more remotely on the mountaintops of Capri, hiding behind his palace's fortified walls. There he kept ever-vigilant watch across the Bay of Naples for signs of a new conspiracy and the approaching armada that would signal it. None ever came.

IN THE MEANTIME, Villa Jovis became adorned by the riches of classical art. Architecturally, it was Rome in miniature. Its marble colonnades and graceful arches brought to mind the venerable legacy of Greece as well as the buildings of the Roman Forum. Luxurious bedchambers and stately assembly rooms were lavished with frescoes. Balconies seemed to levitate a thousand feet over the crystalline sea below, affording breathtaking views of the Bay of Naples and the Italian mainland beyond.

But the palace is perhaps best known to posterity as the site of some of the ugliest and most depraved actions of the time. Rome's prodigious record of intrigue drove Tiberius to paranoia, and his response to perceived disloyalty among his courtiers was ruthless. Executions were a regular feature of life, and not a few victims were thrown from the above-mentioned balconies into the sea below for the sheer amusement of the emperor and his guests. Sexual profligacy also stained the reign of Tiberius, earning him the odious nickname of the Old Goat. He dedicated many of the palace's wall paintings to pornographic subject matter and ordered slaves brought to the island to entertain guests at his debauched parties.

Villa Jovis, finally, was a monument to classical paganism. Its very name brought the ruler of the Roman gods to mind. Jove, known also as Jupiter, was the central deity of the Roman pantheon whose main shrine, the Temple of Jupiter Optimus Maximus back in the capital, was famed throughout the world. The worship of Jupiter on Capri was modest by comparison, but this was compensated for by the personal presence of an emperor who was regarded as divine. Julius and Augustus, Tiberius's immediate predecessors, were both declared gods after their deaths. Tiberius himself was regarded as a god during his own lifetime, and he acted the part.

Moreover, the vigorous cults of violence and depravity Tiberius fostered at court brought attention to important themes in the broader culture of classical paganism. The Roman goddess of sexual love, Venus (whose Greek equivalent was Aphrodite), was regularly honored by the court's nocturnal entertainments. So too was Bacchus (known also as Dionysius), whose cult included drunken orgies and ritualized rape. Indeed, the infamous bacchanalia can be seen as the religious counterpart to—and legitimation of—life at the Villa Jovis.

One day a distant relative arrived on the island to take up his residence at the court. He was the only male survivor of a family wiped out during one of Tiberius's fits of suspicion, and the emperor had ordered him to Villa Jovis to sit at his right hand. His name was Caligula, and he studied carefully as the emperor taught him the art of government. As Tiberius presided at this dark underside of Roman pagandom, the young Caligula took it all in. With an education only the Villa Jovis could provide, Caligula would himself one day subject Rome to frightful acts of violence and depravity, all the while convinced that he too was a god. In fact, more than once he would be discovered in his chambers carrying on a conversation with a statue of Jove.

Tiberius would perhaps have felt satisfaction at the thought of such a legacy, but at the Villa Jovis he does not seem to have seen what was coming. After six years of breathing its atmosphere, the protégé was finally poised to do to his master what had been done to his own family. When the old goat fell severely ill in AD 37, Caligula arranged to have the latest captain of the Praetorian Guard isolate him in his bedchamber behind a locked door. Later accounts differ in the details, but it appears Caligula and his accomplice smothered Tiberius to death. As the young tyrant watched the light fade from the old tyrant's eyes, a new, even darker phase in the history of pagandom was about to begin.

But across the Mediterranean, a thousand miles east of Rome, a very different source for Western values had now come into the world. Three days after His death on the Cross, Jesus had risen from the dead. Before ascending into heaven, He commanded His small band of followers to wait in Jerusalem for the descent of the Holy Spirit. That event, known as Pentecost, would mark the beginning of Christianity. It also marked the beginning of Christendom, a civilization with a supporting culture that directs its members toward the heavenly transformation of the world.

CHAPTER ONE

The Dawn of Christendom

BEFORE HIS PASSION and Resurrection, Jesus spoke often about the kingdom of heaven. In fact, His earthly ministry can be seen as a sustained revelation of this mysterious reality. It is not a kingdom of this world, He stated, just as He, its King, is not of this world. But the kingdom had definitively entered this world through His Incarnation. Members of His body, the Church, participated in the kingdom because they participated in Christ Himself. Wherever the Church was, there was Christ. And wherever Christ was, there was His kingdom.

All that was needed to enter it was a change of heart, or repentance (the Greek word for repentance, *metanoia*, literally means "change of heart"). "Repent," Christ had urged from the first days of His earthly ministry, "for the kingdom of heaven is at hand" (Matt. 4:17).

It is exactly this call to repentance that marked the beginning of His apostles' ministries at Pentecost. On that day the first among them, Peter, issued a sermon that recapitulated all that Jesus had done for the salvation of the world. When he concluded, he was asked by his audience of three thousand Jews what they must do to enter into the kingdom of heaven. "Repent," Peter also admonished, "and let every one of you be baptized in the name of Jesus Christ for the remission of sins; and you shall receive the gift of the Holy Spirit" (Acts 2:38).

Pentecost Icon, Kirillo-Belozersk Monastery (c. 1497)

Christianity and the World

"REPENT"—the call implies a sharp distinction between the world and the kingdom of heaven, a fracture dividing each from the other. And such a division there surely is. There is no way to enter the kingdom of heaven without turning away from the world, or at least from the sinful passions that consume and devastate it. This is why heaven requires a change of heart. It is a kingdom at odds with the kind of earthly existence celebrated by Roman pagandom.

The Sermon on the Mount, for instance, is filled with moral antinomies contrasting the way of the kingdom with the way of the fallen world. In it Christ prefaces descriptions of the requirements of Mosaic law with "you have heard that it was said to the men of old," then goes on to state the contrasting values of heaven. The Beatitudes, especially, reveal an entirely new basis for human life, lifting up virtues like meekness, purity of heart, and poverty of spirit. Christ's call to turn the other cheek in the face of hostility is perhaps the most dramatic example of such values, so countercultural at places like the Villa Jovis of Tiberius.

And yet, Christ did not remove the Church from the world. With her heavenly values, the Church was in fact called to transform the world by her presence within it. This is the mystery of the ecclesiology of traditional Christianity. Members of Christ's body manifest or "image" (that is, become icons of) Christ to the world around them. As the body of Christ, they are collectively the presence of Christ in the world. Christ's personal ministry continues and will continue until the end of time, but only in and through His Church.

It is often observed that Christians are in the world but not of the world, that is, that they do not belong to this world and their calling is beyond it. This is undoubtedly true, but the statement can be misconstrued to suggest that Christians have no place in the world. Some forms of Christianity have even taught contempt for the world and indifference to its condition. But if the above statement is reversed, a different emphasis can be made: that from the beginning, Christians have not been of the world, but they have been in the world. This too is their calling, to be not of the world but emphatically to be in it. For without being in it, they cannot reveal Christ to it.

And so early Christianity emphasized not only the brokenness of the world but also its capacity for redemption. After all, if "God . . . loved the world" (John 3:16), so should they, since God was their heavenly standard of perfection. Traditional Christianity never taught hatred of the world as such. Something like that would one day come in the history of Christendom, but it was a long way from the faith of the first Christians. Jesus observed that the world hated Him and would likewise hate His disciples (John 15:18). But He advocated love for the world, just as He advocated love for one's enemies.

Furthermore, it was His world, for He had created it. And as Genesis 1 recorded, He had declared it "very good" upon its completion. In Adam the world may have chosen death instead of life, but Christ was the New Adam who would plant a life-giving ministry within it.

That ministry was revealed in all its fullness only at Pentecost. Before the descent of the Holy Spirit, the apostles seem only partially to have understood Christ's redemptive plan for the world. His miracles were occasionally seen as ends in themselves rather than signs; His passion was met with incomprehension; and His resurrected body was not easily recognized. Just as a "fullness of time" (Gal. 4:4) was required for the Incarnation to take place, so was it required for the consequences of the Incarnation to be understood. Thus, only when the Day of Pentecost "had fully come" (Acts 2:1) did the Holy Spirit come upon the apostles and fill them with divine wisdom.

Jesus had already indicated the significance of Pentecost when He gathered the disciples around Him on the eve of His death. At that time, He spoke of Himself as a Comforter by foretelling the coming of "another Comforter" (John 14:16 KJV), which was the Holy Spirit. The significance of this statement can be appreciated only in the incarnational context in which it was made. By the end of His earthly ministry, Jesus had revealed that He was the fulfillment of Jewish prophecies about God's Messiah, or Christ. "Comfort ye, comfort ye my people," prophesied Isaiah (Is. 40:1 KJV): This was the ancient promise that God would visit His people and dwell within the world as their Comforter. His prophetic name Immanuel, meaning "God with us," confirmed that He would take His place among men, within their immediate community. Finally born of the Virgin Mary, he became the divine Comforter not only for the Jews, but for the entire human race.

The Incarnation of the Comforter was an act of cosmic enlightenment. This is emphatically proclaimed by the Evangelist John. With the birth of Jesus, divine light pierced the demonic darkness of a truly benighted world—one ruled at that moment by the Emperor Tiberius, whose palace of Villa Jovis represented a microcosm of pagandom's self-destructive passions. But at a deeper level the world was ruled by a power greater than Caesar's. Christian enlightenment was about more than the surface phenomena of statecraft, or of culture and civilization more generally. It was about victory over the "principalities" and "powers" that, according to Paul (Eph. 6:12), were ultimately responsible for its darkness in the first place.

The light broke into the world, but it was not of the world. Through demonic affliction, the cosmos, which had originally been very good, defied enlightenment and fought tenaciously against the Enlightener. Herod's effort to destroy Christ as an infant was only a first attempt. After more than thirty years, Pontius Pilate, appeasing the very Jewish leaders who should have known better, finally achieved what Herod could not, and this because Jesus was now ready to surrender Himself voluntarily to the darkness of the grave.

But before doing so, the Lord gathered His disciples around Him in an upper room in Jerusalem to tell them of the other Comforter who was to come. The Holy Spirit, He stated, would be with them after He departed the world. Like Him, the Spirit came from God the Father. He "proceeds from the Father," Christ declared (John 15:26). As we shall see, later Christian authorities in the West would claim that the Spirit proceeded both from the Father and from the Son. But this was not Christ's revelation on the eve of His Passion. And the point is significant. By declaring that the Spirit proceeded from the Father, Jesus revealed that the same Spirit, as a second divine Comforter, would establish the same unmediated presence of God on earth that Christ did. All of this would take place within the sacramental life of the Church.

After forty days with the risen Christ, the apostles beheld His ascension into heaven, but they remained in the world. Then, ten days later, they received His Spirit. Pentecost thus completed the Incarnation that had begun some thirty years earlier with the Annunciation. Now, in the fullness of historical time, God was with man—spiritually, physically, sacramentally—and would continue to abide with him, "even unto the end of the world."

The Evangelist Luke as Cultural Historian

PENTECOST MARKED THE APPEARANCE of a new civilization and culture that were filled with the light of the gospel. This, at least, is the imagery contained in the earliest history of Christendom, the Book of Acts. This work was written by the Evangelist Luke as a companion to his Gospel. It is properly understood as the earliest history of the Church, but it is more than that. It is also a history of how the gospel revealed by Christ and confirmed by the Holy Spirit became assimilated by Christians living in the world. It is therefore a history of cultural formation in which new beliefs and values were established in society and became normative. And it is a history of

St. Luke the Evangelist. 1650–1700
Egg tempera on spruce, 55 x 43 cm
Ikonen-Museum, Recklinghausen

a cultural transformation in which old beliefs and values were confronted and replaced by new ones.

To be sure, the cultural exchange recorded in Acts did not in every case result in the transformation of pagandom, and Luke was scrupulous in noting this. In Paul's memorable visit to Athens, for instance, that city's highly cultured citizens rejected the bodily resurrection, almost to a person. The belief that the physical world was redeemable and that man's material existence could be salvific was roundly scorned by the

Neoplatonism that prevailed there. But despite such setbacks, the mission of the Church moved forward, and with it the slow consolidation of Christendom.

Luke was particularly interested in culture. He dedicated his twin works to a Gentile named Theophilus, whose Greek name means "lover of God." Theophilus was probably a man of influence, possessing some level of cultural sophistication. He may have been a Roman official who served as a patron of the early Church. For his own part, Luke was no stranger to high culture. He was apparently a physician and, if so, would have possessed an unusually high level of classical education himself.[15] Though it is not recorded in the New Testament, he was also said by early tradition to be the first to paint an image of the Virgin Mary with Christ in her arms, a project that would require considerable artistic training.

It is also significant that the author of Acts revealed a sensitivity to the broader civilization of the Gentiles. This is evident especially in the companion volume to Acts, the Gospel of Luke. There Jesus' lineage is traced to the father of all nations, Adam. Matthew's genealogy, by contrast, terminates with Abraham, the father of the Jews.

What is more, Luke arranged his account in Acts around the theme of evangelization. This links the book directly to Jesus' commandment at the Great Commission to baptize all nations. Luke's story is about the spiritual transformation of the entire world. Accordingly, his narrative begins at Pentecost in the capital of the Jews, Jerusalem, and documents the ministry of the apostle to the Jews, Peter. After shifting at the halfway mark to the ministry of the apostle to the Gentiles, Paul, the story then concludes in the capital of the ancient world, Rome. Holy Scripture is a theandric enterprise, involving both divine initiative and human cooperation. In the twin volumes of Luke and Acts, we can see the cooperative role of the author in the divinely inspired process of composition, shaping his narrative to proclaim the salvation of the entire world.

Luke's story of evangelization documents the appearance of a new civilization in the world. Following his account of the conversion of three thousand on the Day of Pentecost, the author relates ever so briefly that the community of the Church brought forth a distinct approach to wealth and property—namely, that Christians sold their possessions and distributed them to those who had need of them. They held all things in common. The formalized sharing of property is not, of course, an injunction of Christ. The four canonical Gospels all direct his disciples to show charity toward others, but nowhere do they demand the radical distribution of wealth as a principle. The earliest Christians came to this practice by applying the Gospel to their life in a particular time and place within the world, where disparities of wealth among the brethren inspired giving. In other words, it was an early example of a distinctively Christian civilization.

But Luke gives us only a glimpse of this. His intention was not to narrate the history of Christendom as such, but to proclaim the gospel within the context of the Church's early life. All other sources from the first centuries of church history do the same. Only in modern times, really, has an interest in culture and civilization appeared as a discrete subject, distinct from others like government or warfare (which were the main interests of ancient historians). But cultural history is a fruitful offshoot of professional historiography as it enables us to bring attention to important features of the early Church that contemporaries would not have been much concerned about documenting.

Among the useful concepts made available to historians by modern scholarship is that of *subculture*. The term can be used to define a minority group within a larger, dominant society that articulates a distinct system of beliefs and values in contrast with it. This is not necessarily a counterculture, though as we shall see early Christendom was that as well. As a fully developed system of meaning, a subculture, once formed, can provide an alternative basis for cultural life. It can even become the basis upon which a later, dominant culture rests. This was true of the small numbers of Christians who fostered the formation of Christendom in the first century, and it is perhaps also true of those small numbers who seek to revive it today.

Early Christian subculture had four particular sources, four streams that watered it and enabled it to flourish. Each issued from traditional Christianity and became a core value for Christendom. These streams were doctrinal integrity, divine participation, heavenly immanence, and spiritual transformation. Before turning to each in turn, we should note that all were elements of the faith, and their significance was not primarily cultural as such. But the values they contained had a cultural impact. It might be said that these four were the culturally creative principles of ancient Christianity. They contributed to what we will see in this book were the Church's distinctly optimistic views of the world and humanity.

These four sources of Christian subculture relate very broadly to four features of church life listed by Luke in his account of Pentecost. Having related the descent of the Holy Spirit and the immediate expansion of the Church on that day, the evangelist made an important statement about the character of church life thereafter: "they continued steadfastly in the apostles' doctrine, and in the fellowship, in the breaking of the bread, and in the prayers" (Acts 2:42, author's translation).

This statement deserves pause. Most English translations of it lack the definite article ("the") that appears in the original Greek before each of the four nouns. The omission is significant, as the definite article used by the author indicates that each element represented a definite experience. For instance, there was a definite doctrine transmitted by the apostles, not a diverse intellectual deposit from which to draw. There was a definite fellowship, or community, among members of the Church, not an inchoate association of individuals. There was a definite sacrament of this communion, the eucharistic breaking of bread in which non-members did not share. And finally, there was a definite body of prayers used by the Church to worship her Lord, not a merely spontaneous or random approach to worship.

But these often lost articles are not the only point of importance in Luke's description of nascent Christendom. His prefatory words in the verse also provide insight into its character: They "continued steadfastly"—that is, from day one the Church never ceased living out the faith delivered to her by Christ and confirmed by the Holy Spirit. She remained steadfast in her adherence to that faith. She did not waver; she did not compromise. She kept this holy tradition changelessly and handed it on from one generation to the next. Doing so ensured not only the continuity of the faith but the possibility of nourishing a culture with it.

Early Christendom drew all its strength from traditional Christianity. The faith delivered at Pentecost cannot be reduced to a series of principles or any kind of system. But if we use Luke's summary of the Church's life in the second chapter of Acts, we can locate four important sources of the culture it inspired for centuries to come.

Doctrinal Integrity

IN HIS LIST of the essential elements of church life, Luke placed "the apostles' doctrine" in the first position. The integrity of this doctrine was fundamental to the formation of a Christian culture. It could not be compromised by ambiguity or a mixing with the surrounding beliefs of paganism. This doctrine was, in the evangelist's words, the gospel of the kingdom, and its distinction from the values of the fallen world must at all times be defended. A good example of its character is found in the Sermon on the Mount. There Jesus contrasted heavenly values with those "of old." Instead of pursuing retribution, for instance, Christians are to confront evil by not resisting it. In the face of enmity, they are to bless those who threaten them, and even to love them.

This kind of standard was difficult to maintain; it required a real dying to the forces of self-preservation and self-determination that ruled the world. The sacrament of baptism brought attention to this struggle. Through the ritual of dying with Christ which immersion in water symbolized, the spiritually reborn Christian rose to a totally new way of life, one that represented a resurrection into the kingdom of heaven. The two experiences—dying and rising—were inseparable in Paul's account of baptism (Rom. 6:3–5). They joined one to the experience of Christ, who Himself had presented baptism as a second birth that brought one into the kingdom of heaven. The *Didache*, written perhaps in the early second century and only discovered in the nineteenth, echoes this. "There are two ways," it declares in its opening, "a way of life and a way of death. And the difference between them is great." For traditional Christianity, the spiritually untransformed world is entrapped by death. Only by giving way to the gospel of the kingdom can the world find freedom through the resurrection.

Baptism was therefore directly related to a vigorous asceticism that directed one's focus toward the kingdom of heaven. Nothing else could have prepared early Christians for the experience of martyrdom. One of the apostles' immediate followers composed a statement about this. Ignatius of Antioch was a disciple of the Evangelist John. He was killed for the faith in 108 after Roman authorities arrested him and brought him under guard to the imperial capital.

It was a countercultural triumph if ever there was one. As he approached the city, Ignatius famously wrote an epistle to its Christians urging them to stand aside and allow the unjust execution by wild beasts to take place. He did so because the apostolic doctrine he had received through baptism enabled him to see the world and life within it in a different way from the pagans. "Christianity," he wrote,

> *lies in achieving greatness in the face of a world's hatred. For my part, I am writing to all the churches and assuring them that I am truly in earnest about dying for God—if only you yourselves put no obstacles in the way. I must implore you to do me no such untimely kindness; pray leave me to be a meal for the beasts, for it is they who can provide my way to God. I am his wheat, ground fine by the lions' teeth to be made purest bread for Christ.*

Ignatius's readiness for death was in no way morbid. Modern critics of traditional Christianity often see a kind of masochism in the martyrs' lives. Ignatius, however, was radiant with joy as he proceeded toward his death. For him, death in Christ led to true life.

His epistle vividly expresses this sense of life and the impending experience of heaven even now in this world. "Here and now," he concludes, "as I write in the fullness of life, I am yearning for death with all the passion of a lover. Earthly longings have been crucified; in me there is left no spark of desire for mundane things, but only a murmur of living water that whispers within me, Come to the Father."[16] Ignatius embraced death, but not because he despised life. He embraced it because he recognized the existence, even while living in this age, of a life more abundant than that of this age.

Nothing could be more countercultural, and for this reason there would always be great pressure on Christians to compromise or modify the apostolic doctrine. Since cultural integrity depended on doctrinal integrity, compromise would inevitably undermine Christendom's heavenly orientation.

This is why the Church's holy tradition was necessary. Paul had enjoined Christians to hold fast to the traditions he preached, identifying them as both written and unwritten (2 Thess. 2:15). For many years following Pentecost, the apostolic doctrine that Luke said was intact from the beginning was communicated and preserved in such a demonstrably unwritten tradition. Indeed, the entire body of written scriptures ultimately called the New Testament was the result of applying this tradition as a test to the plethora of writings attributed to the apostles and used by early Christians. Some of these were truly apostolic and some were not.[7] Doctrinal integrity was assured by making a distinction between the two by drawing upon tradition.

In addition to joining Christians to the kingdom of heaven, then, baptism established them in the apostolic tradition. In this sense it was a culturally formative sacrament. It initiated Christians into an intellectual community unified by doctrines that defined their relationship to the world around them. These doctrines were not optional. They were a mandatory intellectual inheritance, and the earliest church fathers held them in very high esteem.

Justin Martyr, for instance, during the second century, spoke of those who had chosen rebirth through baptism as a distinct people who accepted the Church's beliefs and values. Being a Christian, according to him, was not only a matter of choosing a new way of life, it was an act of conforming oneself to the very way of life defined by the Church. For this reason, doctrinal pluralism had no place in Christendom. Only those doctrines delivered by the apostles and confirmed by holy tradition were considered a legitimate source of cultural life.

This was already an issue in Justin's time. Roman pagandom was thoroughly pluralistic, and some Christians absorbed their surrounding culture. As a result, they assimilated beliefs and values that were in opposition to

St. Justin Martyr
https://simple.wikipedia.org/wiki/Justin_Martyr#/media/
File:Иустин_Философ,_Афон.jpg

the apostolic tradition. An example was Christian gnosticism, which took a variety of forms but generally taught that every individual has his own path toward salvation. Named for the Greek word for "knowledge" (*gnosis*), gnosticism placed salvation in the hands of the intellect alone. What is more, it tended to favor hidden and cryptic forms of spiritual knowledge discovered through esoteric means and was therefore inherently elitist. Traditional Christianity, by contrast, offered salvation to the whole world, not just a small number of initiated intellectuals. In the second century, Justin saw gnosticism in its early stages and dedicated some of his famous *First Apology* to refuting it.

Even more effective was the work of one of Justin's contemporaries, Irenaeus of Lyons. In *Against the Heresies,* he launched a major defense of the apostolic tradition in the face of gnosticism. This latter work proved to be not only a defense of Christianity but a defense of Christendom. Particularly important for the Church's early culture was Irenaeus's affirmation of the created cosmos.

Gnostics mostly despised the world. They claimed, without basis in the scriptures, that the material universe was a trap for the soul, created by a demigod or demiurge, who, cast down from the highest deity, was responsible for its corruption. Salvation consisted in escaping the world and returning past the demigod to the ultimate godhead that transcended creation. The deity worshiped by gnostics had contempt for the world and stood over it more like the non-incarnate deities of Judaism and, later in the history of monotheism, Islam. For gnostics, traditional Christianity's incarnate Son of God was incomprehensible. Irenaeus refuted these cosmologically pessimistic teachings, emphasizing traditional Christianity's doctrine of the Incarnation and affirming that human salvation was to be worked out through life in the world.

A variation of gnosticism was the teaching of an early Christian named Marcion, whose contempt for the created world and its history led him to reject the validity of the Old Testament. Marcionism brought attention to the gnostic tendency to reject the historical experience of the world and God's immanence within it. In the end, it was a tendency to reject human culture and civilization. By confronting Marcionism, Irenaeus defended not only traditional Christianity's cosmology but its nascent culture too.

So the apostles' doctrine identified by Luke contributed three important things to the Church's emerging subculture. With its emphasis on a baptismal dying to the world, it directed attention toward the kingdom of heaven and the new life it brings to this age. As we saw with Ignatius, this cultivated within Christians a transformational experience even while living in this age. Second, the apostles' doctrine established an intellectual tradition that was corporate rather than individualistic, resisting any tendency toward doctrinal pluralism. Finally, that tradition was cosmologically affirmative and rejected the gnostic assertion that the cosmos is evil. The Old Testament record of God's involvement in history and the New Testament assertion that the Logos is not a wayward demiurge, but the very Son of God Himself, assured believers that the cosmos was good. Only within such a cosmos could a vital, sustainable culture and civilization arise.

Divine Participation

A SECOND MAJOR SOURCE for early Christian culture issued from the corporate participation of its members in the life of God. It is related to what

Luke called in his list "the fellowship." Here the Greek word used is *koinonia,* which is sometimes translated as "communion." It probably did not mean eucharistic communion as such, since Luke next speaks in his list of "the breaking of the bread." What he seems to have meant by the word is that from the Day of Pentecost, Christians lived in a community with a strong sense of identity in which they maintained strong attachments to each other.

This community provided the social network necessary for the rise of a distinctly Christian subculture. It was a community of individuals, but not of individualists. Baptism assured this. To be made a member of the Church meant, as we saw above, to be the recipient and not the author of one's beliefs and values. Indeed, the biblical word "heresy" was coined from the Greek word for "choice." It was what one chooses to believe himself in defiance of the community. The baptismal regulation of individuality was also expressed in the fact that one could not, even in the face of imminent death, baptize oneself. Only another member of the community to which one was being joined could perform the rite of initiation, and that normally with the participation of the entire local assembly.

A vivid example of this is found in a case recorded by Augustine. It occurred soon after the legalization of Christianity, but it was close enough in time to the early period of persecution as to provide a glimpse of the early Church's corporate subculture. An illustrious Roman named Victorinus decided to become a Christian. He was a person of high social rank and education, with a famous reputation as a pagan philosopher. Augustine's account makes a grand impression:

> Here was an old man deeply learned, trained in all the liberal sciences, a man who had read and weighed so many of the philosophers' writings, the teacher of so many distinguished senators, a man who on account of the brilliance of his teaching had earned and been granted a statue in the Roman forum—an honour the citizens of this world think so great.

The Church's twin ideals of individual humility and corporate glory, however, subverted such honors.

Augustine relates how this celebrity had discovered Christianity by reading the Bible and the fathers. Eventually, on his own, he decided that he was a Christian. But his individual conviction was not enough. For a long time Victorinus confided his self-proclaimed conversion only to a Christian friend named Simplicianus. But his friend flatly denied it was real. Only when Victorinus appeared among baptized Christians on the Lord's Day, he was told, would he truly be a Christian.

Initially, Victorinus was contemptuous. "Is it the walls [of the temple] that make Christians?" he mockingly asked. It was a question that might be attributed to innumerable modern Christians, who, claiming to be "spiritual but not religious," see no value in assembling with others for worship. But in the end, as Augustine put it, Victorinus "grew proud towards vanity and humble towards truth."

> *When the hour had come for his profession of faith . . . Simplicianus told me that the priests offered Victorinus to let him make the profession in private, as the custom was with such as seemed likely to find the ordeal embarrassing. But he preferred to make profession of salvation in the sight of the congregation in church. . . . When therefore he had gone up to make his profession all those who knew him began whispering his name to one another with congratulatory murmurs. And indeed who there did not know him? And from the lips of the rejoicing congregation sounded the whisper, "Victorinus, Victorinus!" They were quick to utter their exultation at seeing him and as quickly fell silent to hear him. He uttered the true faith with glorious confidence, and they would gladly have snatched him to their very heart. Indeed, they did take him to their heart in their love and their joy: with those hands they took him.*[18]

This was, as Augustine suggests, a community like no other on earth—one in which love, supported by the spirit of humility, assumed preeminence and prevented the pride of individualism from rearing its divisive head. It was also a community held together by a common commitment to an objective and not pluralistic body of doctrine.

Early Christian communities cultivated the virtue of humility, but that was only the beginning. By subverting the individual ego, they served to empower the greatest of all virtues, charity. And it was this virtue that would become perhaps the most unassailable element of Western culture in the future. Charity would even survive secularization to become, in various forms, a principle of modern society.

As the central virtue of the Church's early community life, charity deserves careful definition. The ancient Greeks, whose language the apostles appropriated, distinguished between various forms of love, such as affection (*storge*), friendship (*philia*), and desire (*eros*).[19] For them, the highest and most noble form was *agape,* or sacrificial love. Its Latin equivalent is *caritas,* which became the root for the English word *charity.* This word would characterize, for example, the love of a mother for a mentally handicapped child, or, to use a modern image the pagan Greeks would have been more comfortable with, of a soldier for his comrades when he throws himself on a hand grenade that would otherwise kill them.

Agape is what God possesses for the human race, even when it rejects Him. The Prophet Hosea reveals the divine character of agape when he is told by God to marry the harlot Gomer and then to continue to chase after her and offer her honor even when she reverts to harlotry. This kind of love is what the New Testament reveals God actually is: "God is agape," states the Apostle John (1 John 4:8).

And if Christians are baptized mystically into the life of God, then they too are called to be love. This is the broader point made by John in his famous first epistle. It is also the Apostle Paul's emphasis in his unforgettable panegyric about love in the thirteenth chapter of 1 Corinthians.

> *Love is patient and kind; love is not jealous or boastful; it is not arrogant or rude. Love does not insist on its own way; it is not irritable or resentful; it does not rejoice at wrong, but rejoices in the right. Love bears all things, believes all things, hopes all things, endures all things. Love never ends . . . (RSV)*

"Love never ends"—this, perhaps, is Paul's most important point. Love is the greatest virtue. But by projecting it into eternity (it "never ends") he indicates that as a virtue it is what enables the human being to participate in the very life of God.

A later generation would call this *deification.* Such a doctrine of salvation was at the heart of early Christian anthropology—the understanding of what it means to be human. Traditional Christianity taught that man is made in the image and likeness of God. Though this image is a mystery and was never defined precisely in the scriptures, there is much in the New Testament that indicates its chief characteristic is agape love.[20]

The Christian community's calling to participate in the life of God through love is powerfully expressed by Christ Himself. Gathering His disciples in the upper room, he issued to them a "new commandment" to love one another. But this commandment was emphatically not that they should love one another in any way that might be convenient to them. It was to love one another "as I have loved you" (John 13:34). Christ said this, of course, on the eve of His sacrificial death on the cross. The Christian community, then, was to be bound together by that very sacrificial love which is of God. What is more, this new commandment in the upper room echoed what Christ had earlier called the Great Commandment: that His disciples should love God with all their being and love their neighbors as themselves.

This element of total, sacrificial love came to distinguish the Christian community from the pagan society that surrounded it. According to Acts and some of the New Testament epistles, a strong commitment to the welfare of the Church's membership was an early feature of the Christian subculture. True religion, insisted the Apostle James, was to care for widows and orphans (James 1:27). I have already noted the early Christian practice of sharing material resources in common for the good of the community. This practice was not limited to individual congregations, however. Paul, for instance, discussed a rather systematic program of collecting goods among Gentile communities and delivering them for the relief of hard-pressed Jewish ones (2 Cor. 8).

It is worth pausing to consider how remarkable such a system was in ancient Rome. Not only voluntarily, but by the command of their God, a network of Christian communities was undertaking to ensure the material welfare of their poor. Those who gave were not only of a different race but would never even see those who benefitted from their largess. As Paul Johnson has noted, nothing like this had ever existed in Rome.[21] And this kind of active charity eventually became institutionalized. The church of Rome, famously, became known not only for the relics of Peter and Paul, but for the vast system of social welfare the pope and his supporting clergy administered there.

Nor was charity limited to fellow Christians. It is clear that the material care of the needy by early Christian communities was extended to non-believers. In the third century, Cyprian of Carthage was known for his efforts to care for the pagans of the city where he was bishop. A contemporary biographer recorded the scene in which Cyprian exhorted his congregation to practice universal charity:

> *The people being assembled together, he first of all urges on them the benefits of mercy. . . . Then he proceeds to add that there is nothing remarkable in cherishing merely our own people with the due attentions of love, but that one might become perfect who should do something more than heathen men or publicans, one who, overcoming evil with good, and practicing a merciful kindness like that of God, should love his enemies as well. . . . Thus the good was done to all men, not merely to the household of faith.*[22]

This is a remarkable document. It would be difficult and probably impossible to find in pagandom anything like it. This practice was only possible because baptism had initiated Cyprian's community into a totally new way of life not of this world. Charity was the ultimate mark of this transformation, enabling them to participate in the very life of their God. It is also poignant to consider the fact that it was precisely those pagans to whom Cyprian showed such kindness who would ultimately torture him and put him to death.

Finally, the subculture's model of community bequeathed to the West one of its most precious ideals, equality. But unlike the enforced equality of modern political theory that leads, in some cases, to totalitarian violence, traditional Christianity introduced a spiritual equality based on mutual respect. This was closely related to the anthropological principle that every human being bears the image of God. Indeed, there could be no possibility of human equality otherwise. Paul gives expression to the belief. There is, he twice declares, "neither Jew nor Greek, there is neither slave nor free, there is neither male nor female; for you are all one in Christ Jesus" (Gal. 3:28; see also Col. 3:11). In Christ, Paul proclaimed, all human beings find an equal dignity. For in Christ all achieve the fullness of their humanity in all its diversity.

In the stratified and unequal world of the Romans, this was a transformational teaching. It provided a reservoir of potential criticism of the social order. The idea of equality would become revolutionary in a political sense only in modern times, when secularization had removed the humility and sacrifice that were taken for granted in such statements. However, even among the peace-loving and deferential early Christians, equality could have a radical social effect, as we shall see in the next chapter.

Indeed, pagans heard rumors about equality among Christians and reacted with fear. Some went so far as to claim that Christians engaged in incest, since husbands and wives were of such a mind as to speak of each other as brother and sister. That this should be a reflection of equality between husband and wife was incomprehensible to pagans, since the relationship between pagan spouses more often resembled that of master and slave. Athenagoras, in his second-century apology for the faith, acknowledged this libel and dismissed it by reminding his pagan audience of the gospel's superior moral law, grounded in the integrity of the apostolic doctrine. "Our account lies not with human laws," he declared,

> which a bad man can evade. . . . but we have a law which makes the measure of rectitude to consist in dealing with our neighbour as ourselves. On this account, too, according to age, we recognize some as sons and daughters, others we regard as brothers and sisters, and to the more advanced in life we give the honour due to fathers and mothers.[23]

Heavenly Immanence

THIS BRINGS US TO a third important source of the early culture of Christendom: the sacraments. The third element Luke lists as a characteristic of church life is "the breaking of the bread." Communion in the Body and

Blood of Christ was, from the start, a normative experience for Christians. It was also the heart of a larger sacramental tradition. The sacraments were a way of recognizing that God did not remain aloof from His creation but became incarnate, filling the world with heavenly immanence.

The doctrine of the Eucharist was at the center of this teaching. Christ had declared that He was the bread of life, which "came down from heaven" to nourish and sustain those who dwell on earth. He emphasized that through communion with His disciples He was not offering perishable bread that sustained life only for a time and could not stave off death. Indicating His body, He rather elaborated the sacramental consequences of the Incarnation:

> This is the bread that comes down from heaven, that one may eat of it and not die. I am the living bread which came down from heaven. If anyone eats this bread, he will live forever; and the bread that I shall give is My flesh, which I shall give for the life of the world. (John 6:50–51)

Those who literally ate His flesh and drank His blood would participate immediately in the life of heaven. That His meaning here was literal is indicated by the fact that several would-be disciples abandoned Him because of such a "hard saying." They understood Jesus to be talking literally, not symbolically, and when they acted on this belief, Jesus did not protest that they had misunderstood Him. Later on, Paul emphasized the reality of Christ's Body in the Eucharist and warned believers to discern it properly (1 Cor. 11:29).

Early fathers of the Church likewise asserted the literal reality of consuming Christ's Body and Blood in the Eucharist. They often did this in the context of a defense against heresies. Justin Martyr, as we saw above, was an early opponent of the gnostic tendency to diminish the earthly context for salvation. In his *First Apology*, he put it very simply:

> For not as common bread and common drink do we receive [the eucharist]; but in like manner as Jesus Christ our Savior, having been made flesh by the Word of God, had both flesh and blood for our salvation, so likewise have we been taught that the food which is blessed by the prayer of his word, and from

which our blood and flesh by transmutation are nourished, is the flesh and blood of that Jesus who was made flesh.[24]

This statement, made by one of the best-educated and most culturally engaged of all early Christians, says much about the background of early Christian culture. There is nothing common, nothing mundane about the sacrament of communion. And this is so because it communicates the very divinity of God. Justin's statement here about the Eucharist also brings attention to baptism in that it claims merely to hand on what "we have been taught"—that is, the continuous tradition of the Church, unbroken after (in Justin's time) more than a century of her history.

That sacramental tradition had been attested to earlier in the second century by Ignatius of Antioch in his struggle against the heresy of docetism. This was the teaching that Christ's incarnate body was not truly physical but only appeared as such. The root word *dokesis* in Greek means *apparition*, and the heresy might also be called *apparitionism*. This heresy would be echoed loudly in a later age, when a form of it known as iconoclasm tried unsuccessfully to eradicate all images of Christ within Christendom.

As then, so docetism in Ignatius's time was fundamentally a rejection of the Incarnation. Ignatius recognized this and struggled to confront it. In his *Epistle to the Smyrnaeans*, he writes that the docetists "absent themselves from the eucharist and the public prayers, because they will not admit that the eucharist is the self-same body of our Savior Jesus Christ."[25]

The apostolic tradition was attested also by Irenaeus toward the close of the second century, again in the context of the recurrent struggle against docetism. In *Against the Heresies*, he had the following to say about Christian apparitionists who denied the bodily reality of the eucharist.

> *How can they say that the flesh, which is nourished with the body of the Lord and with his blood, goes to corruption, and does not partake of life? . . . For we offer to him his own, announcing consistently the fellowship and union of the flesh and spirit. For as the bread, which is produced from the earth, when it receives the invocation of God, is no longer common bread, but the eucharist, consisting of two realities, earthly and heavenly; so also our bodies, when they*

receive the eucharist, are no longer corruptible, having the hope of the resur-
rection to eternity.[26]

The early Church believed forcefully in the reality of the Eucharist, and this belief shaped her understanding of the created world. The Eucharist was the chief of the sacraments and was thus an anchor for her cosmology of heavenly immanence.

But the sacraments were not limited to the Eucharist in the early Church. We have already mentioned baptism, which enabled a Christian to live out the apostolic doctrine. It was also the necessary gateway into eucharistic communion. No one but baptized members of the body of Christ were admitted to the divine banquet. The *Didache* states this with perfect clarity. No eucharistic communion was possible outside the body, since the body of Christ was the presence of Christ on earth. And one could only be a member of it who had through baptism died with Christ and been raised in His resurrection. "No one is to eat or drink of your eucharist," the early-second-century document declared, "but those who have been baptized in the name of the Lord."[27]

Justin, likewise, immediately before his statement about the reality of the Eucharist quoted above, observes that "no one is allowed to partake but the man who believes that the things which we teach are true, and who has been washed with the washing that is for the remission of sins, and unto regeneration, and who is so living as Christ has enjoined."[28] It is noteworthy here that Justin not only documents the early Church's restriction of eucharistic communion to the baptized, but articulates the doctrinal and moral requirements of that communion. Only the man "who believes that the things we teach are true" and "who is so living as Christ has enjoined" may partake.

As Justin noted, baptism represented a "washing that is for the remission of sins." And this washing was physical as well as spiritual. Throughout His ministry, Christ honored His creation by making use of it in working the salvation that could only come from Him. One particularly vivid example of this is the healing of the man born blind in John's Gospel. Only with Jesus' spittle and the dust of the earth made into clay were the man's eyes healed.

Baptism likewise made use of the material world created by God, and with even greater emphasis. In this sense, it was a guide to the early Church's cosmology. That the healing of the world would come from the Creator was little surprise to Jesus' followers. That it would come through the sacramental appropriation of the physical world, however, was more startling.

One of the earliest writers to remark on this mystery was Tertullian, who lived into the third century. He wrote a treatise on baptism that opens with a theologically rich reflection on the providential role of water in God's saving plan. It reads so much like a praise of the material substance that at one point the author felt it necessary to apologize midsentence and remind the reader of the real purpose of water: to bear the Holy Spirit to man.

But along the way Tertullian cannot resist describing the numerous ways prior to the institution of baptism in which God communicated His grace to the world. It was over water that the Spirit hovered at the creation; it was water that cleansed the world in the time of Noah; it was water that served to drown Pharaoh at the exodus of the Jews from Egypt, which, it might be noted, was a type of Christ's Passion and Resurrection vividly remembered in the early Church.[29] Tertullian reflects that "it is not to be doubted that God has made the material substance which he has disposed throughout all his products and works obey him also in his own peculiar sacraments." His conclusion, then, is "that the material substance which governs terrestrial life acts as agent likewise in the celestial."[30] In other words, God had joined earth to heaven through the sacramental power of water.

The principle of heavenly immanence imbued early Christian subculture with a deep respect for the cosmos. This not only enabled it to affirm that the world was very good, but to draw all forms of human activity—social organization, artistic production, and even government—into a process of spiritual transformation.

Spiritual Transformation

IF GOD WAS PRESENT in the sacraments of the Church, with all of creation participating in the experience, prayer and worship served to order and regularize the principle of heavenly immanence. And even more than that, by integrating worship into the rhythm of the natural world, traditional Christianity served to transform it.

Christ Himself had offered an example of regular, heartfelt prayer to His heavenly Father. He also frequented the Jewish temple during the established holidays that had, for centuries, provided a scripturally regulated pattern of true worship. Indeed, ancient Judaism was not, as is often said, merely a "religion of the book." It was also a religion of the temple, and a great deal of its holy book, the Old Testament, was dedicated to elaborating divinely commanded feasts, fasts, and liturgies. Early Christian worship sprang out of this holy tradition. Therefore, Luke considered this worship normative to church life, and listed "the prayers" as the fourth and final mark of that life.

Christian worship had actually started even earlier. The Gospels tell of the disciples gathering together on the very day of Christ's Resurrection—the first day of the Jewish week—when the risen Lord made His presence known among them. Then, one week later, according to John, the disciples were gathered together again in what might be called a proto-liturgy, an occasion when Christ imparted to them the gift of the Holy Spirit. But it was, of course, only at Pentecost that the Spirit was given in all His fullness. When that day had "fully come," Acts declares, the apostles "were all with one accord in one place." We are told that prior to Pentecost, it was the practice of the apostles and possibly Mary (compare Acts 1:14 with Acts 2:1) to assemble on the first day of the week in prayer. After Pentecost, this apostolic proto-liturgy became the model for Christian worship throughout the world.

What made the liturgy complete now was the offering of Christ's Body and Blood during the course of it. But the regular assembly of Christians in order to participate in the Eucharist was itself significant. The consolidation of a regular pattern of worship created conditions under which Christendom's nascent civilization could begin to flourish.

The service at the heart of Christian worship occurred on the first day of the weekly calendar inherited from the Jews. According to the Gospels, this was the day of the week on which Christ rose from the dead. It became known as the Lord's Day, and its observance is documented in the

New Testament (Rev. 1:10). According to the calendar of pagan Rome, it was known as *dies solis*, the Day of the Sun. Christians did not cease to use this moniker in public, but among themselves a strong preference for "Lord's Day"—*kyriake* in Greek and *dominicus* in Latin—soon took hold.

What is more, the Christians self-consciously distinguished this day from the Jewish Sabbath. Though Christ's followers were initially inclined to participate in the established Jewish worship, by the end of the first century we can see clear signs that membership in the Church made one a participant in a totally new liturgical experience. As Ignatius put it, "those who used to live according to the old order of things have attained to a new hope and they observe no longer the Sabbath but Sunday, the day on which Christ and his death raised up our life."[31] If the old covenant had prescribed a day of rest, the new day of worship called Christians to action. This vitality is suggested in the very order in which the Lord's Day fell within the seven-day week. It was the first. It was the day on which, according to the cosmologically rich first two chapters of Genesis, God had begun the creation of the world.

The Lord's Day was, in fact, the day on which time itself had been created. Before this first day there had been only eternity; after it, "there was evening and morning, one day" (Gen. 1:5 OSB). The Lord's Day, then, was a day that represented a link between earth and heaven, between the cosmos and its Creator.

But if the first day of the week was the first day of the old creation, it was also the first day of the new creation. The divinely arranged weekly cycle of time inherited from the Jews was now seen in a new light. The cycle pointed to Christ's work to re-create the creation, a work that culminated with His death on the cross. It was a work solemnized when, with His very last words, He declared His divine-human ministry completed. For this reason, the seventh-day Jewish Sabbath that fell only a day after Christ's death could in no way serve Christians as a day of worship as such, for it was a day of rest. On that day God had once, at the beginning of time, rested; and on that day too His Son rested, buried in a tomb.

Christ rose from the dead not on the seventh day of the week, but on the first. And so the first day came also to be for Christians the "eighth day."

There is, of course, no eighth day in the Jewish calendar. That is the point behind the term's symbolism. For the Lord's Day resets, as it were, the old covenant's method of measuring time. It propels the earthly calendar beyond itself into the kingdom of heaven. And with this, the created world is reset to accommodate that kingdom.

The Lord's Day thus served to reveal the spiritual transformation of the world. In the early second century (if not earlier), for instance, the *Epistle of Barnabas* imagines Christ declaring, "It is not the Sabbath now celebrated that pleases me, but the Sabbath which I made, and on which, after bringing all things to their rest, I will begin an eighth day, that is, a new world."[32]

Some Christians were so inspired by this experience of paradise that they were actually prepared to die for it. In 258 Pope Sixtus II was beheaded in Rome by soldiers when he refused to comply with a ban on worship at the catacombs, being actually pulled from his episcopal chair during what appears to have been a Lord's Day eucharistic assembly. In another case, a group of what one historian has called Lord's Day martyrs were arrested in Carthage in 304, under Diocletian's persecution, for their refusal to desist from assembly on Sundays. There were nearly fifty in all. When they were placed on trial, their priest insisted on their need to assemble on that day, for, as he put it, doing so "is a law for us." A reader in whose home the assembly had been discovered agreed, adding that "we cannot live without celebrating the Lord's Day." A virgin named Victoria placed her martyr's declaration within the context of Sunday worship: "I attended the meeting, because I am a Christian."[33] "I am a Christian": The famous formula of Christ's witnesses during these centuries was spoken before pagan magistrates, but it was implied simply in the act of assembling on the Lord's Day.

The cosmological character of early Christian worship was not limited to Sundays. In fact, all of earthly time came to be infused by heavenly worship. By the second century the celebration of Christ's Resurrection had become an event on the annual calendar. It was linked to the timing of the Jewish Passover, though in Rome it was carefully scheduled to take place after Passover and on a Sunday. With time the period of celebration after Pascha grew, as did a period of fasting before it. This preliminary period eventually became the Great Fast. Calendrical fasting was already a normative and universal feature of the early Church, documented at the beginning of the second century by the *Didache,* which acknowledges the practice of fasting on Wednesdays and Fridays.

In addition to the annual and weekly calendars, even the daily calendar was being transformed by Christianity. Writers like Tertullian instructed believers to measure their days with prayers at certain hours. Aware that they were in the world but not of it, he urged them to "snatch a moment from business" to bring sanctity to life in this age. Other writers recommended nighttime prayer vigils. Hippolytus of Rome, author of the third-century *Apostolic Tradition,* connected all-night vigils with the eschatological experience of Christ's coming. And he added a cosmological twist to this form of prayer:

> *The ancients who have passed the tradition on to us have taught us that at this hour all creation rests for a moment in order to praise the Lord: the stars, the trees, the heavens stop for a moment in union with the souls of the just.*[34]

This beautiful vision of a cosmos brought into mystical harmony with God through the prayers of His saints on earth is a good expression of the Church's early experience of cosmological transformation.

That experience is documented in the earliest known hymn composed for Christian worship, *Phos Hilarion* ("O Gladsome Light"). It is suggestive that this third-century composition used in evening worship is as cosmological as it is christological. It speaks of the Son of God. But it also likens Christ to the light of the candles that were used in evening worship at a time when there was no electricity. "Now that we have come to the setting of the sun and behold the Light of evening . . . " a phrase from one rhythmic English translation reads. The "Light of evening" is, of course, Jesus Christ. And He is powerfully experienced—beheld—in worship timed for the darkening of evening, after the natural sun has set and the supernatural Sun has revealed Himself.

CHAPTER ONE

Experiencing Paradise

CHRISTENDOM BROKE LIKE THE DAWN over pagandom, and its culture had one principal goal: to bring man into an experience of the kingdom of heaven while living on the earth. This experience can be called "paradise." Its focus was not the paradise lost to Adam and Eve. That is described in the first three chapters of Genesis. That primordial paradise was an obscure reality. Known also as the Garden of Eden, it was a place of communion with God at the beginning of time. Centered on the mysterious Tree of Life, it was an experience of knowing God. But its duration was apparently quite brief. As soon as we are told of its establishment it is destroyed by the decision of Eve and Adam to live without divine communion, to be nourished by something other than God. The result was expulsion from the garden and the stationing of an angel with a flaming sword outside its gates, barring reentry.

The primordial paradise of Adam was lost forever. However, in the

Adam and Eve in Paradise
Cathedral Basilica of Saint Louis

"Second Adam," Jesus Christ, the apostles claimed that what had been lost due to the Fall was recovered, and even more, that in Christ communion with God assumed a fullness never known to Adam. Christians continued to live as Adam's descendants within a fallen world. But as the Church, they were given the experience of divine communion as a pledge of the eternal kingdom of heaven. Life in the world could thus become an experience likened to paradise. It was not the primordial blessing, but one incomparably greater insofar as it involved participation in the life of God through Christ and the Holy Spirit. It is what can be called an eschatological paradise, one grounded in the ultimate (Greek *eschatos*) salvation of the human race.

Being eternal, this paradise could not be established or institutionalized on earth by any action of men. Indeed, because of the sinful brokenness of the world, it could be entered fully only at the end of time, following the Second Coming of Christ. But unlike the primordial paradise, this one did not remain obscure to those who had been initiated into the life of Christ. Its verdant beauty was already visible from the distance of this world.

As the first century came to a close, the Apostle John wrote about this paradise. The Theologian reserved it for the final chapter of his Revelation—the last book of a Bible that had opened with an account of the primordial paradise. For John, the eschatological paradise was infinitely greater in glory, though he made clear allusions to its prototype, Eden. By divine inspiration, he saw

> *the river of the water of life, bright as crystal, flowing from the throne of God and of the Lamb through the middle of the street of the city; also, on either side of the river, the tree of life with its twelve kinds of fruit, yielding its fruit each month; and the leaves of the tree were for the healing of the nations. There shall no more be anything accursed, but the throne of God and of the Lamb shall be in it, and his servants shall worship him; they shall see his face, and his name shall be on their foreheads. And night shall be no more; they need no light of lamp or sun, for the Lord God will be their light, and they shall reign forever and ever. (Rev. 22:1–5 RSV)*

It was this paradise, awaiting the consummation of time yet already present in the world, that Christendom manifested.

And as long as it was irrigated by the waters of traditional Christianity, Christendom's culture remained vigorous. But if the soils in which it grew became desiccated by pessimism about God's presence in the world and the possibility of man's communion with God, it would suffer its own kind of Fall. This is what happened long after the story told in this volume, when the eleventh-century division of Christendom created conditions for the rise of a new culture in the West, one that became estranged from paradise. But until then, for a full millennium, the original Christian culture remained the heart of a truly paradisiacal Christendom.

CHAPTER TWO

Beyond the Catacombs

I T IS OFTEN SAID that Christian civilization arose only after the Roman state adopted Christianity in the fourth century, and that before then there was no Christendom, only Christianity. In his massive and erudite six-volume history, for instance, Warren Carroll stated that before Constantine "Christendom still awaited its founder."[35] A Christian civilization with a supporting culture was impossible, the conventional narrative goes, without access to political power.

This is not true. From the beginning of her history the Church cultivated distinct beliefs and values that created a unique proto-civilization—however small—and a subculture to animate it. It is true that in its earliest form Christendom had almost no immediate impact on the world. Indeed, it would take nearly three centuries before it succeeded in influencing the world on a large scale. But, as I argued in the previous chapter, Christendom was founded at Pentecost, and its founders were not emperors but the faithful members of local parish churches. While not numerous, these Christians began to spread out across Roman pagandom in a network of culturally creative communities.

I will address the advanced forms of Christendom that arose from state support of and mass conversion to Christianity in the next chapter. In this one, I would like to show how, before political support was afforded it, traditional Christianity cultivated what the West would one day recognize as its fundamental cultural values.

Subterranean Christendom

THE NASCENT CIVILIZATION of early Christendom was confined to an extremely small part of the Roman population and forced to exist on the fringes of society. It is symbolized in part by the catacombs, those underground burial chambers in which the faithful were in some cases compelled to gather outside the city limits of Rome. Unlike the halls of Villa Jovis—vaulted on cliffs overlooking the sea, attracting the powerful and ambitious, and decorated with pornographic murals—the claustrophobic, underground corridors and chapels of the catacombs revealed a civilization rooted in values very different from those of pagandom. Here humility, poverty, and chastity ruled. Here Christians adorned their walls with paintings and statements about their faith in a God who emptied Himself by descending from heaven to earth, taking on the form of a servant and rescuing the human race from the despair of sin.

It was here that was found what may be the earliest emblem identifying Christians, the ICHTHYS, or symbol of a fish. Ichthys is the Greek word for "fish." As an acronym, however, it was intended among secretive early Christians as shorthand for "Jesus Christ, Son of God, Savior." Another important emblem was the CHI-RO, or representation of the superimposed first two Greek letters of the name "Christos." The catacombs were also home to some of the earliest iconography, though this began at a somewhat later date than the ICTHYS or CHI-RO. The Catacomb of Saint Priscilla, for instance, contains third-century depictions of Christ as the Good Shepherd and of the Virgin Mary.

The iconography of the Roman catacombs is matched by that of a house church at Duro-Europos, in modern Syria. This is an example of a place where regular Christian worship took place. It was built openly on the borderlands of the Roman Empire, far from the threat of persecution. As such, the house church is rather an exception to the conditions of early

Christendom. But its images represented values that were typical. Here Christians assembled every week on the Lord's Day, Sunday, to commemorate the Resurrection of Christ.

Though mostly looted and demolished by the Islamic State in the early twenty-first century, the house church at Dura Europos contained numerous images painted as early as the third century. These include a representation of the Myrrh-Bearing Women approaching the empty tomb of the risen Christ. Interestingly, two other unearthed images depicted the healing of the paralytic and the Samaritan woman at the well, both of which became themes in the paschal commemorations of the Eastern Church.

The Christendom of the early Church was founded on the experience of paradise, and this was represented especially by the Resurrection of Christ. Indeed, the catacombs themselves were not just burial places for Christians who went to their deaths in the hope of the resurrection. They were also shrines for the relics of those Christians who consciously died in witness to that hope.

We know with certainty that early Christians venerated the remains of these martyrs, or witnesses (the Greek *martyria* literally means "witness"). The work known as the *Martyrdom of Polycarp*, written in the middle of the second century, is evidence of this. The earliest martyrology outside the New Testament, it does not conclude its account with the saint's death. Rather it ends with the faithful gathering his relics and placing them in a "suitable place" for veneration. It even adds the detail, significantly, that at the place where the relics lie the faithful will "gather together in joy and gladness" every year to remember the saint's hope in the kingdom of heaven. From the beginning, the early Church's liturgical calendar was rooted not only in weekly assemblies on the Lord's Day but in annual saints' holidays as well.

Perhaps the most arresting image of this liturgically borne hope is also found in the Catacomb of Priscilla. In one chamber used most likely as a chapel, a wall is adorned with a mural of a woman standing in worship, her hands upraised in the classical *orans* posture. Significantly, the images that surround her indicate that she is part of the eucharistic assembly of the Church, enjoying communion with its risen Lord.

Wall painting of woman in prayer
By Kristicak - Own work, CC BY-SA 4.0, https://commons.wikime-
dia.org/w/index.php?curid=38106244

Here in the cata-
combs and in other
liturgical havens scat-
tered throughout
the Roman Empire,
Christians unknow-
ingly laid the foun-
dations of a West yet
to come. For it was
here that they mani-
fested all four of the
elements of Chris-
tendom discussed in the previous chapter. They would have been amazed
to learn that they were the founders of a civilization, and not only because
of their statistically insignificant numbers. The thought that Christianity
would transform the world was amazing because for the most part they did
not really expect anything from the world. They were, by all indications,
hated by it.

Persecution tended to come in waves. Since it lasted for nearly three centuries—a third of a millennium—we should not think of it as an unrelenting
and uniform experience. The earliest opponents of the Church were Jews
living in and around Jerusalem. The Protomartyr ("First Martyr") Stephen
is reported in Acts to be the first victim of anti-Christian violence committed by these, his own people. Soon, however, Gentiles joined in, and Acts
describes some of the attacks directed against the Apostle Paul when he was
far beyond the reach of religious authorities in Jerusalem.

Early hostility toward Christianity led to a dispersion of Christians from
the city where Pentecost had occurred. Interestingly, this experience seems
from the start to have inspired the faithful. The author of Acts, the Evangelist Luke, stated that in response to the first widespread persecution, "those
who were scattered went everywhere preaching the word" (Acts 8:4). In
other words, rather than retreat or surrender, they became even more committed to the spread of their faith. What is more, not only did hostility fail

to defeat the Church, but she grew in numbers in response to her ordeals. Again, Luke notes that in the wake of the persecution that followed the martyrdom of Stephen, "a great number believed and turned to the Lord" (Acts 11:21).

As time passed, even more memorable persecutions occurred. By the end of the first century, the Roman state itself began to lead the way. Emperor Nero was the first to conduct a widespread persecution of Christians. Apparently in order to find scapegoats for the great fire that consumed much of Rome in AD 64, he rounded up Christians and had them tortured and killed. He is said to have lit up his garden with torches made by impaling Christians on stakes and lighting them afire. Others were beheaded. Some were crucified. Among his victims were the Apostles Peter and Paul.

Subsequent emperors periodically followed Nero's example. In many cases it was not the imperial government that led the way, but the pagan population. One of the best-documented persecutions occurred under Marcus Aurelius in the Gallic town of Vienne in 177. In this town alone, four dozen martyrs were put to death in a single episode of violence.

By the end of the second century, Roman emperors recognized that in the persecution of Christians they could achieve two valuable political ends. They could eliminate socially despised and religiously isolated subjects. In addition, they could supply victims for the blood sports that had come to characterize much of pagan Rome's entertainment industry. As an outgrowth of the cruel and histrionic statecraft pioneered by Julius Caesar and expanded at the court of Tiberius, Roman rulers used public shows to pacify the masses of disadvantaged citizens while providing a ferocious disincentive to sedition. The system of publicly funded blood sport was finetuned at the gladiatorial contests, where rulers such as Caligula and Nero seated themselves prominently as royal spectators. For truly dangerous revolutionaries, the state reserved the instrument of crucifixion. In the aftermath of the notorious Spartacus rebellion, for instance, the road leading to Rome had been lined with no fewer than six thousand crucified slaves. Roman statesmen were connoisseurs of cruelty, and Christians very often paid the price.

Not that Christians would have made good revolutionaries, of course. Famous for their obedience to the Roman state (Romans 13:1: "Let every soul be subject to the governing authorities"), they could only rarely be accused of actual subversion. But as the empire began to waver during the troubled third century, emperors became ever more insistent on public displays of political and religious conformity. This found expression especially in the ritual cult of the emperor. Some rulers had long been recognized officially as gods. Augustus was the first, but a slew of tyrants followed him into the ranks of pagan deities.

The spectacle of what might be called imperial divine self-awareness was often odious. Caligula, as we have seen, preened himself in front of a statue of Jupiter, believing he was, if not equal to the king of the gods, at least a member of his inner circle. On one occasion, he is said even to have erupted in anger and threatened Jupiter. In the meantime, Caligula had the palace remodeled to include a shrine dedicated to himself, in which priests offered daily sacrifices. (His preference for animal victims was predictably extravagant: they slaughtered peacocks before him.)

But Caligula was by most accounts mad, or nearly so. Saner emperors were more circumspect about their presumed divinity. In one case the spectacle was almost comical. Emperor Vespasian, on his deathbed, was reported to have mumbled cynically, "Oh dear, I think I'm becoming a god."

Whether they truly believed in it or not, pagan Rome's rulers came to insist on allegiance to the cult of the emperor. Their subjects were expected to enter temples dedicated either to the living emperor or, more commonly, to one of his many predecessors, and to make a sacrifice before his statue. The state did not really care what its subjects believed. Rome, as the heir to Hellenistic civilization, celebrated religious diversity as a part of its pluralistic culture. But a sacrifice to the emperor was proof that whatever convictions one held, he was prepared to accommodate them to the demands of the worldly order. And with these demands, faithful Christians could of course never comply.

And so state-sponsored persecution ravaged the Church off and on for some two hundred and fifty years. One of the most poignant episodes occurred just as the third-century decline of the empire was beginning. It was launched by Emperor Septimius Severus and represented a particularly fierce attack on Christianity.

Severus had come to power at a critical time in the history of the Roman state. The second-century period of growth and prosperity marked by what historians call the Five Good Emperors came to a nasty end with the Year of Five Emperors, named for the sequence of usurpers who, in the single year of 193, used violence and deceit to seize the throne. The ancient and revered Senate had ceased even theoretically to influence imperial succession. Now power fell into the hands of those prepared to kill for it. The bloodletting was halted only when Severus had one of the Five, Emperor Didius Julianus, killed. He then set about establishing a secure political basis for what by comparison would be a long reign.

The persecution of the empire's Christians was part of this program and is memorably documented in a spectacle that occurred in the Roman city of Carthage. There, in 203, Severus had a group of Christians rounded up and brought to the central amphitheater. The occasion was the celebration of his son Geta's birthday. To mark the event, Severus ordered that Christians be brought out before the crowds and, for everyone's amusement, executed. Two of the condemned were a young aristocratic woman and her slave girl, who were catechumens.

Their names were Perpetua and Felicity. We have little documentation about the early Church, but remarkably, their experience at the hands of Severus is documented by a diary that Perpetua kept in prison while awaiting punishment. She recorded that before the public execution, her pagan father visited her and implored her to renounce her faith in Jesus. He pleaded with her by reminding her of her social status, her youth, and her family's love for her. If she would only submit to the state's demand to sacrifice before the imperial cult, she could have all of these good things restored.

She refused. And when the day of execution came, she and Felicity together marched bravely into the arena to meet their end. A Christian editor of Perpetua's diary who was an eyewitness recorded what happened. Because of their obstinacy, the authorities decided to subject the two

Saints Perpetua and Felicity
Nick Thompson; Capella Arcivescovile (Archiepiscopal Chapel), Ravenna.

women to as cruel a death as possible. The pagan spectators who had come to amuse themselves with blood sport would surely have approved. Crucifixion was typically reserved for criminals and in any case would require more time than the imperial birthday party could afford. The decision was therefore made to throw the two prisoners to wild beasts. First a bear, then a leopard, and finally a raging bull were unleashed on the young women. None fulfilled its purpose, however, and Severus's son became impatient. So in the end, the two women were slain by the executioner himself.

But in the martyrdom of Perpetua and Felicity there was something inauspicious for an increasingly tired pagandom. It was not merely the unnecessary victimization of innocent Christians who otherwise would have done the empire no harm. The spectacle struck at the very core of its pagan values. In the Carthaginian arena, true majesty proved to belong not to the cruel emperor and his coddled son. It belonged to the Christian martyrs and their faith in something and Someone not of this world, even in the face of certain death.

The spectacle of their death was characterized best by a comment made by the posthumous editor of Perpetua's diary. He described the two women's entrance into the arena as a procession, "as if on their way to heaven." As they went, they did something no one among the crowds expected. They bore witness to Jesus Christ as the Lord of heaven, yes. But they also bore witness to His kingdom, to heaven itself. They were filled with the experience of paradise.

In the face of Roman society's inexorable estrangement between rich and poor, this noblewoman and her slave girl walked into the arena actually holding hands. And before the end came, they may have turned to one another and exchanged what early Christians called the kiss of peace, the gesture of love and harmony that had broken into a hopelessly divided world when the Church appeared at Pentecost. The act revealed to the assembled crowds a vision of society totally different from the one they knew. For those who attended the spectacle of killing at Carthage's amphitheater in 203, an obscure, persecuted, but vibrant and inspired new civilization came momentarily into view.

In the Arena

WHAT, IF ANYTHING, the throng of Carthaginian spectators knew about Christianity is any historian's guess. But it cannot be denied that the presence of Christians in public arenas brought attention to their beliefs and values. The fact that they were being condemned precisely for their faith, and not for any other violation of Roman law, assured this. This anomaly could only have stirred curiosity in a society increasingly fascinated by exotic religions. Whether in the public arena or at home by the hearth, many Romans would have come to know at least something about the faith of the Christians.

There are numerous ways in which Christianity would have proved fascinating. Both its vision of the world and man's place within it—its cosmology and anthropology—were unlike anything pagandom had known. Christianity claimed that there is only one God, whereas paganism recognized many. It claimed that this one God had created the world in goodness and that He had created man in His own image and likeness. Paganism looked on the world as a spiritual prison house and imagined the gods anthropomorphically in man's image. Christianity claimed that God loved the world sacrificially and, because of that love, became human so that He might enable humanity to participate in His divinity. For paganism, the doctrine of the Incarnation would have caused astonishment and quizzical inquiry.

Christianity would surely have gained the attention of contemporaries through the actions of its followers. Here a core moral teaching of Christ was important: "be merciful, just as your Father also is merciful" (Luke 6:36). More even than its views of man and the world, Christianity's moral teaching was inspirational and provocative. It opened up avenues of human relationship and experience that had never before existed. Many Romans obviously rejected the gospel. But many—and, with the passage of time, an ever-growing aggregate—ultimately came to sympathize with the gospel and even to embrace it because it inspired such exemplary behavior among Christians.

This point has been made forcefully in recent years by the sociologist and historian Rodney Stark. As a scholar writing against the backdrop of a modern, secularistic disdain for Christian influence in society, he has documented a wide range of improvements that resulted when Romans converted to Christianity. His *The Rise of Christianity,* in particular, provides numerous examples of how the Church's subculture ultimately won the heart and mind of pagandom, and I will be referring to this book repeatedly in what follows.[36]

Some of the most powerful impressions of Christianity upon pagans may have been made in public arenas such as that at Carthage. Very likely, there were those who looked on the image of the slave girl Felicity holding her wealthy mistress Perpetua by the hand before both were killed, and could not shake it from their minds after leaving to go home. It must have been what cultural anthropologists call a "liminal experience," that is, a kind of shock to one's system of values that results in an unexpected transition to a new way of thinking and being.

We know that the blood sports enjoyed by Romans featured various types of criminals—escaped slaves, murderers, insurgents—but we do not know of any others selected because of their religious affiliation. This extraordinary detail is often passed over without comment by historians. Hundreds of thousands, possibly more than a million, Roman subjects attended the public games in the centuries following the addition of Christianity to the list of offenses punishable by exposure to lions and other deadly animals. In the two and a half centuries between Nero's palace garden massacre and Diocletian's blockbuster death spectacles, pagans were confronted by the image of the stalwart, even heroically faithful Christian martyr who had lived in submission to the law and harmed no one. His only offense was that he had been a worshiper of Jesus Christ. By their deaths, then, these martyrs were witnesses not only to their Lord, but to the subculture that His Church was forming within pagandom.

While we can only speculate on the impressions this mass of the population may have formed about Christianity, we certainly know something about the values they brought with them to the arena. The spectacles they attended were framed by the popular morality of the age. Within that system, mercy and compassion were largely absent. Mercy was considered a virtue by some ancient writers, but only within tightly drawn limits. Much of the time, it was seen as an obstacle to virtue, especially when it stood in the way of honor.

The classic epics of Homer, for instance, celebrated virile passions such as conquest and vengeance. We may think of Odysseus in the great eponymous epic returning home after years of unexplained absence to find his wife Penelope surrounded by a host of suitors, and slaughtering them all to a man, feeling absolutely no remorse. Such violence is presented by Homer as an act of moral honor. The exercise of mercy, and even more of forgiveness, would have been disgraceful by the values of the epic.

Later Greek philosophy largely reinforced Homeric contempt for mercy. An aversion for it can be found, for instance, in reflections on slavery. As an institution, slavery highlighted the moral question of how to relate to the vulnerable and suffering. By the time of the fifth-century Golden Age of classical Greece, it was a systemic part of Athenian society. For his part, Plato accepted slavery as inevitable and considered it appropriate in all societies. Even the ideal state he detailed in *The Republic* appears to have assumed the existence of slavery, though it is not mentioned by name.

More forcefully, Aristotle taught that slavery was "not only necessary, but expedient." He advocated it because he was convinced that the powerful have a moral right given to them by nature to subjugate the weak. And for Aristotle, it was the natural order of things, not a transcendent deity, that determined good and evil. For both philosophers, then, an amelioration of slavery would be unethical because it would subvert a social order that took for granted the legitimate domination of some by others. The Romans, having adopted so much else from the Greeks, largely maintained this view. Their society relied heavily on slavery, and it is no surprise that they perpetuated the classical defense of it.

More than this, however, the Romans agreed with their Greek moral teachers that the very question of mercy for the vulnerable and suffering in society was problematic. Compassion for the weak, they believed, was an emotional state that disrupted the function of reason. As such, compassion was in most cases treated as a vice. A truly virtuous Roman was one who could look at the suffering of others without wincing, feeling entirely free of any moral bond with them.[37] Obviously, such a view was implicit in the public games taking place in Rome's numerous arenas. Observing the slaughter below them, the crowds appear to have felt not the slightest sympathy with the victims.

And so the contrasting views of Christians were all the more provocative. Christians were called to imitate their God, whose first characteristic was love. And those pagans in the audience who knew something of the actual activities of Christians knew that they lived out this commandment.

There were, to be sure, numerous slanders against the Christians that misled the populace. As early apologetics reveal, Christians were occasionally accused of horrendous moral infractions. Their practice of referring to spouses as brother or sister led to the charge of incest. Their gathering at the eucharistic meal led to that of cannibalism. And, of course, their refusal to sacrifice to the pagan gods could earn them condemnation as atheists. But for the skeptical or open minded, the reality of Christian morality could be readily discovered.

It would have been hard to miss. The Christians, as we have seen, dedicated themselves to caring for the poor in their own midst. And there is evidence that their mercy regularly overflowed the banks of parish life. Cyprian's admonition to fulfill Christ's commandment to love one's enemies by caring for the pagans as well as the Christians was noted in the previous chapter. As a result, good was done to all men, and many were the pagans who knew this.

Others were aware, as they pondered the spectacles of the arena, that it was the Christians, and really only the Christians, who in times of plague organized care for the sick. The third century was a time of recurring epidemics. One of the most devastating occurred midcentury. In the great city of Alexandria, home of pagan learning and also of the earliest Christian schools, a large part of the population died.

The bishop there was named Dionysios, and in 260 he composed a paschal report about the life of his diocese. The now-annual commemoration of Christ's Resurrection was an appropriate occasion to reflect on the death that surrounded the population of the city that year, both Christian and pagan. It was an occasion, Bishop Dionysios insisted, in which the former are called to be witnesses to the latter. And apart from the memory of those who had actually experienced martyrdom at the hands of the pagans, he could find no better witnesses to the gospel than the many Christians who voluntarily and at great personal risk chose to nurse the city's plague victims. His words about them are worth quoting at length.

> *Most of our brother Christians showed unbounded love and loyalty, never sparing themselves and thinking only of one another. Heedless of danger, they took charge of the sick, attending to their every need and ministering to them in Christ, and with them departed this life serenely happy; for they were infected by others with the disease, drawing on themselves the sickness of their neighbors and cheerfully accepting their pains. Many, in nursing and curing others, transferred their death to themselves and died in their stead. . . . The best of our brothers lost their lives in this manner, a number of presbyters, deacons, and laymen winning high commendation so that death in this form, the result of great piety and strong faith, seems in every way the equal of martyrdom.*[38]

It is interesting to speculate that pagan survivors of this epidemic may later have attended public games in Alexandria in which Christians—perhaps even some who had nursed these same pagans back to health—were thrown to lions for public amusement.

By the Hearth

I HAVE IMAGINED the impact Christian witness likely had on at least some pagans who attended shows in the public arenas. But what many saw in public, even more viewed in private. Moving from the arena to the hearth, from public encounters to domestic relationships, we can document even more ways in which catacomb Christendom slowly began to win the West.

We can do this because there is overwhelming evidence that Christianity spread largely through interpersonal relations. There is so very little direct documentation of the reasons individual pagans or even groups of pagans chose to convert to Christianity in the early centuries. This is noteworthy. In our age of personal blogs and autobiographies, of self-conscious life narratives, it is perplexing to find that the ancients left almost nothing behind that directly relates their motivation to convert. Historians are thus left to find indirect evidence and to rely on a reasoned historical imagination. Happily, the results of this method are convincing. They are also fascinating.

Such conclusions often center on the role of women, who appear to have represented a majority within the Church. No church membership censuses were taken, of course, but there is indirect evidence that women outnumbered men by a significant margin. One such piece of evidence cited by Stark is an inventory of garments stockpiled for an internal parish charity in North Africa during the first decade of the fourth century. The inventory suggests that women outnumbered men there by about five to one. While such a statistic is by no means universally applicable, it illustrates the consensus historians long ago reached: that early church membership was predominantly female.

This is hardly surprising, because Christianity dignified women. In the ancient world, women enjoyed very little of the status and honor they would one day have in Christendom. And there were two broad reasons for this, one anthropological and the other institutional.

Anthropologically, paganism assigned a low value to women. Classical philosophers were nearly unanimous in regarding female humanity as naturally inferior to male. In his *Politics*, Aristotle considered women thus, concluding they had no legitimate claim to equality of any kind, whether political, social, or intellectual. In fact, he regarded femininity as a "deformity" of masculinity. Plato, the idealist, tended to be less categorical. But in *The Republic*, he indicated that women are not only physically inferior to men but morally and spiritually of less value as well.

As Athenians, both philosophers contributed moral principles to their city-state's institutional expression of female inferiority. Athens denied all rights to women, treating them essentially as political non-persons. Girls were married to men who on average were twice their age. As children they had no rights; as married women they effectively became the property of their husbands. Women were excluded from much of public life because they were considered a hindrance to a good social order. They were not educated. Their assigned role consisted exclusively in bearing children for their husbands, who could divorce them for any reason whatsoever (their recourse to divorce was by comparison extremely limited). Lacking any other social significance, women were consigned in many cases to the household gynaeceum, the inner room or rooms of the family's dwelling. There, attended by female slaves, the Athenian housewife lived a remote and socially insignificant existence.

Classical paganism's moral and institutional disdain for female humanity had an even darker expression. Greek and Roman civilization was steeped in a culture of infanticide, and the victims of it were predominantly girls.

Again, the twin pillars of Greek philosophy provided the moral basis. For his part, Aristotle actually advocated a legal requirement that no children born with deformities should be allowed to live. As for sexually selective infanticide, he seems to have left that to the discretion of parents. Plato, likewise, argued in *The Republic* that infant homicide is a necessary part of the ideal civilization. Not only children born with physical defects, he indicated, but those lacking a normative level of intelligence were to be eliminated. Plato's anthropological vision is interesting in this point; it opened the way to the principle of sexual selection. He argued that if a human being lacks the capacity to reason, he is not really a human being at all, but rather subhuman. As such he—or in this case she—is potentially unworthy of life. Since female humanity for Plato was already inferior to male, the practice of killing newborn girls in particular would therefore be justified.

The Romans assimilated such views. Seneca, the great stoic authority on virtue, wrote about the social benefit of killing deformed and unwanted children, grouping it with the elimination of rabid dogs. It can be noted that moral and philosophical arguments in favor of infanticide were not the result of custom alone. Pagans felt strongly about them. Tacitus, for instance, expressed sharp moral indignation upon learning of Jewish bans on the practice. He would of course have felt the same when confronted by Christianity's opposition to it.

Philosophy aside, there was actually a large measure of hypocrisy in the ancients' practice of infanticide. The victims were usually exposed, that is, placed in an outdoor environment where they were sure to perish. Instead of killing the child outright, the parents could consider themselves guiltless of direct murder, allowing their offspring to die indirectly from the elements, or hunger, or wild animals.

In other cases infants were simply strangled or drowned. Two archeological sites on opposite sides of the Roman Empire have recently revealed the scope of infanticide before the rise of Christendom. In Palestine, a port town named Ashkelon contains an ancient Roman sewer that actually became clogged with the bodies of some one hundred newborn infants. In Britain, a second-century Roman villa near Hambleden has been found to contain a similar number of victims. Because the latter was a burial site in which the skeletons were all concentrated together and largely intact, it has been possible to use infant growth rate benchmarks to determine the exact stage of development at death. The conclusion is that these infants were probably not the victims of premature birth or postpartum disease but of intentional violence only moments after birth.

The widespread practice of infanticide was closely connected, of course, to that of abortion. In the absence of effective birth control methods, abortion was simply one way of eliminating unwanted children. And though there was no ultrasound or genetic tests to detect what kind of child the fetus was, parents showed a readiness to eliminate it as an act of pre-Christian family planning. The philosophers who provided moral justification for infanticide used the same argument for abortion. Aristotle urged abortion on "any parents who have children in excess," and Plato, even more inclined to social engineering, speculated that state personnel could ideally manage decision-making about the fate of unwanted children.

By contrast, traditional Christianity from the beginning universally and consistently forbade all forms of abortion and infanticide. Though New Testament scripture recorded no direct ban on the practices, the Church's broader tradition did. It appeared in innumerable statements beginning as early as the second-century *Didache*. There was no ambiguity about the position of early Christians on this issue. Hippolytus, Athenagoras, Minucius Felix, and of course the moral firebrand Tertullian all provided an explicit witness to the Church's tradition.

What is particularly significant about the practice of infanticide is, again, the fact that the victims were most often female. Had parents been equipped with the technology of ultrasound, no doubt abortions too would have been more numerous.

With classical culture's contempt for the female sex, parents—women as well as men—were often inclined to retain boys and kill off girls.[39] For them it was simply a matter of euthanasia, or "good killing." According to pagan anthropology, society derived more benefit from boys than from girls. Families that accumulated girls therefore often felt obligated to eliminate them for the good of the family and society. This was given legal expression in the basic code of Roman law known as the Twelve Tables. While it authorized the killing of both sexes when born with deformities, it empowered the paterfamilias, or male head of household, to select newborn females in particular for the sole reason that they were female.

The practice of sexually selective infanticide was so widespread in pagandom and so socially acceptable that parents could speak to one another about it as if they were discussing simple household economy. We have a letter fragment preserved on papyrus from Alexandria during this time. It was written by a husband to his wife while he was away from home on the ancient equivalent of a business trip. In it, he reports the small events that have occupied his attention while away from his wife and regretfully announces the need for his journey to continue a little longer. This is unfortunate, he observes, because she is due to give birth back at home. "I ask and beg you," he therefore writes, "to take good care of our baby son, and as soon as I receive payment I shall send it up to you." He then continues, "If you are delivered of a child [before I come home], if it is a boy keep it, if a girl discard it."

The ease with which this pagan man communicated his decision to kill his child is breathtaking, even today. Our post-Christian Christendom still retains, in most cases, a respect for the lives of boys and girls once they are born. This may be changing.[40] But in the ancient world infants were killed with a shrug of the shoulders. And the personalities who made such decisions were by no means outwardly sinister. The letter quoted above actually ends with an expression of strong spousal affection. "You have sent me word," the husband notes dotingly, "not to forget you. How can I forget you? I beg you not to worry."[41]

Given its disregard for the female sex, pagandom had a hard time retaining its women after they came into contact with the Christian subculture. For women, the gospel was good news indeed. Not only had Genesis declared that they shared equally with men in the image of God, but the New Testament presented a totally new vision of female humanity. This was, to be sure, a part of the larger anthropology of traditional Christianity. But its newness was most dramatically experienced by women.

Women featured prominently in the Gospels. Luke's brought special attention to the dignity and piety of the Virgin Mary at the Annunciation. She, along with the Disciple Whom Jesus Loved, courageously stood alone at the Cross in John's Gospel. The Book of Acts, too, places her in a position of honor, as she was with the apostles in the upper room where the Holy Spirit descended at Pentecost.

The Virgin Mary was said to have been uniquely blessed "among women," but she was only one of many women who accompanied Jesus during His ministry. Some, like Martha and Mary, became His particularly close friends. It was a group of women who discovered the empty tomb and who first announced the Resurrection. Because of this, one of these "myrrhbearing women," Mary Magdalene, soon came to be dignified with the titles "Equal to the Apostles" and even "Apostle to the Apostles."

In his epistles, Paul declared twice that men and women share in a spiritual equality. Sacramentally joined to Christ by baptism, both also share in the fullness of divine life. And while in one place Paul admonished women not to teach in the community, throughout his epistles he made it clear that women frequently assumed positions of church leadership. In addition to the female diaconate of people like Phoebe (which was probably non-liturgical and limited to the care of women only), Paul assigned considerable honor to several female Christians. And some he even seems to have assigned the responsibility of teaching. Priscilla, along with her husband Aquila, not only accompanied him on his missionary journeys as an assistant but contributed to the apostolic ministry of defending doctrine. In Ephesus, she and her husband corrected the neophyte Apostle Apollos, pulling him aside and revealing to him "the way of God more accurately" (Acts 18:26).

It is no wonder, then, that women joined the Church in comparatively large numbers after coming into contact with the gospel. By the beginning of the third century, women seem to have represented the majority of the Church's membership. This is remarkable, because it was also a time when among pagans they were noticeably in the minority. The common practice of female infanticide had assured this. But as a majority within the Church and a minority without, they were uniquely positioned to play a role in a miraculous century of church growth.

Historians have long known that the Roman Empire entered a prolonged decline in population by the end of the second century. Incessant warfare, famine, and plague all contributed to it. But a low birth rate was also to blame. There were far fewer women than men, and fewer women meant fewer births. Fewer births resulted in the incapacity of Roman society to replenish its population.

Remarkably, as pagan society withered, Christendom thrived. The third century saw Christians finally emerge from being a statistically irrelevant part of the population to claiming, by century's end, some ten percent of it. And it was female Christians who played a key role in the process of evangelization.

Since women were in short supply within the broader society, the Church's "surplus" of them meant they were likely to intermarry with pagan husbands. It is true that some patristic sources even from this early time expressed disapproval of intermarriage. There was reasonable concern that the woman's zeal would begin to fail in the face of a pagan husband's disapproval. Stark has observed one such statement by Tertullian. But he notes that the famous Christian moralist also disapproved of women wearing cosmetics. Since it is likely that his latter concern grew out of an existing practice from which women were not easily dissuaded, the same may be said of his ban on intermarriage. In other words, by objecting to intermarriage the author revealed that it was indeed happening, and on a scale large enough to warrant his published objections. Such statements are prescriptive rather than descriptive, and Tertullian likely would not have made them had there not been an existing issue to address.[42]

But whether they entered mixed marriages already as Christians, or made a marriage mixed by converting within it, women were one of the main transmitters of Christianity to pagan men. The result was a quiet evangelization that had momentous effects on the world around them. Within their homes, gathered by the hearth, wives collectively were in a position to witness Christianity on a scale far greater than that of martyrs in the arena. They may have lacked the large public audience of Perpetua and Felicity, but they more than made up for this through the personal influence they exercised within an ever-multiplying system of mixed marriages.

That women exercised a spiritual influence on their pagan husbands cannot be doubted. We have few descriptive sources to draw upon, but the abundance of prescriptive writings indicates that the Church expected wives to hold to the highest spiritual standard. Both Peter and Paul had attested to this. Peter charged them to be examples of piety to their husbands for their husbands' sake, while Paul claimed that Christian wives actually sanctify their non-believing spouses.[43]

We have considered ways in which the Church's teaching about female dignity would have ennobled women. It would also have affected their husbands. No doubt there were many boors among the latter who would have remained unmoved by Christian piety. Not a few would have resented the claims to spiritual equality. But within the mixed marriages that only increased during Rome's third-century demographic crisis, a significant number of men would have found it impossible to resist their wives' superior morality (combined, as it must have been, with Christian humility).

We can, perhaps, reasonably expect that within the domestic intimacy of marriage, one particularly noteworthy virtue slowly took root. This was sexual integrity, a key feature at the heart of what the West would become.

At first, the ideal of chastity must have seemed dubious, even ridiculous, to pagan men. But with time, it assumed a power within Christendom that would not be broken until modern times.

Sexually speaking, pagan Rome was a man's world in which male promiscuity was broadly celebrated and institutionalized. A relatively high percentage of men never married, preferring a lifelong sequence of mistresses and prostitutes over the responsibilities of a single wife. Those who did marry did so late in life but preferred virginal brides, typically in their early teens.

Though monogamy was an ancient social norm backed by the threat of criminal punishment, married men were culturally quite free to visit prostitutes and in many cases even keep extramarital concubines. Rome's culture of male virility encouraged not only numerous and frequent heterosexual relationships but homosexual ones as well. There was no social stigma attached to same-sex relationships, and many sources from the period speak of it as a completely normal way of life. To gain social approval, a man would typically engage in such an act with someone of lower social rank, particularly a slave. Slaves, it can be noted, were legally unprotected from all forms of sexual exploitation and abuse.

The Christian virtue of sexual purity, or chastity, offered a radically different cultural ideal. It redefined the purpose of human sexuality and linked it to salvation. It also contributed to a new definition of personal integrity, linking the body inseparably with the soul. This had been inconceivable to the ancients, who looked on the soul as eternal but the body as a disposable source of mere pleasure. What is more, chastity was a virtue that applied to men as well as women. Pagan sexuality, on the other hand, was for the most part a system of double standards that encouraged indulgence in men and abstinence in women. Finally, by directing sexual relations toward an exclusively monogamous marriage uniting one man and one woman for the duration of their lifetimes, it provided an opportunity to experience the divine, sacrificial love of God Himself.

This radical vision of sexuality was grounded in Christian anthropology and not, as modern detractors have claimed, in a system of mere precepts and regulations. In the aftermath of the sexual revolution, a secularized Western culture has come to see such regulations in a negative light, as unnecessary barriers to human happiness and fulfillment. This secularized Christendom regards the body as the ultimate point of reference in determining human fulfillment.

Traditional Christianity was more complex. It hallowed the spirit, but it also hallowed the body. For Christians, the body was an integral part of the human person, created by God and destined for eternal glory in the resurrection. Paul insisted that the body would rise from the dead, just as Jesus' body had.[44] And because of this, it was a matter of great concern to Christians how the body was treated in earthly existence. This is why, for instance, they never cremated it upon death. As Jesus' body was carefully and lovingly anointed and buried, so were those of all of His followers. What, the Christians might have asked, would the Resurrection of Christ have been like if His body had been burned to ashes, as was the custom then among pagans? As a general rule, to intentionally disfigure or destroy the body was considered a sin.

This is why Paul rebuked the Corinthians so strongly for their licentious sexual behavior. For through it they were corrupting their bodies, which were called to purity. Corinth, it might be noted, was notorious in the ancient world for the promiscuity of its citizens. The city was dedicated to Aphrodite, the goddess of erotic or sexual love. Public worship was centered on the city's main temple, which was served by a host of ritual prostitutes that at one time reached a thousand in number.

"Corinthian morality" was an epithet throughout the Roman Empire, and Paul appears to have had this in mind when he rebuked those who visited prostitutes. As his words reveal, his objection resulted from a belief in the sacramental holiness of the body. "Do you not know," he asked,

> that your bodies are members of Christ? Shall I therefore take the members of Christ and make them members of a prostitute? Never! Do you not know that he who joins himself to a prostitute becomes one body with her? For as it is written, "The two shall become one flesh." (1 Cor. 6:15–16 RSV)

The act of sexual intercourse, Paul indicated, unites one person to another in a way that transcends the mere physical act itself. This is why it has no legitimate place in human relationships outside of marriage.

Significantly, in the verses above Paul was not quoting the Old Testament, which, like paganism, allowed a man to divorce his wife (though not she him). He was quoting Jesus, who, in Mark's Gospel, paraphrases the account of Adam's marriage to Eve in Genesis, but then adds "What therefore God has joined together, let no man put asunder" (Mark 10:7–9; cf. Gen. 2:24). Jesus was responding to a Pharisee who asked if it was indeed acceptable for a man to divorce his wife. The answer was no. In other words, the Gospel's new commandment of sacrificial love extended to men who, for whatever reason, found themselves disinclined to care for or live with their wives. But now, by loving their wives as themselves, they could experience union with God. Marriage had become an experience of paradise.

Christendom's transformational imperative was bringing light to the benighted world of pagan Rome. It was enabling pagans to experience marriage as a sacrament, a mystery of the kingdom of heaven on earth. Once again, it was Paul who had most fully revealed this in the New Testament. He presented an image of marital union that transcended earthly exigencies like economic security, mutual affection, or sexual gratification. To be sure, none of these were renounced in Christian marriage. But the cross of sacrificial love was now placed at the center of the relationship between husband and wife. The wife was called to live in a loving, voluntary obedience to her husband, and the husband was called to live in a loving, self-emptying service to his wife.

And what was most remarkable, the monogamous marriage relationship (which even pagan Romans were expected to honor) no longer involved only two persons. The divine Person of Christ Himself was a third presence within it, sacramentally offering Himself to the couple and through their love for each other raising them up to heaven.

What human heart, jaded by the promiscuity and license of Roman culture, could remain indifferent to this exalted vision of marriage? What pagan man could sustain his culture's low esteem for women when his wife radiated the light of a superior moral vision? How could the possibility of paradise not draw him away from the paltry beliefs and values of his past?

Some men, no doubt, would have reacted with contempt, divorcing their strange and inconvenient Christian wives to start over with "normal" pagan ones. It appears from contemporary sources that this was not uncommon. Justin Martyr relates the story of one woman who tried sincerely to win her husband over to the gospel only to have him abandon her and return to a life of wanton promiscuity.

On the other hand, many were the men who found in their Christian wives an inspiration that pagan marriage, with its aimless sexuality and debased standard of love, utterly lacked.

A Century of Miraculous Growth

IT IS SOMETIMES SAID in our time that church growth is not about numbers. This is certainly true in one sense. Inner, spiritual growth is the ultimate measure of evangelization. But numbers matter too.

They certainly mattered for Luke, who had carefully counted "about three thousand souls" (Acts 2:41) who converted on the Day of Pentecost. And as time advanced, so did the numbers of Christian converts. This inevitably brought persecution, which resulted in still more growth. Because of a persecution wave in Jerusalem, Luke notes, Christians dispersed to other cities and there continued to grow in number. His victorious evangelical narrative concludes not with numbers, however, but with symbolism: By the end of Acts, Christians have expanded far beyond the limits of culturally provincial Jerusalem to engage even the court circles of the imperial capital of Rome itself. We may assume that a pattern of slow but steady growth characterized the Church during the remainder of the first century.

That Christianity was a religiously compelling but statistically still insignificant presence in the empire at the beginning of the second century is suggested in one of the few statements by contemporaries we have about this matter. The document is a letter by the Roman civil servant Pliny the Younger, dating to about 112. Pliny the Younger was the nephew of the famous author Pliny the Elder, who had been born during the reign of Tiberius and perished during the eruption of Vesuvius in AD 79. Pliny the Younger became a Roman statesman and served as senator, then consul, and finally as advisor to Emperor Trajan. His final state appointment was to the Province of Bithynia on the southern Black Sea coast, where he served as governor. It was in that office that the pagan statesman composed a letter to Trajan describing his efforts at suppressing Christianity at the beginning of the second century.

In his letter, Pliny made three significant observations about the Christians in his province. The first was that they were zealous for their faith and obstinate in keeping it. This perplexed the governor, who claims to have given them numerous opportunities to return to paganism. The second point is that they represented a religion that was by this time well known in the empire and growing. As he put it, "the contagion of this superstition has spread not only to the cities but to the villages and farms."

However, in addition to these two points about the strength and influence of Christians, Pliny indirectly suggests that the faith was still little known and probably rather limited in its adherence. This can be inferred from the fact that he was writing to the emperor for instructions because of his general ignorance about Christianity and Roman policies toward it. Since Pliny was a highly placed and experienced member of the imperial administration, with many years of service in the capital itself, it is hard to believe he would never have encountered Christians or discussed policies toward them if they had been a numerically significant part of the population. That he confesses ignorance about the matter suggests the opposite.

A century later, however, Tertullian could claim that the Christian population of the empire was now quite substantial, particularly in the cities. Of course, we have no contemporary statistics, no sources providing anything like an exact measure of its strength. No membership censuses were kept within the Church, and the imperial government, while used to conducting censuses for tax purposes, had no particular interest in monitoring religious affiliation. What most historians can say, however, is that after yet another century, in 300, the membership of the Church must have comprised, at the least, some ten percent of what many believe was an imperial population of around sixty million. That puts the Church's share at about six million. Greater estimates have been put forward, but most present scholarship—Christian and secular—is comfortable with the conservative figure of ten percent.

In his well-received study of the empire's Christianization, Rodney Stark provides a simple yet compelling model for how the ten percent figure could have been reached. Drawing from sociological studies of particularly successful modern cults such as the Mormons, he determined that a growth rate of some forty percent per decade (or 3.42 percent per year) was achievable. Taking the widely accepted figure of six million Christians in 300, he then applied his growth model, working backward. The result is a list of mathematically determined estimates ranging from one thousand Christians in AD 40 to 7,530 in 100, to 217,795 in 200, and to 1,171,356 in 250. This brings the estimate for the year 300 to the magic number of 6,299,832. Extending the model forward beyond 300 results in an estimate of 33,882,008 in 350, a generation after Emperor Constantine's conversion. At that point, the Christian population of the empire had become a majority.

Stark's growth model is elegant in its simplicity. Moreover, it self-consciously avoids any claims about growth that rely on supernatural assumptions. This, clearly, is not how Luke or the later apologists interpreted growth. They declared unselfconsciously that the Holy Spirit was at work in bringing large numbers of converts into the fold. The Acts of the Apostles has in fact sometimes been dubbed the Acts of the Holy Spirit. But such claims do not win sympathy in the scientific study of church history.

And in this sense, the third century, which began with the persecution of Severus and ended with the conversion of Constantine, can to a Christian only appear miraculous. During this century, the Church emerged from the obscurity of the catacombs to become a public presence, surpassing a million members by midcentury. Her prestige surged as her members cared for the empire's plague victims and offered a vision of marriage and the sanctity of life that helped solve its population decline. And, as irrational reactions by pagans claimed more and more innocent lives, the "blood of the martyrs," to paraphrase Tertullian's famous adage, became "the seed of the Church." In other words, persecution generated growth.

To many, that growth seemed unstoppable. It was surely advanced by the readiness of many Christians to enter into and participate in the society that surrounded them. While they may have been baptized into radically different beliefs and values than their pagan neighbors harbored, and withdrew secretly on the Lord's Day to worship behind closed doors, at the same time they seem to have held the view that it was their calling to engage the world around them.

A remarkable expression of this sentiment is found in the anonymous second-century *Epistle to Diognetus*. This work exudes a missionary, even gregarious spirit. It observes that normative Christians are externally no different from their pagan neighbors. They do not live in a separate community, do not dress or speak differently, do not follow peculiar customs. "But," the author declares,

> *inhabiting Greek as well as barbarian cities, according as the lot of each of them has determined, and following the customs of the natives in respect to clothing, food, and the rest of their ordinary conduct, they display to us their wonderful and confessedly striking method of life. They dwell in their own countries, but simply as sojourners. As citizens, they share in all things with others, and yet endure all things as if foreigners. Every foreign land is to them as their native country, and every land of their birth as a land of strangers. They marry, as do all [others]; they beget children; but they do not destroy their offspring. They have a common table, but not a common bed. They are in the flesh, but they do not live after the flesh. They pass their days on earth, but they are citizens of heaven.*[45]

Christians living in pagandom engaged the world around them, but remained always faithful to the kingdom of heaven.

As this work reveals, evangelistic engagement with Rome's pagan population was especially active in cities. It was there that Christian missionaries had planted the earliest demographic roots. True, Jesus had moved within primarily rural communities, but soon after Pentecost His apostles concentrated their missionary work on the empire's biggest cities. Jerusalem was naturally the first, where James appears to have served as the overseer, presiding as he did at the time of the important Apostolic Council. Antioch was next, where tradition places Peter for many years prior to his visit to and martyrdom in Rome. Paul would follow him to the capital, but not until missionary journeys had planted parish networks in cities that included Ephesus, Philippi, and Thessalonica.

Christianity was of course not the only alternative to the gods and goddesses of ancient Rome. By the beginning of the third century, the empire's urban population had become used to many new religions and lived in an atmosphere of teeming religious pluralism. All of this, interestingly, bears resemblances to the post-Christian Christendom of our time, where the motto "celebrate diversity" has replaced spiritual transformation as a moral imperative.

Religious pluralism was not particularly comforting for Rome's people. A dizzying array of deities arose, so great that no one could possibly appreciate or understand them all. Those who tried were forced to minimize their involvement in one cult in order to make space in their lives for others. This syncretism led to a growing superficiality lamented by numerous contemporaries. In fact, it became common to hedge one's loyalties by participating in multiple religious cults at once. In Egypt, one wealthy benefactor built temples to the traditional gods Jove, Minerva, Mars, Fortuna, Hercules, and Sula, but in the spirit of diversity opted to build one to the Persian deity Mithra as well. Another man served simultaneously as a priest in no fewer than four religiously disparate temples, perhaps like some Christian pastors of today who seek enrichment through non-Christian "spiritualities."

Religious pluralism brought spiritual confusion to Rome. For a still powerful and proud empire, this was a curse and in no way a blessing. By the early fourth century, some within the government were beginning to feel a need to intervene in public life and arrest the confusion.

The Great Persecution

TRAGICALLY, ONCE AGAIN the Roman state decided to use Christians as scapegoats. By the end of the third century, the Church had grown very large indeed, no longer feeling confined to the subterranean existence of early times. Some of her members were recognized public figures, including members of court. A swelling self-confidence was expressed by the fact that the Church was now openly building temples where her members gathered publicly on a weekly basis. According to the contemporary historian Eusebius, known for his hyperbole, this was the ultimate proof of the Church's impending victory.

> *What approbation the rulers in every church unmistakably won from all procurators and governors! How could one describe those mass meetings, the enormous gatherings in every city, and the remarkable congregations in places of worship? No longer satisfied with the old buildings, they raised from the foundations in all the cities churches spacious in plan. These things went forward with the times and expanded at a daily increasing rate . . .*[46]

Numbering some six million members, erecting temples throughout the empire, and enjoying a presence at the imperial court, the Church now had a subculture that was moving beyond the catacombs.

And then came one final blow. It was a persecution campaign that went further than any before it. Subsequently known as the Great Persecution, it was launched by Rome's last great pagan statesman.

Diocletian came to power in 284 by the same means as so many other Roman emperors—murder. He had been present during the journey of a Roman army from campaigning in Persia, when the Emperor Numerian was assassinated by a conspirator named Aper. The event was particularly strange, as Aper had Numerian killed secretly and his body sealed within the imperial litter for the duration of the journey. Finally, the army arrived in the town of Nicomedia, where, to everyone's horror, the litter was opened and Numerian's decomposing body exposed. The ambitious Diocletian now proved more adroit than Aper. He gathered the garrison together and denounced Aper as the assassin. His crocodile tears impressed the men, who acclaimed him

Emperor Diocletian
Underground of Diocletian palace, Split, Croatia. ©Cesarz - Shutterstock

Numerian's rightful successor. As they shouted their devotion to him, he raised his sword in the air and plunged it into the hapless Aper.

Diocletian inherited an empire in trouble, and he knew it. His entire reign was dedicated to rebuilding it. The most ambitious expression of this project was to reorganize its administration into western and eastern halves, with a system of four emperors ruling in collaboration with each other. Naturally, Diocletian assured that he would be the senior partner in the arrangement. The tetrarchy, as this system came to be known, was the first step toward what, after Constantine, would become a distinct empire centered in the East.

Having completed the new administrative arrangement, Diocletian appointed co-emperors for the West and East. He himself assumed office in the East, and established the Greek city of Nicomedia as his capital. In the West he appointed as one of his subordinates a man named Constantius.

This illustrious general had some time earlier taken as a wife—or possibly a concubine—a Christian woman named Helen. The union appears to have been a happy one, though after many years Constantius would leave her for a more politically advantageous marriage to the daughter of the senior emperor of the West, Maximian. But Helen's spiritual qualities deeply impressed Constantius, and, like many other pagan husbands in mixed marriages, he developed a strong respect for the Christian faith. And in the meantime, Helen bore him a son. In an act of submission to Diocletian, Constantius agreed to send the boy to the senior emperor's court in Nicomedia to live there as a political hostage. The son's name was Constantine.

During the first part of his reign, Diocletian showed a tendency toward the religious toleration of Christians. They were increasingly found in positions of public influence, and a trio of them named Dorotheus, Gorgonius, and Peter actually helped administer the imperial court. It was said, in fact, that Diocletian's wife and daughter were converts. But as these early years passed and Rome's endemic troubles persisted, Diocletian decided to alter his religious policies. He seems to have come under the influence of contemporary polemics against Christianity by pagans such as Porphyry, whose *Against the Christians* had just appeared. He was also increasingly susceptible to the influence of his subordinate emperor in the East, Galerius. The latter was fiercely opposed to the growing legitimacy of Christian culture and had begun using anti-Christian policies to advance his own political interests.

In 302, Diocletian met with Galerius, Porphyry, and other opponents of Christianization at his court in Nicomedia. The purpose of the meeting was to resolve the problem of Christendom's growing legitimacy and cultural influence in public life. There was real concern that by refusing to participate in the pagan sacrificial system, Christians were creating an alternative political culture. For centuries, Romans had regarded the regular sacrifices to the pagan gods as the reason for their ascendancy in the ancient world. Continued prosperity demanded that animals and libations continue to be offered in the public temples on a regular basis. And if a significant part of the population categorically rejected this custom and refused to sacrifice, the gods would in turn abandon the Romans. Was not the crisis of the previous century, which had seen the pagan population shrink and the Church grow, proof of divine displeasure?

The meeting of 302 was convened to find a solution to this impending calamity. And because its participants believed the hour was late and the threat overwhelming, they resolved on a merciless plan of action. The Christians of the empire, they concluded, must be totally eliminated.

Only one preparation remained to be made before the emperor and his advisors could proceed with their plan. A suppliant was dispatched to pagandom's most sacred shrine, the Oracle of Delphi near Athens. Since the time of Homer, this had been the site of pagan humanity's surest contact with the divine. The temple stood on the side of a mountain and was served by a priestess. She sat on a tripod within a dark, subterranean chamber of the temple, breathing fumes that emanated from a cleft in the rock beneath her. During a certain period of the year, she accepted questions from the suppliants who traveled from throughout pagandom to query her. It was believed that when she spoke, she was inhabited by Apollo himself.

Diocletian's suppliant arrived soon after the Nicomedia conference, and when he questioned the Oracle about putting the empire's Christians to death, the shaman ecstatically though cryptically answered in the affirmative. His plan thus confirmed, Diocletian launched the greatest organized persecution of Christians before modern times.

There are wide disagreements about the actual numbers of Christians killed or injured during the Great Persecution, as this event came to be known. Historically, Christian historians have measured casualties in the tens or even hundreds of thousands, though without ever insisting on a specific number. The lives of saints, many of them written years later, were very comfortable citing high figures. In one event, no fewer than twenty thousand martyrs were said to have been killed on a single day in Nicomedia alone. There can be no doubt the event actually occurred. It was triggered by the fact that Christians had boldly decided to build a temple in the eastern capital and to locate it within view of the emperor's palace. Diocletian resolved that the Christian temple had to go. On Christmas Day, his army surrounded it and burned it to the ground with the congregation locked inside.

It is not necessary here to establish definitively how many Christians were killed during the Great Persecution. What is important is to understand what this event meant in the history of Christendom. It revealed a growing crisis in the identity of Western civilization on the eve of Constantine's conversion to Christianity. In this sense, it was a kind of culture war, though one in which the pagans fought with swords as well as pens.

This combination of rhetoric and violence is particularly visible in the case of one of the martyrs, Katherine of Alexandria. Her life begins with a mother who, like many other women of the age, converted to Christianity after learning about it from a missionary. This woman remained married to her pagan husband, and it is hard to believe her piety did not have an effect on him. It certainly affected her daughter. Katherine, upon learning about Christ from her mother, made the decision to convert herself. After her baptism, she refused to remain quiet as her mother had and began to speak openly of the faith. This was well noted by her contemporaries, for her father was a wealthy and powerful magnate. The young woman achieved even greater distinction by her physical beauty and her brilliant mind. But as a convert to Christianity, she ceased to be inspired by the pleasures of the world. Power, wealth, philosophy, and beauty were forgotten as she directed her gaze toward heaven.

Eventually, her life relates, she was confronted by Maxentius, one of the tetrarchy's subordinate emperors, during his visit to Alexandria. The city was the cultural capital of the empire and the site of a developing conflict between paganism and Christianity. It was the renowned center of Neoplatonism, on the one hand, and of the earliest Christian schools on the other. It was here that theology had been born in the scholarship of apologists such as Clement and Origen.

Maxentius had come to Alexandria at least in part to promote the Great Persecution, but when he ordered public sacrifices to the pagan gods, Katherine confronted him as a missionary herself. In deference to her beauty and wealth, he hesitated. At first he tried to seduce her. Such an act was consistent with pagan morality and, as we noted in the previous chapter, with the precedent of earlier emperors such as Tiberius and Caligula. Indeed, contemporary testimonies about Maxentius's character fully support this detail in the life. When seduction failed, however, he sought to discredit her by compelling her to answer for her faith before a team of pagan intellectuals. There were many of these available at short notice in such a city. To the amazement of all, she not only withstood their arguments, but was said actually to have spoken with such learning about Rome's culture that these philosophers ultimately converted to Christianity. This was too much for Maxentius. The pen gave way to the sword, and Katherine was beheaded.

For all its violence, the Great Persecution was a failure. Even under a leader as visionary and vigorous as Diocletian, Roman pagandom in the early fourth century was not what it had been. Christendom had had three full centuries to supplant it, at first slowly and haltingly, but then with greater energy as conversions proceeded apace. Then, during the second half of the third century, Christendom became unstoppable.

Too many had by now converted to the new faith. And too many more pagans stood behind their Christian fellow-citizens, friends, or spouses. There was considerable sympathy for their counterculture. The fact that Christians were still in the minority was not very significant. They were a minority in numbers, but in spirit they were becoming a majority. As the life of Saint Katherine attests, they simply overpowered their pagan opponents with the majesty of their doctrine and the dignity of their deaths.

By 305, Diocletian realized as much. And so Rome's last great pagan statesman did something unprecedented. He abdicated his power and retired to his native Dalmatia, where he spent the remainder of his life farming cabbage. It was not a happy existence. Political reports continued to reach him at his villa, and the news was always bad. The continued failures of the persecution and the final collapse of the tetrarchy revealed that his vision of a revitalized pagandom was impossible to achieve. His final days thus passed in depression, and in 313 he killed himself.

It was the same year that Constantine, now emperor in the West, finally brought the Great Persecution to an end by legalizing Christianity.

CHAPTER THREE

From Rome to Byzantium

WITH THE COLLAPSE of the Great Persecution, it was clear that Christendom was in the world to stay. Diocletian had failed to eradicate it, and with his abdication the political will to preserve pagandom largely abdicated as well. Immediate successors like Galerius and Maximinus tried halfheartedly to revive the persecution but could attain no lasting results. There was too much popular sympathy and even support for the Christian subculture. Indeed, Galerius finally cancelled the persecution in his territories and, on the point of death from an excruciating case of stomach cancer, actually appealed to Christians to pray for him and the good of Rome.

The psychological effect of the persecution's failure must have been great. But even greater would have been the realization that the Church was growing at a phenomenal rate. By now she claimed as members well more than ten percent of the empire's population. And her growth showed no signs of slowing. Just the opposite. What is more, whatever she may still have lacked in numbers, her dynamic counterculture more than compensated for in spirit.

It is often asserted that the conversion of Emperor Constantine at this time was the event that caused the rapid transformation of Rome's religious demographics, resulting in an empire that was predominantly Christian within a century. But the historical record supports another interpretation.

Christianity did not take over the empire because Constantine converted to it. Constantine converted to it because it was taking over the empire.[47]

For three centuries, the Church had been laying the foundations of a highly developed civilization. Much of Christendom was already in place. Its culture possessed a strong sense of identity—much stronger than that of pagandom—and it was sustained by a living experience of the kingdom of heaven. This experience inclined it toward a dissatisfaction with the existing world but not a rejection of it. In fact, because of the Incarnation, the Christian faith looked precisely to the world as a place in which, through the Church, Christ made Himself present. This principle of heavenly immanence defined the Church's cosmology and directed it toward a transformation of the world.

And so the time had finally come for the Roman state to enter Christendom. In his conversion, Constantine was boarding a ship that had been sailing for a long time and had reached a momentous stage in its journey. It had successfully traveled the difficult journey from Jerusalem to Rome. Now it was time to navigate the waters from Rome to Byzantium.

The Conversion of Emperor Constantine

IT IS WORTH REFLECTING for a moment on the conversion of Constantine. The Roman world was no doubt stunned when it learned of this event. But it would not have seemed too far-fetched a possibility within the context of Constantine's own family. His mother, Helen, as we have seen, was a Christian herself. She was a convert and had taken considerable risks in living in a union with Constantius under the watchful eye of Diocletian. Almost nothing is known about Helen's interactions with her son during his childhood, but given the strong moral character she exhibited in later years she must have had, like so many other Christian women in mixed marriages, a formative influence within her household.

As for Constantine's father, Helen's influence appears to have led him to sympathize strongly with the Christians of the empire. He was one of the tetrarchy's subordinate emperors, and during the Great Persecution he

Saints Constantine and Helen
Icon of Saints Constantine and Helen at the Greek Orthodox Church in Cana, Israel.
©Gellia - Shutterstock

distinguished himself as the one partner who in his own territories refused to enforce Diocletian's harsh dictates.

During these years of persecution, the young Constantine found himself in Nicomedia, at Diocletian's court. He was forced along with his mother to observe the cruelties suffered by Christians in the East, where the violence was greatest, and to bide his time. Eventually, he knew, his period of political captivity would come to an end, and he would join his father in the West. It was a long wait. After Diocletian's abdication, he was transferred to the custody of Emperor Galerius, an even more ruthless enemy of the Christians. Then one night, after his dissolute new master had fallen into a drunken stupor, Constantine decided to act. He approached Galerius with a veiled request to leave the court on a pretense. Obtaining permission, he then flew toward the frontier in a wild ride through the night. Along the way, he disabled the horses at each post station to prevent pursuit. When Galerius awoke the next morning, Constantine was long gone, and he was soon reunited to his father in Gaul.

Constantine accompanied Constantius to Britain, where an uprising threatened. As the campaign advanced, however, Constantius suddenly died. He had enjoyed the devoted loyalty of his soldiers, and they now hailed Constantine as his father's successor. The new emperor accepted their acclamation. But he knew his title would remain contested until he confronted his main rival for mastery of the West, a usurper named Maxentius.

This tyrant had made a name for himself in Rome, where he established a stronghold based on military alliances and heavy taxation. However, the people of this greatest of all Christian cities did not trust Maxentius, and when he declared war upon the upstart Constantine, they naturally favored his enemy.

This led to one of the great battles of the ancient world, not in numbers but in significance. Constantine led his army south into Italy and camped on the northern side of the Tiber River near the Milvian Bridge, not far from Rome. The following morning he would meet his enemy Maxentius and the civil war would be decided.

That night, Constantine witnessed a vision in the sky. Historians have long puzzled over it, not least because it was recounted only years later by sources that had not been present at the time. What is more, those sources disagree over what exactly appeared before Constantine's eyes. One described an image of the Chi-Ro emblem and another the cross. Whatever the exact symbol was, Constantine was also said to have heard the words, as if from God Himself, "By this sign, conquer."

By this point Constantine had come a long way from the paganism of his ancestors. Raised by a Christian mother, supported by a sympathetic pagan father, he had become more and more influenced by Christianity as his youth advanced. As a sort of intermediary faith, he had recently expressed interest in the supreme god Sol Invictus, the Unconquerable Sun. This semi-monotheistic cult had gained a large following in Rome, and one emperor, Aurelian, had even placed its god at the top of the pagan pantheon. But the faith of his mother continued to draw Constantine. And now, on the eve of a battle that promised to decide his fate, he accepted as divine revelation the sign that appeared above him in the sky. The following morning he went into battle as a self-proclaimed Christian.

The resulting Battle of Milvian Bridge occurred in 312. During it Maxentius made the rash decision to meet Constantine's army on the north bank of the Tiber River instead of remaining within the safety of Rome's walls. In addition to the stone Milvian Bridge (which still stands to this day), he had ordered the construction of a smaller pontoon bridge in case a hasty retreat was needed. In the face of a devastating counterattack by Constantine, just such a contingency arose. However, as Maxentius and his men scrambled back across the river, the flimsy structure gave way underneath them. Maxentius fell into the water and was drowned, along with many of his men. Those stranded on the north shore were slaughtered.

Nothing now stood between Constantine and Rome. He entered the next day to the cheers of its citizens, many of whom were Christians. How fully he himself was committed to the faith at this point will never be known. Despite the Battle of Milvian Bridge, he continued in subsequent years to honor the cult of Sol Invictus by having the Sun God depicted on coinage, and he was not baptized until the very end of his life. Nevertheless, upon his victory over Maxentius in 312, Constantine embarked on a political course that brought unprecedented and lasting prestige to the Church. Along with the birth of the Church at Pentecost and the Great Persecution, his reign was a watershed moment in the history of Christendom.

During his reign, Constantine did much to establish Christianity in the Roman Empire. His first act, just a year after defeating Maxentius, was to issue the famous Edict of Milan. This formally terminated the persecution of Christians throughout the empire. Constantine was not yet in full possession of its territories, however, and new campaigns against another emperor of the East, Licinius, were required before the edict could fully take effect.

The Milan Edict created a legal order in which Christianity was tolerated along with the other religions of Rome. There was as yet no legal preference given to Christianity, though Constantine's other actions made clear his personal preference for it. He forbade the offering of pagan sacrifices by provincial governors, for instance. This was not so much to eliminate pagan worship as to open the way for Christians to begin filling regional political offices, since sincere Christians could not and would not assume an office that required pagan worship.

Constantine also passed a series of laws that favored Christianity and gave support to its cultural values. Crucifixions, long the most hideous form of public execution, were now formally abolished to honor the memory of Christ's Passion. Gladiatorial shows were also banned, as they were a reminder of the Roman state's erstwhile mistreatment of Christians. These shows were also the most flagrant example of pagandom's contempt for the virtue of mercy.

Constantine did not abolish slavery, nor would any Christian ruler until modern times. But he did ban one of its most abusive features, the absence of culpability when a master murdered a slave. The state now granted slaves its protection from arbitrary killing, elevating the values of the gospel over those of Aristotle. Perhaps most noticeably, the Church was favored when Constantine issued a law honoring Sunday, the Lord's Day, as the official weekly day of rest. Now Christian laborers would be assured of the opportunity to assemble together to worship whether their masters favored it or not.

Constantine not only worked to sanctify the Roman state; he worked to sanctify its public spaces, too. Though he had won the city of Rome in his war against Maxentius, he was disinclined to remain long in a city so filled with the monuments of pagandom. Every street he walked down, every square he saw was littered with temples to what he now recognized as false gods. Amphitheaters like the Coliseum reminded him of the innumerable martyrs his predecessors had put to death for public amusement.

Indeed, at this point Constantine may have shifted his understanding of who exactly his predecessors were. Were they Augustus, Tiberius, and Diocletian? Or were they Ignatius, Katherine, and Helen? It is fascinating to ponder the effects his conversion would have had on his personal identity. Constantine was perhaps the first Christian in history to be confronted so starkly by the gospel's countercultural challenge to the establishment. And to resolve the matter he decided to build a new capital for a Christian Rome.

The city of Constantinople was officially named New Rome, but inevitably it came to bear the name of its founder as well. It was built on the ancient Greek city of Byzantium, and historians have come to call the Christianized Roman Empire it ruled by that name. It was not only religious reasons that made Constantine select this site. Byzantium had a highly defensible location and access to commerce between Europe and Asia. But it was above all a capital that would lack pagan temples. Instead, its public spaces would be marked by Christian temples, and Constantine constructed two in particular that became important architectural monuments to Christendom. For the moment the more preeminent was the Church of the Holy Apostles, where he gathered the relics of Christendom's founders. The other was Hagia Sophia. Originally a relatively small church, it would one day, two centuries later, be rebuilt as the greatest temple in the world.

To these Constantine added temples in other cities of his empire. After his mother, Helen, made a pilgrimage to Jerusalem to discover the True Cross on which Jesus was crucified, he ordered the construction of a church on the site of the empty tomb. This came to be known in the East as the Church of the Resurrection, or Anastasis, and in the West as the Church of the Holy Sepulcher. Finally, back in Rome Constantine ordered the construction of a church to house the relics of Saint Peter; this church became known as Saint Peter's Basilica.

Constantine's most enduring act of establishing Christianity, after the Edict of Milan, was to gather the empire's Christian bishops at a council in the city of Nicaea in 325. This, the First Ecumenical Council, was assembled to resolve the question of Christ's identity. An Alexandrian priest named Arius had gained a large following by claiming that Christ was a great man but not divine. This doctrine, known later as Arianism, deviated from traditional Christianity as bishops such as Athanasius of Alexandria understood it. The result was tremendous strife within the Church.

Since Constantine now regarded the population of the Church as essentially that of the empire, he convened hundreds of bishops from throughout the realm, at state expense, to resolve the issue. Much has incorrectly been made of the emperor's role in the Council of Nicaea, with claims popularized in recent years that he dominated the discussions and issued orders to the bishops to determine the outcome. The only thing he was determined to do, in fact, was to allow the bishops an opportunity to reach a conciliar decision. That they did, and they enshrined it in a statement of belief that came to be known as the Symbol of Faith or Nicene Creed. Its precision in defining Christ as "of one essence with the Father" is a sign of how very important apostolic doctrine was in early Christendom.

Thus Constantine began the long and ever-incomplete process of integrating Christianity and government. He fell short of this goal on numerous occasions, sometimes notoriously. The case of his second wife Fausta and his son Crispus is an example. We will never know with certainty what was behind the decision, but in 326 Constantine ordered the executions of both. A possible explanation for the otherwise capricious and senseless act is based on indications that Fausta may have resented Crispus, the issue of Constantine's first wife, and to orchestrate his downfall slandered him with the charge of seeking to seduce her. Constantine, a strict moralist when it came to sexuality, became outraged and ordered his son's execution. Soon after this, however, he ordered Fausta's death. This execution may have resulted when the emperor discovered, too late, that the accusation against his son was totally fabricated by Fausta, and that she herself may have seduced the youth. Overcome with agonizing regret over his first action, he ordered her to be drowned in a hot bath.

Such occasions of violence on the throne may be the reason Constantine deferred his baptism until the end of his life. He apparently held the belief that if he, as ruler, committed sins after his baptism they would not as easily be remitted.

In any case, he finished his life's journey as a member of the Church. As he approached the end, his thoughts turned ever more toward the memory of his now-departed Christian mother. Helen had been the first to share Christianity with him, and the image of her lifelong meekness must have been a comforting salve for a man haunted by acts of manipulation and violence. It was certainly an inspiration.

While Constantine had been feeding his ambitions at the side of a father who had abandoned her for political gain, Helen had been living out her life in modest obscurity. While he had been destroying his rivals for supreme power in the world's greatest empire, she had been planting charities for the well-being of the poor. While he had been erecting an urban monument named for himself, she had been visiting the city of Christ's death and Resurrection. We know that the fragments of the True Cross Helen sent to her son in Constantinople were received with great devotion. Perhaps it was then that Constantine began to plan his baptism. In any case, following Helen's example, he expressed the desire to make a pilgrimage to Jerusalem and to use the occasion to be baptized in the Jordan River.

Alas, he never fulfilled the intention. But his final days were spent on a journey that brought him to his mother's native town at the eastern end of the Sea of Marmara. To honor her memory, he had renamed the town Helenopolis. No pagan emperor had ever so publicly dignified a woman. He had followed this with the dedication of a church there in memory of Saint Lucian, one of the Great Persecution's last martyrs, who had died at Nicomedia when Helen was living there. He was one of her most beloved saints.

It was during a visit to Helenopolis in 337 that Constantine fell ill. He called for the local bishop, Eusebius of Nicomedia, and received the triple immersion of Christian baptism at his hands. The contrast this deathbed act made to those of his imperial predecessors could not have been more dramatic. As they lay dying, Roman emperors from Augustus to Tiberius to Vespasian to Diocletian had fancied themselves gods, and the pagan priesthood had been devoted to acknowledging them as such. Now, the Roman emperor submitted himself to a Christian priest who claimed to serve only the one true God.

The founder of Christian statecraft died on the Day of Pentecost, still wearing his white baptismal robe.

The Sanctification of the State

WE HAVE SEEN how traditional Christianity assigned a redemptive purpose to the world. The Church had been placed in the world to sanctify it and to bring it into a correct relationship with God. According to the Gospel, the world existed in a corrupted and demon-riddled condition. But since God had become man and had joined Himself eternally to His creation, He had opened the way toward reconciliation between that creation and Himself.

The Church was therefore given a ministry of sanctifying the world. All areas of human life became subject to this ministry. They included the relationships established through marriage, for instance, but they also included other relationships such as those that were social or economic. The sanctification of the world extended to the time of the calendar and the space of places of worship. Art was sanctified, too, as was language when used in worship. The Greek letters *chi* and *ro*, when joined intentionally to honor the name of the Savior, became holy. Even the material creation received a special honor in the sacraments. Water, as Tertullian had indicated so eloquently, became the means of working the world's redemption. Wheat became Christ's very Body and grapes His Blood.

Could not that realm of human culture and civilization known as government, then, also participate in the sanctification of the world? With Constantine's conversion, even this part of the creation now came within the scope of the Church's cosmic ministry.

Statecraft was, to be sure, a problematic area of human life from the Church's perspective. This was not because the Bible provided no guidance for conducting government. The Old Testament was filled with both righteous and unrighteous examples of it. Even the New Testament made reference to the government, enjoining Christians in most cases to be submissive to it.

What was difficult for the Church was the place of violence and coercion in government. This could not be sanctified because it was not part of God's original creation but a sinful corruption of that creation. This had been more than evident in the Roman government's treatment of Jesus at His judgment and crucifixion. It was evident also in the pagan government's policies of persecution, which had only recently come to an end with the Edict of Milan. Now that the government was in the hands of a Christian, though, many wondered whether Constantine would be able to live like a Christian and apply to his actions the gospel commandments of mercy and forgiveness.

Constantine's conversion to Christianity earned him many enemies, not all of them pagans. Many have been Christians, and curiously more of them live in our time than in his. There is very little suggestion that fourth-century Christians, many of whom had barely survived the recent persecution, resisted the idea of a Christian sovereign or had scruples concerning his legitimacy. Indeed, just the opposite is true. What we actually see is a chorus of contemporary approval and support.

But in much later times, the first Christian emperor has become the object of widespread criticism and even condemnation. He is sometimes presented as a foolishly credulous ruler who saddled the Roman state with an apathetic religion at a time when domineering values were needed. Others have seen him as a cynical statesman who appropriated Christianity in order to co-opt the Church. And there are many more who have simply been scandalized by his acts of political violence, such as his decision to execute his wife and son.

Among modern Christians, however, an even more damning and influential indictment is made. This is often expressed by the term *constantinianism*.

The word has been given wide circulation especially by modern Protestants who regard the rise of a Christian state to be a betrayal of the Church's true vocation.

Early expressions of this idea are to be found during the Reformation, when Roman Catholicism's official hold on European statecraft represented an obstacle to reform. More than this, all that was considered wrong with Western Christianity at that time—the papacy, clericalism, monasticism, sacramental worship—was traced back to the fourth century, when the Church "fell" into worldliness and superstition. Constantinianism became a catchphrase for much that was wrong with post-apostolic Christianity, supporting the historically ignorant view that between the age of the apostles and the time of Martin Luther stretched an unmitigated period of graceless idolatry.

Modern theologians have given constantinianism a more sophisticated meaning. Some have used it to describe a form of Christianity that in their view has become a bulwark for politics and an obstacle to the gospel. Christian pacifists like Stanley Hauerwas have been particularly drawn to this line of criticism, claiming that the rise of a Christian state led inevitably to the collapse of the original meaning of Christian identity. As Christians flooded the Church in order to become better integrated into Rome (or Byzantium, or England, or America), their commitment to the gospel dissolved. The result of this approach is a kind of retroactive puritanism, a tendency to purge the past of those elements of historical Christianity that modern, largely Calvinist models of faith cannot accommodate or tolerate.

What is more, such criticisms are often based on a skewed account of the history. With Constantine, the Church surely did enter a period in her history marked by recurring temptations toward political servility. Below I will discuss a particularly noxious form of this known as caesaropapism. But that is not the only or most important outcome of his conversion.

One theologian who has recently come to the defense of Constantine's legacy is Peter Leithart, himself from a Reformed and therefore Calvinist background.[48] In addition to reviewing a range of historical details and nuances often ignored by his fellow Protestant critics, Leithart gives special attention to the sacramental character of traditional Christianity. He notes that pagan Rome was a civilization of blood sacrifice. Every city had elaborate public rituals in which animals were slaughtered as offerings to the gods for the well-being of the state. The public games were effectively human sacrifices. The belief was that the political order could not exist without sacrifice.

What Constantine did, remarkably, is to replace blood sacrifice with the Church's liturgical, bloodless sacrifice. For the first time in history, human civilization depended on the sacramental presence of the Incarnate God. The Eucharist brought an end to sacrifice. Nothing more could be done by human beings once the Son of God had offered Himself on the Cross. All they could do was to follow Him there, taking up the cross by loving one another. "I require mercy and not sacrifice," Jesus had repeated from the Prophet Hosea (Matt. 12:7, quoting Hos. 6:6). In fact, love was the one way the Christian could enter into the event of Christ's Passion, offering himself as a "living sacrifice" (Rom. 12:1).

Completely refuting the claims of Constantine's detractors, then, Leithart notes that by abolishing public sacrifices and establishing eucharistic worship throughout the empire, Constantine effectively opened the way for replacing his subjects' allegiance to the earthly state with an allegiance to the kingdom of heaven.[49] Rome was now, at least in principle, a "eucharistic *civitas*" whose model was not an earthly order but an eschatological one, or, in other words, paradise.

It might be noted that Leithart does not stop here but goes on to offer a chilling reflection on what happens when the Christian state so constituted does indeed fall from its sacramental foundation. It degenerates into what he calls "nihilistic politics." In modern times, he observes, secularism prevents the state from honoring a higher power, whose existence it rejects either formally or in practice. Neither Christianity's bloodless sacrifice of the Eucharist nor paganism's blood sacrifices of animals and humans have any formal legitimacy. But the state still requires a kind of sacrifice through acts of public devotion and submission to it. And in the post-Christian Christendom of the twentieth century such acts again assumed an almost

ritual form when millions were put to death in the "sacred name" of the pro-
letariat, the master race, or even the autonomous individual.

Christendom Holds Its Breath

THAT THE CHRISTIAN STATE founded by Constantine the Great failed
to be perfectly Christian is revealed in the events that followed his death in
337. Since Constantine had executed his eldest son and potential heir, Crispus (along with his wife, Fausta), years earlier, the succession went to a triumvirate of much younger sons, all named monotonously after their father.
Constantine II (aged 21), Constantius II (aged 20), and Constans (aged 17)
divided the realm between them. But within a few years, the eldest among
them attacked the youngest and was defeated and killed by him. Then Constans himself was killed during an insurrection, leading to the consolidation
of the entire empire under Constantius. But as Diocletian had shown, Rome
was too great a territory for one man to rule alone, and Constantius decided
to make a cousin named Julian his subordinate emperor. Julian, however,
chafed at the arrangement and went to war against his patron. Before the
armies met in 360, Constantius died, leaving Julian the sole emperor.

Constantine's sons had shown an alarming inclination toward Arianism,
and many of the empire's Orthodox may have breathed a sigh of relief on
Julian's accession. But the sigh was cut short by what happened next. Julian,
who had been raised a Christian and was even an ordained reader, suddenly
and unexpectedly renounced his faith. He became, to posterity, Julian the
Apostate.

The reasons may have had something to do with the fact that Christians
had viciously murdered his family. In the aftermath of Constantine's death,
Constantius—Julian's future patron—had ordered the massacre of almost all
male relatives to preclude rivalry to the brotherly triumvirate. The act was
not particularly remarkable and actually had an established place within
the political culture of pagan Rome. As we saw, for instance, Tiberius had
treated the family of his own protégé and heir Caligula similarly. The massacre of potential rivals was certainly an effective way of securing power

Emperor Julian the Apostate

and would prove depressingly commonplace throughout the history of Byzantium.

The hypocrisy of Constantius's Christian statecraft notwithstanding, Julian announced that he had become a pagan. In spite of his carefully chosen Christian tutors, as a youth he had fallen in love with classical mythology for both its literary qualities and its religious values. He had even made a pilgrimage to Ephesus to study secretly under a neoplatonic philosopher named Maximus. Julian then traveled to Athens to partake of classical paganism at its source. While residing in the city, he formed incongruous friendships with two fellow students who would go on to play an important role in the Church, Basil the Great and Gregory the Theologian. It was in Athens that Julian finally renounced Christianity. He would even go on to immerse himself in a basin of bull's blood as a ritual act of renouncing his baptism.

In a certain sense Julian the Apostate was, to paraphrase his modern admirer Friedrich Nietzsche, a spirit born before his time. He was the West's first convert from Christianity to paganism. He was also the only ruler in Christendom openly to renounce his faith until the French Revolution.

Julian was not content to practice paganism in the confines of his court. Just the opposite. He saw himself as a heroic, godlike restorer of pagandom. It was said that he actually considered himself the reincarnation of Alexander the Great, who had spread Hellenism throughout the world. Julian not only advocated the public reintroduction of pagan cults but wrote tracts on how to promote them among his subjects. It was a new culture war.

Sharing the classical contempt for mercy and humility, Julian regarded Christianity as a cultural disease that had infected the entire empire. His cultural program, based on paganism, would bring healing through education and, when necessary, violence. He especially emphasized certain principles that would make paganism competitive against Christian cosmology. One was charity. He lamented the fact that pagans were always outdone by Christians in providing for the material needs of their people. The second principle he appropriated was heavenly immanence. In books such as *On the Gods and the World,* he and court intellectuals countered the Church's sacramental worship and advanced a program of new rituals that would emphasize man's immediate experience of the divine in this life. In a short time, Julian had begun to organize an integrated imperial cult with priests appointed directly by him to advance the civic faith. He also reintroduced the persecution of Christians.

One of the strangest expressions of Julian's cultural program was a project to rebuild the Jewish temple in Jerusalem. As a former Christian, he was aware that the destruction of the temple by the Romans had been prophesied by Jesus. By rebuilding it, he believed he could undermine the Christian faith and bolster Judaism as an alternative to it. The project was a complete failure. Even non-Christian sources from the time reported that efforts to restore the foundation were met with setbacks so perplexing and mysterious as to appear divinely ordained.

Julian did not live long enough to be disappointed, however. As construction reached a dead end, he was in the East on a campaign against the Persians. With characteristic boldness, he led his soldiers in defending against a Persian attack, and while charging into the enemy line was struck by a spear. It penetrated his liver, and the enormous quantity of viscous blood that erupted from the wound signaled that he would not recover. Having been dragged from the scene by attendants, he died in his tent. A contemporary report stated that in his death agony he raised his eyes toward heaven and conceded, "Thou hast conquered, O Galilean!"

It is hard to know what would have become of Constantine's legacy had Julian the Apostate reigned as long as his predecessor in cultural warfare, Diocletian. As it was, he died less than two years after becoming sole emperor. Not until modern times would another internal political assault on Christendom occur. For now, with all its flaws and shortcomings, the legacy of Constantine was assured.

CHAPTER THREE

Symphony and Caesaropapism

THAT LEGACY WAS CHARACTERIZED by a close relationship between the emperor and the bishops. This was not, emphatically, a relationship between "church and state." There was no actual relationship between Church and state at this time because the state was a part of the Church. The distinction between the two realms, so common in the secularized political ideology of modern Christendom, would not have made sense in Byzantium. Only after its model of statecraft was discarded in the West after the Great Schism did the distinction become a possibility.

For now, Byzantium offered Christendom a model of statecraft that came to be known as *symphony*. The emperor, as head of the state, was expected to rule in harmony with his Church's bishops. Appropriating the enormous political machinery of Roman autocracy, he would issue laws, raise taxes, support the clergy, and suppress heresies for the supposed benefit of the Church. He would be afforded many prerogatives in church life, but in the end he was expected to know his place as a layman with a layman's ministry—however unique that ministry may have been. Like all ideals, symphony often miscarried, and we will consider some notorious examples below. But it remained the political heart of Christendom for more than a millennium.

Symphony found early expression at the end of the fourth century during the reign of one of only two other Byzantine emperors to receive Constantine's illustrious epithet. Theodosius the Great came to power as a champion of Christian statecraft, but he went even further than Constantine the Great in establishing it. Along the way, he showed particular care to work with the bishops and, when expected, to defer to them.

This was apparent in the face of heresy. Like Constantine, Theodosius was alarmed by the continued disagreements among his subjects about the person of Jesus. Arianism had gone underground after the First Ecumenical Council but had reemerged during subsequent years. By the end of Constantine's reign, the emperor had actually shown sympathy for advocates of Arianism such as Eusebius of Nicomedia, the bishop who baptized him. As we saw, Constantine's son Constantius had favored the heresy. And in the years after Julian's death, it found support in the reign of an emperor named Valens.

Like Constantine, Theodosius desired an empire in which his Christian subjects shared a single faith defined by the bishops. To achieve this, in 380 he issued the Edict of Thessalonica, declaring that only one form of Christianity was to be considered "catholic" by the government. His definition of catholicity is interesting. It identified the Apostle Peter with the true faith. It also traced that faith down to Theodosius's own generation by identifying it with certain contemporary bishops who were linked to the apostolic teaching of Peter. No doctrinal definition of catholicity was offered, so venerable were these bishops and their jurisdictions. Rome was one of these jurisdictions, but it was not the only one. Alexandria was also identified as a standard of catholicity. Rather than assert submission to Rome, then, Theodosius was claiming that the catholic Church was conciliar and looked to more than any one territorial bishop for her identity.

In promoting unity, Theodosius also followed Constantine's example by calling for an assembly of the empire's bishops to clarify the Church's teaching about the person of Jesus. Hundreds of bishops came to Constantinople in 381 to constitute what came to be known as the Second Ecumenical Council. Its main achievement was the augmentation of the Nicene Creed. The council's definitive statement of the faith included clauses about the Holy Spirit proceeding "from the Father," and about the unity of the "one, holy, catholic, and apostolic Church." Though Arianism would continue for years to come, and even be reborn in modern Christendom among a body called the Jehovah's Witnesses, the Second Ecumenical Council marked the effective end of this heresy's influence within the Byzantine state.

Theodosius was prepared to use the coercive resources of the state to support the Church's struggle against heresy. He was also ready to use these resources against paganism. While Constantine had assured toleration of non-Christians in the Edict of Milan, his successors had not been so generous. Constantius had formally forbade public sacrifices. And Gratian, Theodosius's immediate predecessor, had ordered Rome's ancient Altar of Victory dismantled and the Vestal Virgins disbanded. For his part, Theodosius set his eyes on the temple of Serapeum in Alexandria.

This temple to the god Serapis was one of ancient Rome's most revered pagan shrines. As Christianity advanced and the old religion retreated, pagans had grown increasingly restive in the great Egyptian city. When the local bishop dismantled a temple of Dionysius and paraded its idols through the streets to discredit paganism, an anti-Christian riot broke out. After attacking Christian temples and the worshippers in them, a mob of pagans withdrew to the huge Serapeum and turned it into an armed fortress. Along the way they seized additional Christians in the streets and once behind the Serapeum's walls, tortured them. Some they even crucified on the walls. Theodosius initially offered clemency to the brigands if they surrendered. When they did not, he ordered the temple seized and destroyed, many of its defenders being killed in the process.

Though paganism would continue to limp along with ever-decreasing influence, as a cultural force it was by now largely spent. The destruction of the Alexandrian Serapeum is a significant signpost in this historical transition. Pagandom was fading fast, and there would prove to be no going back until modern times.

Another dimension to the principle of symphony appeared during the reign of Theodosius. If the ruler correctly recognized his place within the Church, he was supposed to be subject to interventions by the bishops in cases of misrule. This, it must be said, almost never happened, so awesome was the status of Roman autocracy. But even Eusebius, in a panegyric on the life of Constantine, made the emperor's legitimacy contingent on his fulfilling the will of God.

In 390 an actual test case for the legitimacy of symphony arose. In that year, Theodosius gravely overstepped his role as a defender of the peace when a riot broke out against the government in Thessalonica. In a rage, he ordered a summary massacre of all the citizens involved. The result was the deaths of thousands, many of whom were innocent.

In pagan Rome there would have been no legitimate recourse against the autocrat. It was, after all, his empire. But in Christendom he was now morally accountable. Bishop Ambrose of Milan therefore stepped forward to chastise the emperor. Recalling the prophet Nathan's intervention against King David, who had used his royal power to kill unjustly, Ambrose ordered

Theodosius to repent of his sin before again receiving communion. He even barred the emperor from his cathedral until his penance was completed.

Theodosius finally submitted, and an important precedent was set. In the centuries ahead, the principle of symphony would imply a moral accountability that provided Christendom with a kind of religiously based moral constitution. Nothing like this had ever occurred in the world before, and the moral absolutes of traditional Christianity were responsible.

The principle of symphony was central to Theodosius's policies of protecting the Church from heresy and pagan violence. But it was an ideal always in danger of distortion. Eventually it would open the way for imperial mismanagement of church affairs and even for the imposition of heresy. Before that happened, however, Byzantine autocracy's capacity for mischief exposed itself in a more petty manner, in an episode that involved a vain empress, a grasping eunuch, and a morally uncompromising churchman.

After Theodosius's death, the eastern half of the empire was ruled by his son Arcadius. A man of little will and even less vision, Arcadius had married a woman named Eudoxia. She was his opposite. Their union was a strange one, even more so because it had been engineered for the political gain of a court eunuch named Eutropius. Castrated men had recently become a common sight at the Byzantine court, as Eastern practices of maintaining political integrity were

St. Ambrose of Milan

beginning to seep into imperial politics. The Church's teaching against the practice of bodily mutilation, like her teaching about mercy toward one's enemies, was frequently disregarded in the disorienting atmosphere of high politics. By law eunuchs could not rule, and by definition they could not produce successors. So they became a trusted if not completely respected part of court culture.

Eutropius was a particularly ambitious example. He appears to have arranged the murder of his chief rival for influence over Arcadius and then to have put himself forward as an adviser when the question of marriage was raised. He knew of the equally ambitious Eudoxia and offered her his recommendation to Arcadius in exchange for a lifetime of court influence under her. She took him up on the offer, but then decided after the wedding to shorten Eutropius's lifetime. When he realized that she had played him and not he her, he fled the court and took up sanctuary in the capital's chief cathedral.

Hagia Sophia was not yet the architectural wonder it would one day be, but it did contain one of Christendom's spiritual wonders. His name was John Chrysostom, and he was the archbishop of Constantinople. He had come to the capital from Antioch, where he had distinguished himself with his fine oratory and brilliant insight into the scriptures. He was also known as a moral stalwart, fearless in challenging the wealthy and powerful members of his congregation. "If you have two pairs of shoes at home," he told his wealthiest parishioners, "then you have stolen one of them from the poor!"

Inspired by the heavenly standards of the gospel, Chrysostom was simply uncompromising. In Constantinople, he had already earned the suspicions of Eudoxia, who resented his patent disregard of private property and the majesty of the imperial court. So when a terrified Eutropius arrived at the cathedral one day seeking episcopal protection from imperial tyranny, Chrysostom provided it.

Eudoxia was enraged. She began to poison Arcadius's views of John. Then, knowing the archbishop had enemies within the church hierarchy, she manipulated a council of bishops known as the Synod of the Oak to have him deposed. In 403 this body ruled that John was a heretic. She now sent him into exile from the capital. However, no sooner had he departed under armed guard than Eudoxia, then pregnant, suffered a miscarriage. Intensely superstitious, she ordered his return and the restoration of his office.

But the fickle empress could not tolerate Archbishop John for long. Soon after his return, she erected a gilded statue of herself on the square directly in front of the cathedral. The ceremony of the idol's unveiling occurred on a Sunday, the Lord's Day, at the moment when John was presiding at the eucharistic service in Hagia Sophia. This was too much for John. Soon after, Byzantium's most eloquent bishop preached a homily designed as a chastisement of the empress. Its subject was the fall of John the Baptist in the face of female iniquity at court. "Again Herodias is enraged, again she dances," he declared. "Again she seeks John's head on a platter!"[50]

This time Eudoxia, with the cowed Arcadius looking over her shoulder in silence, ordered John's permanent expulsion from the capital. He was sent under armed guard to the most distant part of the empire, Armenia. Once the honored and beloved archbishop of Byzantium's capital city, he ended his life as a disgraced exile. Exhausted and exposed to the point of sunstroke, he finally died on a remote, dusty trail while being driven relentlessly by his guards. Nevertheless, his final words, "Glory to God for all things," were those of faith and gratitude.

The story of John Chrysostom's fall from favor is not a story of ecclesio-political symphony, but of ecclesio-political malfeasance. It was the story of Eudoxia's improper use of imperial authority to silence a critic and eliminate him from the capital. But an even graver distortion of symphony emerged within the Byzantine state later in the fifth century. It arose not from intentional malfeasance, but from misfeasance—that is, from the mistaken conviction that forcible action against the bishops was in the genuine interest of the Church.

The name that has been given to this idea by posterity is *caesaropapism*. The word is deeply anachronistic. Coined as late as the eighteenth century by a Protestant named Justus Boehmer, it carries a peculiarly anti-Roman theological prejudice. This is all the more remarkable in that the word is applied almost exclusively to the record of Eastern Christian statecraft.

Caesaropapism obviously has its roots in two words, *caesar* and *papism*. The first identifies the agency of the emperor and the second that of the popes. The image is of a ruler who demands supreme control over the Church in a way comparable to that of the medieval popes, who for Boehmer's generation constituted the ultimate example of the misuse of power. This image has no historical place in early Byzantine statecraft, as papal supremacy would not emerge for centuries to come. But the word has caught on in the modern historian's vocabulary, and in fact, it captures better than any other word the tendency of some Byzantine emperors to arrogate control of church policy and, in the face of episcopal resistance, to cause harm.

An early expression of this tendency occurred in the middle of the fifth century. In 451 the Fourth Ecumenical Council held at Chalcedon had alienated a large part of the empire's Egyptian and Syrian population, which subsequently broke from the catholic Church. Again, the conflict was about the person of Christ. The Orthodox resolved at the council that Jesus possessed both divine and human natures, and that each remained intact after the Incarnation, "without confusion." This "two natures" position was rejected by the monophysites, or "one nature" party, which now withdrew from communion. The division was worsened by the fact that the monophysites had long felt themselves to be second-class citizens within the Greek-dominated Byzantine Empire.

Byzantium's emperors initially supported the Orthodox position. But as time passed, they realized that the loss of the empire's southern population to heresy was a severe threat to their rule over that area. So, in order to encourage reintegration of Syriac and Coptic subjects, Emperor Zeno decided in 482 to issue unilaterally an edict known as the *Henotikon*. It declared that there were in fact no real doctrinal grounds for division after all, and in defiance of the recent council's resolutions ignored totally the question of Christ's person.

Such an action was consistent with Byzantine precedent; Theodosius, as we saw, had issued the Edict of Thessalonica about catholicity in a similar manner. In that case, however, the Orthodox bishops had supported him. They did not support Zeno. They had rallied behind the late Pope Leo of

Rome, who had written a document called the *Tome* used at the council and accepted in a conciliar way by its members. The bishops now regarded Zeno's statement as a negation of that conciliar definition of the faith.

By this time, however, the emperor had considerable leverage in the appointment of the Church's leading bishops. The patriarch of Constantinople was understood to be thoroughly dependent on the emperor's favor, and even the distant bishop of Rome was not customarily enthroned until after the emperor had confirmed his nomination.

In Constantinople, the patriarch at this time was Acacius. He was thoroughly subservient to Zeno and in fact may have been the actual author of the *Henotikon*. He now was condemned by Pope Felix III of Rome for his failure to resist the emperor and his apparent refusal to submit to the decisions of the council at Chalcedon. It was no easy matter to excommunicate Acacius, however, as he enjoyed the emperor's protection in the capital. Just as the power of Empress Eudoxia could result in John Chrysostom being deposed and ejected, so the power of Emperor Zeno could be used to protect Acacius from the Church's Orthodox bishops.

Pope Felix therefore appealed to a group of monks in the capital known as the "Sleepless Ones," a name given in honor of their rule of continual prayer and worship. These monks had tended in the past to side with the papacy on the matter of enforcing Chalcedon. They now expressed a readiness to help in the struggle against the *Henotikon*.

The plan that resulted was almost comical. Knowing of the extreme danger involved in confronting Acacius directly, the monks devised a way of passing on the pope's excommunication without, they hoped, being detected. On a day when the patriarch was due to celebrate the Divine Liturgy, the monks gained access to the altar. There they stood reverently behind Acacius until the right moment presented itself. One of them then produced the bull of excommunication from his pocket and artfully pinned it to the back of the patriarch's vestments. The monks quickly departed unnoticed from the church and fled back to their monastery.

By the time the patriarch was alerted that he was serving the liturgy with a bull of excommunication on his back, it was too late to confront those who had served it. The Acacian Schism, as it came to be known, would last until 519.

Two Visions of the Christian State

IN THE MEANTIME, Byzantium inspired two distinct visions of the Christian state. They were in some ways complementary and in others completely different. Both would endure for centuries to come. The first was that of Eusebius of Caesarea. The second was that of Augustine of Hippo.

Eusebius is often called the father of church history because of his famous and valuable narrative of the Church's first three centuries. This title is not correct and betrays an academic and even secularist prejudice. The Evangelist Luke is the father of church history, by virtue of his narrative known as the Acts of the Apostles. Luke's work is by no means lacking in what professional historians consider rational inquiry and the empirical use of sources. It is true that it is not scientific in the sense that it does not suspend faith in the supernatural forces that influenced church history. But in our postmodernist era many an historian has insisted that a purely "objective" or disengaged approach to the past is impossible in any case. Be that as it may, Luke was no less rational than professional historians in his careful arrangement of a narrative (discussed in chapter one above) consisting of a thematic beginning, middle, and end. And he was scrupulous in his presentation of evidence, the acquisition of which required tireless research (a process he alludes to in the preface to his Gospel).

But if Eusebius is not the father of church history, he is the next in line to undertake it seriously. His *Ecclesiastical History* is a massive account of the Church's experience all the way to his own time, when Emperor Constantine converted to and then legalized the faith. Eusebius was the author of many kinds of writing, but this work is what has made him famous. Less well known is a shorter work he composed on the thirtieth anniversary of Constantine's accession to power, entitled *Oration in Praise of Constantine*. It is this work and not his *History* that best reveals his view of the new Christian state. To understand the work's significance, it is helpful to consider the world in which Eusebius lived as a bishop.

That world had been, prior to Constantine, one of social ostracism and perpetual danger for Christians. The Great Persecution had ravaged the Church, claiming the lives of many of Eusebius's contemporaries. When Eusebius assembled with several hundred fellow bishops—at Constantine's expense—during the Council of Nicaea, many had scars from their tortures, and a few were missing limbs or eyes. The psychological impact of the Church's sudden, unexpected change of fortune on any Christian writer of the time would have been great. Indeed, as Eusebius appears to have published early editions of his *History* prior to the Edict of Milan, the sections that precede the Edict sometimes betray a tragic mindset. Those that follow, on the other hand, are comparatively triumphalistic.

Eusebius became an immediate and enthusiastic supporter of Constantine. It is hard to imagine how he could not have done so. However, his praise was not without reserve and certainly not without scruple. It is important to assert this, for some historians have viewed Eusebius as a kind of flunky, a "court bishop" who found shelter in the emperor's favor and cynically accommodated his teaching to justify royal power. His namesake Eusebius of Nicomedia, whom we met at Constantine's baptism, is more vulnerable to that charge. The latter appears to have been as much a politician as an overseer of the Church. An obstinate Arian, even after Nicaea, he used his influence to have the great Athanasius exiled. As for Eusebius of Caesarea, access to the throne did not sway his behavior or his presentation of the faith. Indeed, while critics treat him as little more than an appendage of the court, it has been shown conclusively that he actually stood in Constantine's presence on but four separate occasions.[51]

His high praise of the emperor, then, was probably due to the emotional impact of the Edict of Milan. By the end of his life, following the death of Constantine, Eusebius recalled the memory of the heir to Diocletian peacefully summoning the Church's bishops to the capital and humbling himself before them. He remembered the emperor hosting a banquet for the bishops and moving about the hall in order to converse with them. It was a paradisiacal image for the old bishop, who had lived through the worst years of martyrdom the Church had ever known. "One might have thought," he reflected, "that a picture of Christ's kingdom was thus shadowed forth, and [the banquet] a dream rather than a reality."[52]

But the reality was that the Roman Empire had become—or was at least fast becoming—an example of the Church's heavenly transformation of the world. This, the latest and perhaps greatest of the Church's cosmological projects, is the basis for the bishop's views about Christian statecraft. They are most fully expressed in his *Oration*.

The work is rather tedious, insofar as its thirty-some double-columned pages read as an unremitting celebration of Constantine's various accomplishments. But as an example of classical panegyric, that is what it was expected to do. Although it is titled an "oration," it is inconceivable that it could ever have been delivered verbally. Not even Constantine could have endured that. But from this work can be extracted certain points that together represent a coherent and compelling vision of the Christian state that had now come to manifest itself in the world.

Eusebius's vision is one of heavenly immanence and further elaborates the sacramental approach to human culture we observed in chapter one. Nevertheless, it rests on the conviction that the world is good insofar as it is the creation of the transcendent God. The oration's first point establishes God's transcendence, which after centuries of emperor-worship was something new.

> Today is the festival of our great emperor. . . . [But] he who presides over our solemnity is the Great Sovereign himself [that is, God]; he, I mean, who is truly great; of whom I affirm (nor will the sovereign who hears me be offended, but will rather approve of this ascription of praise to God), that He is above and beyond all created things, the Highest, the Greatest, the most Mighty One; whose throne is the arch of heaven, and the earth the footstool of his feet.

Having established from the start the transcendent sovereignty of God over his creation, which includes human rulers, Eusebius declares that this God is everywhere present within it. The entire cosmos is sustained by this immanence. "Does not the universal frame of earth acknowledge him her Lord, and declare, by the vegetable and animal life which she produces, her subjection to the will of a superior Power?" The entire natural world sings praises to its Creator. "The rivers, flowing with abundant stream, and the perennial fountains, springing from hidden and exhaustless depths, ascribed to him the cause of their marvelous source. . . . The duly measured fall of winter's rain, the rolling thunder, the lightning's flash, the eddying currents of the winds, and the airy courses of the clouds, all reveal his presence to those to whom his Person is invisible." Though transcendent, then, God has become present in the glorious majesty of the natural order.

Eusebius's cosmology is not limited to nature, of course. As plants, animals, and even the elements praise God through their proper activities, so men praise him by living within a well-ordered state. At its head is the Christian ruler, caring above all for the salvation of his subjects. But more than this, as a member of the Church he actually participates sacramentally in the restoration of the cosmos. Pagan rulers defiled their office with blood sacrifices and immoral behavior. But in the person of Constantine, the Christian emperor rules "as an act of thanksgiving to [God] by whom he has thus been honored." The ultimate sign of his sacramental service as ruler is to participate in the mercy of God, to imitate "his Divine philanthropy by his own imperial acts."

What is interesting here is that Eusebius, rather than the sycophant he is sometimes depicted to be, establishes rather clear conditions under which the ruler may fulfill his cosmological purpose. "He is indeed an emperor, and bears a title corresponding to his deeds; a Victor in truth, who has gained the victory over those passions which overmaster the rest of men: whose character is formed after the Divine original of the Supreme Sovereign, and whose mind reflects, as in a mirror, the radiance of his virtues." Such a ruler lives by a virtue determined by God, and, as Eusebius adds, is engaged in continual prayer to him.

The Eusebian vision of the state, then, was one in which Christ's incarnate presence in the world was manifested by a righteous political order. The emperor was, like King David of old, subject to divine law, and his virtues were measured not by human standards but by transcendent ones. He participated sacramentally in the salvation of the world and, "by bringing those whom he rules on earth to the only begotten Word and Savior renders them fit subjects of his kingdom." Finally, Eusebius's is a vision of heavenly immanence in which members of the Christian state are able "to anticipate even here the commencement of a future existence."[53]

Eusebius was not alone in reflecting on the significance of early Christian statecraft. A century later, Augustine of Hippo did the same thing. This time, however, the results were very different. In *The City of God*, he put forward a vision of the Christian state that juxtaposed a society of the elect with one attached to purely worldly ends. The two societies overlapped each other, but one was destined for paradise while the other was consumed by the passions of self-love and violence. Augustine's dualistic conception of the world was comparatively pessimistic, lacking Eusebius's confidence in the Christian state.

One of the reasons for this was the sharp division between the world and the kingdom of heaven that had been cultivated by North African theologians in the past. The greatest of these theologians was Tertullian. He had urged Christians to sever completely any ties to a world dominated by pagans. "What has Athens to do with Jerusalem?" he once famously asked, censuring the whole of classical culture. So hostile was Tertullian to worldly entanglements that he harbored sympathy for a schismatic group known as the montanists, whose extreme asceticism appealed to him.

By Augustine's time, this heresy had largely disappeared, but Tertullian's dualism in distinguishing between the world and the Church persisted in other forms. The Donatists, for example, advocated removal from the catholic Church due to what they regarded as her compromising policy of readmitting repentant apostates.

Augustine was not the only heir to the uncompromising spirit of Tertullian. He lived at a time in which the glow of Constantine's peace with the Church was beginning to fade. The decades that had elapsed since Eusebius's euphoric tricennial oration had brought deep uncertainties about the political state of Christendom.

On the one hand, a string of rulers—beginning with Constantine's

Tertullian
https://commons.wikimedia.org/w/index.php?curid=445137

own sons—had deviated from Orthodoxy and done harm to the Church as a result. Another had abandoned the faith altogether and tried, unsuccessfully, to turn the empire back to paganism. And even the steadfastly Orthodox Theodosius had acted like a pagan tyrant in subjecting the people of Thessalonica to imperial vengeance. Indeed, it was Ambrose of Milan, the very bishop who had excommunicated Theodosius over this deed, who catechized and baptized Augustine.

To make matters worse, Augustine now found himself bishop of a provincial city on the North African coast, tracking with apprehension the advance of barbarian armies throughout the remnants of the Western Roman Empire. In 410, news of Rome's fall to the Visigoth Alaric reached him. Then, twenty years later, the Vandals arrived at his own city's gates and began their siege.

In this context Augustine wrote his most famous work. *The City of God* is the summation of a life of theological reflection, unlike the rather occasional *Oration* of Eusebius. Augustine was a highly creative theologian, one of the most brilliant in history, and towered over the Greek historian. For this reason a comparison of the two is rather lopsided. Nevertheless, since each gave expression to views on government that would influence Christendom for centuries to come, a comparison is merited.

We have seen that Eusebius viewed the Christian state as an extension of the kingdom of heaven. The ruler manifests the presence of God in this world—"even here"—serving essentially as a minister of His kingdom. Despite its grounding in the doctrine of the Incarnation, Augustine was deeply suspicious of such a cosmology. He preferred rather to emphasize the world's brokenness and therefore separation from God. Even when he did assign to this life the possibility of experiencing divine communion, it was a fleeting experience. "The Supreme Good of the City of God," he wrote,

> is everlasting and perfect peace, which is not the peace through which men pass in their mortality, in their journey from birth to death, but that peace in which they remain in their immortal state, experiencing no adversity at all. In view of this, can anyone deny that this is the supremely blessed life, or that the present life on earth, however full it may be of the greatest possible blessings of soul and body and of external circumstances, is, in comparison, most miserable?

Misery is the normative condition of this world. Even if one does acquire a blessed sense of divine peace, it is "rather by future hope than in present reality."[54] The joy of paradise is thus projected into the future and largely removed from this age.

This is all very pessimistic in comparison to Eusebius. However, it is also more attentive to Pauline doctrine about the sinful passions. Augustine's view of the world was profoundly influenced by his circumspection about evil desire, or concupiscence. The Fall was always lurking in the human heart and effectively polluted every sector of civilization. While purification of the passions through ascetical struggle was possible at an individual level, it was beyond foolish to think that it could have an impact on society as a whole. In this way, an element of subjectivity entered into such reflections about the world. Rather than an objective manifestation of paradise, as with Eusebius, experience of life in the world was related to and at some level determined by the spiritual condition of the individual.

Thus, the divine peace about which Eusebius spoke could only be a fleeting taste of paradise, not a sustained experience of it. And when it made its appearance—"even in this life"—it did so only "through faith." True peace must await the end of time, when it will be known "through open vision." By opposing faith to vision, Augustine was reducing the experience of divine peace to something of an abstraction, something that could be intellectualized but not fully known under the conditions of this age.

The distinction between this age and the one to come was perfectly consistent with the Christian tradition, and Eusebius would have accepted it as such. The bishops' differences were rather of emphasis. Augustine was forever minimizing the experience of paradise in this age. "Peace here and now," he insisted, "is such that it affords a solace for our wretchedness rather than the joy of blessedness. Our righteousness itself, too . . . is nevertheless only such as to consist in the forgiveness of sins rather than in the perfection of virtues."[55] Solace and not joy; forgiveness and not perfection: such was the modest potential of this world, even after the Incarnation.

But Augustine's pessimism was also the source of his marvelous and lasting influence in the history of Christendom. It provided him with a realistic insight into the limitations of the world and the need for a transcendent source for its renewal. This was something Eusebius, the exuberant apologist of Christian autocracy, was simply unable to appreciate. It was reinforced by the dualism Augustine inherited from Tertullian. And it was, after all, an important theme in traditional Christianity. We have noted in chapter one the contrast between the world and the kingdom of heaven in the Gospels. We have also noted in chapter two the theme of earthly homelessness in early writings such as the *Epistle to Diognetus*.

Augustine picked up this theme and elaborated it into a full-blown cosmology. The world can never be a home to the Christian, he claimed, and by extension the earthly city can therefore never accommodate the City of God. "God's City lives in this world's city," he admitted, "as far as the human element is concerned; but it lives there as an alien sojourner."[56] The principle of peregrination, then, of a dissatisfied alienation from the world, came to determine his view of this life.

The City of God therefore comes to represent the human community set apart from the city of the world. Where Eusebius tended to merge the two,

Augustine divided them. But the City of God is not disconnected from the city of the world, and this is the brilliance of Augustine's cosmology. The heavenly community becomes, as it were, a judge over society and at the same time the source of its renewal. It becomes the purpose, or, to borrow from the Greek language that Augustine did not speak, the *telos* toward which it strives. And this sense of purpose or teleology would energize Christendom in the centuries ahead, restlessly urging it toward higher levels of moral and spiritual achievement. Augustine's theology, in short, would one day become for the West the dominant expression of Christendom's transformational imperative.

Justinian

BUT AUGUSTINE LIVED a long way from Constantinople, and the Byzantine establishment found the more celebratory cosmology of Eusebius more to its liking. By the end of the fifth century, the Roman Empire had completely collapsed in the West. Ruled from Constantinople since the early fourth century, it now faced a flood of invaders against which it could not defend itself. The greatest of these were the Goths, peoples who had migrated into southeastern Europe from Germany and Scandinavia.

Ironically, the Goths had converted to Christianity under the influence of Ulfilas, a missionary supported by Constantinople. He was an Arian, though, and the two main Gothic tribes, the Ostrogoths and Visigoths, came to see Orthodox Byzantium as an enemy. During the fifth century they overran the Danube and established a tenacious presence in the West. In fact, it was the Visigoth Alaric who, for the first time in history, actually conquered Rome itself in 410. No foreign army had done so in the twelve hundred years that had elapsed since the founding of the city. The psychological blow to *romanitas* was incalculable. From Palestine, the words of Jerome upon receiving the news were representative of an entire civilization: "My voice sticks in my throat; and, as I dictate, sobs choke my utterance. The city which had taken the whole world was itself taken."

After a century of the empire brooding over this loss, a powerful ruler

Emperor Justinian (Shutterstock.com)

assumed the throne in Constantinople. Justinian, like all Byzantine emperors, was indeed a Roman. There had been no break in the political identity of the empire's rulers after they became Christians and moved to the Greek East. Official documents were still signed by the "Emperor of the Romans" until the final days of the Byzantine state. Documents were, for the time being, still issued in Latin rather than Greek. And the capital city's official name was, after all, New Rome.

So when he came to power in 527, Justinian set out immediately to reverse the conquests of the barbarians in the West. Under his able general Belisarius, two main military campaigns were waged, first against a Germanic tribe related to the Goths, known as the Vandals, in northern Africa, and then against the Ostrogoths themselves in Italy. The latter Gothic War was particularly costly and led to vast destruction and the depopulation of the peninsula. By the time the Old Rome had been rejoined to the New, the city's population had plummeted to less than 100,000.

In the long run, historians consider Justinian's wars of reunification largely a waste of lives and resources. They were certainly a waste of time. Within a generation a new barbarian tribe known as the Lombards would cross the Alps to conquer large territories in Italy. This left only part of the

peninsula in Byzantine hands. Rome itself, along with the important administrative city of Ravenna, would remain firmly connected to Constantinople
for another two hundred years. The largely Greek southern peninsula would
remain Byzantine longer. As for northern Africa, another fate awaited it
under one of Justinian's successors, Emperor Heraklios.

For the time being, Justinian appeared to have done much to strengthen
the Byzantine Empire. But the empire was not just a territorial state. It was
administrative reality too, the political heart of Christendom. In fact it
was precisely during Justinian's reign that one of the earliest self-conscious
expressions of Christendom as a unique political civilization began to appear.
This took the form of *sancta respublica*, Latin for "Holy Commonwealth."

Justinian has gone down in history as the earliest codifier of Roman law,
his *Codex Justinianus* (*Code of Justinian*) being the most famous of his writings.
For him, Christendom was a civilization in which religion, culture, and politics were all closely integrated—the inevitable consequence and even necessary outcome of the cosmology that accompanied the Great Commission.
Earlier emperors had issued laws about the place of Christianity in the state,
but none was as systematic as Justinian in assimilating the government to a
Christian vision of the world.

Justinian legislated on nearly all aspects of Christianity, including, especially, the place of the clergy in society. His goal in doing so was not so much
to place restraints on the clergy, as later rulers in the medieval West would
do, but to clarify the nature of their authority and that of the state. His
vision of the Christian state can be defined as either one of symphony or
one of caesaropapism. He would have been comfortable with the former
term, for it was he who coined it. In his *Sixth Novella*, a sort of addendum to
the *Codex*, he put forward what historians consider the classical view of the
relationship between clergy and ruler.

> *There are two greatest gifts which God, in his love for man, has granted from
> on high: the priesthood and the imperial dignity. The first serves divine things,
> while the latter directs and administers human affairs; both, however, proceed
> from the same origin and adorn the life of mankind. Hence, nothing should
> be such a source of care to the emperors as the dignity of the priests, since*

it is for their imperial welfare that they constantly implore God. For if the priesthood is in every way free from blame and possesses access to God, and if the emperors administer equitably and judiciously the state entrusted to their care, general symphony (symphonia) will result and whatever is beneficial will be bestowed upon the human race.[57]

As John Meyendorff noted, the doctrine of symphony here cannot be separated from the context of assigning appropriate, God-given ministries to the clergy and the emperor.

In other words, it is not a symphony between Church and state, or even between clergy and ruler. It assumes that the two are one, and that the purpose and identity of both groupings is identical. This was the dominant view of the state in early Christendom. Only with time, after the rise of an ecclesiastically "transcendent" entity, the reform papacy of the eleventh century, would the concept of a distinction in purpose be conceivable. Then a new Christendom would assign to the clergy a new role, one of supervision and earthly transcendence. And when that view collapsed during the Protestant Reformation, the result would be—again after centuries had elapsed—one in which the clergy have no legitimate role to play in political life at all. For the time being, however, Byzantine Christendom remained a civilization in which the government and the clergy enjoyed a common experience of heavenly immanence.

But this is not to say that all was well. It never is in a broken world, and while Byzantine civilization cultivated a strong attachment to the kingdom of heaven, it was not the kingdom of heaven itself. With its refusal to distinguish between imperial state and catholic Church, Byzantium helped undermine the prophetic ministry of the clergy. In such an atmosphere, clerical resistance to imperial injustice and immorality was unlikely.

We have seen how Theodosius, after ordering the massacre of his subjects at Thessalonica, was confronted by Bishop Ambrose of Milan and compelled to undergo penance for the deed. A similar scenario unfolded under Justinian in 532, when an uprising called the Nika Riots broke out in the capital's Hippodrome. The emperor was very nearly forced to flee the city as a result. After he recovered his nerve, he reacted with ferocity. The result was the death of nearly thirty thousand citizens. This time, no bishop of the stature of Ambrose stepped forward to speak truth to power. The imperious Christian ruler, perhaps like God Himself, simply appeared to them unapproachable.

Justinian did not hesitate to approach the bishops, however, when they failed to support his policies. He had launched his reign as a staunch Chalcedonian, only to soften his attitude toward the monophysites with time. This led to tensions between him and the Orthodox bishops, especially the distant and occasionally defiant pope of Rome. When Justinian tried to win the sympathy of the monophysites by condemning a group of their adversaries, a fissure erupted between him and the Orthodox clergy that was not easily closed. The law in question, known as the Three Chapters, posthumously anathematized a group of three theologians whose writings were deemed particularly unacceptable to the monophysites. The goal was to win their goodwill and draw them back into the catholic Church, rather as Zeno's *Henotikon* had sought to do.

It too failed, though not as miserably. Zeno had never obtained the approval of the papacy, which ultimately excommunicated the subservient Patriarch Acacius of Constantinople. With dizzying self-confidence, Justinian did something that Zeno would never have dreamed of doing. He sent emissaries to Rome, not to persuade Pope Vigilius to accept the Three Chapters, but to abduct him and place him under house arrest until he did. The pope was transported to Constantinople, where he spent nearly the remainder of his life under constant duress for his reluctance to support the legislation. After eight years as a prisoner of the capital, he did finally sign his name to the document. Only then was he free to return to Rome, but he died during the journey. If any acts deserve the label caesaropapism, this affair is surely one of them.

Justinian's policy toward the bishops could be tyrannical. However, his reign marked a high point in other aspects of Christian government. Under the influence of his wife, Empress Theodora, he passed laws that gave greater support and honor to women in the Western world. New measures against infanticide served particularly to protect female infants. The property rights of women were increased, and women convicted of adultery were to be spared the age-old penalty of death. Perhaps most dramatically, Theodora, who unlike Rome's pagan empresses exercised direct rule much of the time, took a special interest in caring for marginalized women, especially prostitutes. She officially forbade sex slavery (the slave population was and would remain very high for centuries to come) and used the resources of the crown to help women escape prostitution. Unlike Christian lawmakers in a nihilistic modern Christendom, Justinian was not shy about legislating morality.

He also did not hesitate to use the state's material resources for the expansion of Christian culture. This was most notable in his building projects. Throughout his empire, he erected Christian temples and monasteries as visual confirmation of the sanctification of the world. In the distant Sinai Peninsula of Egypt, he established a large monastery at the foot of the mountain where Moses beheld God in the burning bush. It became a monument to traditional Christianity's cosmology of heavenly immanence. It still stands this day, known as the Monastery of Saint Katherine.

In the West, in the administrative city of Ravenna, Justinian presided over the consecration of three temples of great cultural significance: San Vitale, Sant'Apollinare in Classe, and, confusingly, the latter's namesake Sant'Apollinare Nuovo. The iconography of the second temple was particularly expressive of Christian cosmology. It featured an image within the apse (the half-dome ceiling above the altar) of the Transfiguration, the event in Christ's ministry that perhaps more than any other emphasized the theme of heavenly immanence. In the icon a nimbus cross with Christ at its center hovers in the upper register, flanked by the prophets Moses and Elijah, with whom Jesus spoke during the event. Below are three lambs symbolizing the apostles Peter, James, and John, who beheld it. The entire lower half of the icon depicts a verdant scene of earthly glory, where plants, animals, and Saint Apollinaris all join together in praise of the Incarnate God.

In Constantinople, Justinian built or rebuilt no fewer than thirty Christian temples, including those of Saint Irene and Saints Sergius and Bacchus. His most famous reconstruction project, however, was Hagia Sophia. The original church with this name had been burned down during the Nika

Riots. Located on a promontory overlooking the Bosphorus, the site offered Justinian the opportunity to create a monumental statement about Byzantine Christendom. Clearly, the precedent of the Jerusalem temple built on Mount Zion was in the back of his mind. For when the church was completed only five years later, the emperor was reported to have exclaimed, "O Solomon, I have outdone you!"

CHAPTER FOUR

When the West Was Still Eastern

J USTINIAN'S WARS OF RECONQUEST failed to prevent the long-term
political division of Christendom. In the short term, however, they
helped preserve the cultural bond that united the Roman Empire of the
East and the Old Rome of the West. This bond was expressed by the term
romanitas, a term used for the culture of Rome. It described a composite
way of life that included a centralized government, urbanism, and the rich
intellectual heritage of Latin and Greek philosophy. In later years, it also
included Christianity.

Christian Romanitas

NOWHERE WAS CHRISTIAN ROMANITAS more in evidence than in the
East. The New Rome that was Constantinople had within two centuries of
its founding become the West's ultimate example of urban splendor, equal
to Old Rome in the days of Augustus. The city contained multiple palaces
and the famed Hippodrome, where chariot races had come to replace the
blood sports outlawed by Constantine. Surrounded by a huge earthen wall,
Constantinople would remain impregnable to enemy armies for nearly a
millennium.

Elaborate cisterns assured residents of a regular supply of water, and merchants enjoyed an inexhaustible supply of goods delivered from distant ports through the easily defended harbor called the Golden Horn. Architects erected Christendom's greatest temples, and painters adorned them with mosaics and frescoes that no other artists on earth could match. Scholarship flourished, rendered mainly in Greek, though court life continued through the time of Justinian to be conducted in Latin. The Christian ruler called himself—and was called by others—the heir to Augustus and the "Emperor of the Romans."

Back in Old Rome, there was no fundamental disagreement with this. Those who inhabited the former capital emphatically thought of themselves as members of a unitary Christian empire ruled from Constantinople. But while their eastern compatriots enjoyed military security and prosperity, they faced uncertainty. Justinian's armies had destroyed the Ostrogothic regime in Italy, but in doing so they had also destroyed much of Italy. The aristocracy was nearly bankrupt, and famine was a constant danger.

To make things worse, Constantinople began to turn its attention toward threats from Persia, signaling a decline in military support to Italy. As this occurred, Western Rome was confronted by a new power known as the Lombards, who began to encroach on Italy from beyond the Alps. The city's identity as the political, economic, and cultural center of the empire had clearly become a thing of the past. Even its architectural monuments— once the pride of the empire—were now crumbling into ruin from lack of resources.

Beyond Italy, in lands long ago assimilated by the Roman Empire, discontinuity was even more extreme. In the regions of Gaul and Spain, for instance, a century of barbarian conquest had shattered the empire's administrative unity. There, romanitas totally lacked what Peter Brown has called the "wide horizons" of Eastern Christendom.[58] Local societies were cut off from the imperial center and fell under the influence of provincial elites. But as limited as their vision of Christian romanitas necessarily became, the western regions of the former empire retained one feature of its former universality—the papacy.

It is precisely to the time when the western territories of the Roman

Empire were being dislodged that we can date the papacy's earliest claims to a jurisdictional reach throughout the West and even in some cases beyond. As the political element of Christian romanitas began to dissolve during the fifth century, an ecclesiastical element was conceived to replace it. The bishop of Rome became in certain ways a substitute for the absent and largely impotent Byzantine emperor.

This development was particularly noticeable in the case of Pope Leo the Great, who claimed, largely without precedent, that the papacy exercised jurisdictional preeminence (*principatus*) throughout the universal Church. Such a claim suggested a rivalry with the emperor, who was by now accustomed to the role of guarantor of the ecumenicity of the Church within his empire. He therefore refused to accept the pope's innovative use of the title.

The papacy's claim also dismayed Eastern bishops, who were accustomed to a tradition of ecclesiastical governance known as conciliarity (or synodality)—that is, one that is council-based and consensual. With the rise of Byzantium there had been five recognized centers of church leadership, each represented by a preeminent bishop, or patriarch. This pentarchy included, in the first position, Rome, then Constantinople, and after that the ancient sees of Alexandria, Antioch, and Jerusalem. It would be a long time before Leo's novelty of Roman universal preeminence would create a sustained challenge to the pentarchy, but his model of a distinctly papal romanitas proved consequential.

For the time being, this model was supported by the outcome of the Fourth Ecumenical Council held in the city of Chalcedon in 451. As we have seen, Leo provided to the assembled bishops his famous *Tome*, the most important theological text used to clarify Orthodox doctrine about the Person of Christ since the First Ecumenical Council. The *Tome* stated that because of the Incarnation, Christ possessed two distinct and unconfused natures, divine and human. Bishops holding to a doctrine that Christ possessed only one nature, known as monophysites, were accordingly anathematized by Chalcedon, lending prestige to the papacy.

A sense of jurisdictional preeminence also lay behind Leo's notorious objection to one of the council's resolutions, Canon 28. This ruling assigned to Constantinople the same administrative status as Rome, due to the fact that the former had now superseded the latter as the empire's political capital. The canon and Leo's reaction against it reveal a sharp disagreement that was emerging between East and West on the question of Rome's jurisdictional authority. The bishops of the East obviously regarded Rome as preeminent within the pentarchy, but in terms of moral authority and prestige rather than administrative oversight. Using a simple political logic, the East considered Constantinople, as the new capital, naturally similar in status to Old Rome.

Leo, on the other hand, argued for Roman preeminence on administrative grounds. He was one of the first to claim that because the Apostle Peter had died in Rome, the bishop that ruled there was Peter's unique heir. Here Leo appropriated a term used first by Cyprian of Carthage, who had spoken of the "chair of Peter" (*cathedra Petri*). Cyprian was a Latin father and is doubly significant because he had actually distinguished himself during the third century as an opponent of papal administrative overreach. Citing Peter's primacy in the Gospels, he had argued that all bishops share equally in the apostle's authority, and that no bishop, even that of Rome, has jurisdictional authority over another.

Ironically, Leo now came to use the term "Peter's chair" to assert a unique authority for the bishop of Rome. This was an innovation. Nowhere in the New Testament had Peter's primacy ever been defined in administrative or jurisdictional terms. On the contrary, at the important Jerusalem Council, the principle of conciliarity, not petrine primacy, had led the apostles to their important resolution against the requirement of circumcision (Acts 15). Paul himself had even noted Peter's fallibility in the matter of ecclesiastical leadership (Gal. 2:11). Peter was said to be "first" (*primus*) in the Gospels (Matt. 10:2), but the character of that status remained totally undefined.

Peter's successors in Rome had occasionally exercised influence beyond their immediate jurisdiction. In the second century, for instance, Clement of Rome sent an epistle to the church in Corinth. Much is often made of this example of early "papal" (the term was in fact not used widely until much later) authority. However, the fact that Clement's epistle was anonymous indicates that at this time there was simply no sense that he possessed authority in the name of the Apostle Peter or through his office or chair. Otherwise, Clement would have identified his office in order to invoke that authority.

Gregory the Great

LEO'S PAPAL MODEL of Christian romanitas was an historical anomaly when it appeared in the politically chaotic fifth century. Once imperial rule of Italy was restored by Justinian in the sixth century, it drifted back into relative obscurity. Its eclipse was particularly evident during the pontificate of Gregory the Great, whose prestige came to surpass even that of Leo.

Gregory belonged to a long line of popes known for close ties to Constantinople and deep respect for a universal romanitas that encompassed the West and the East. Indeed, he had spent seven years of his early life in New Rome as the papal *apocrisiarios,* or envoy. This office had become an important means of testing future popes and provided them with valuable experience in the eastern capital. When Gregory was elected pope in 590, he therefore brought an intimate knowledge of Eastern Christianity to the papacy.

In fact, the two and a half centuries that followed Justinian's reconquest have come to be known among historians as the period of a "Byzantine papacy." During this period, popes were required to obtain imperial approval in Constantinople before their elections could be confirmed in Rome. What is more, many of the popes were of Greek origin, imported either from the East or from Byzantine southern Italy.

Gregory, however, was not one of these. He was thoroughly Roman, the descendant of a long line of eminent patricians. In fact, one of his ancestors appears to have been a pope himself. But Gregory's aristocratic lineage by no means left him indifferent to Rome's commoners. As a young man he had been selected to serve as the city prefect, an office that introduced him to the nearly limitless needs of Rome's poor. He soon left this post to become a monk. As heir to an ancestral estate on the city's Caelian Hill, he had the means of establishing a monastic community on the site in which the

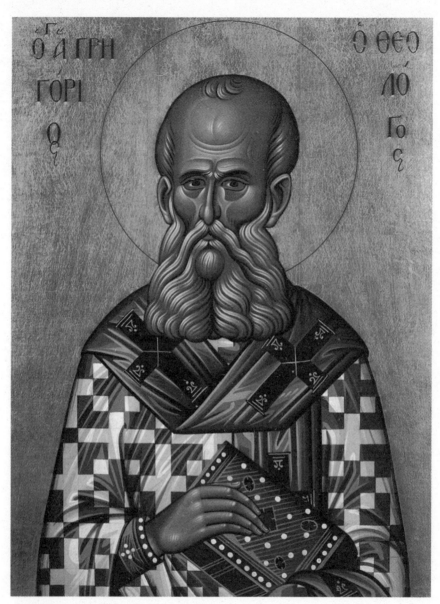

St. Gregory of Nazianzos, the Theologian
Copyright 2001 TheoLogic Systems, Inc.

refinements of a Latin education were as important as ascetic struggle. Then, following his sojourn as papal envoy to Constantinople, Gregory returned home to find himself elected to the papacy.

Gregory the Great is regarded as one of the most significant popes in the early history of Christendom. He was the first monk to be elected to the office, and his ascetical piety left a deep imprint on it. He was the first pope to write prolifically, earning, alongside Ambrose, Jerome, and Augustine, the distinction of being one of four "doctors" of the Latin Church. His *Dialogues,* documenting in four volumes the lives and miracles of Italian saints, became widely read and contributed greatly to the formation of a distinctly Western piety. Throughout the long work, Gregory presents a cosmology in which God is sacramentally present in this world, filling it with His awesome splendor. As his biographer George Demacopoulos notes, "in Gregory's theological view of the world, God remains active with his creation through visible and invisible ways. . . . For the holy man, the ascetic, and all those who have committed themselves to a life of spiritual growth, the mysteries of God's intervention in the world are a source of comfort and hope."[59]

The second volume of the *Dialogues* was dedicated exclusively to the life of Benedict of Nursia, whose monastic rule would become the most widely followed one in the West. Here especially the imprint of Eastern piety can be detected. Having read and absorbed the lives of Eastern saints like Anthony of Egypt while in Constantinople, Gregory resolved to provide equivalents for a Latin audience. According to Andrew Ekonomou, the pope "would create in Benedict of Nursia an Italian Antony, giving the afflicted peninsula and the entire West a superhuman figure whose sanctity could match that of 'the patriarch of Eastern monks'."[60] Gregory also enacted reforms of the Western liturgy, and it is to him personally that the dominant style of medieval singing known as Gregorian chant is attributed. Finally, he dispatched missionaries to Britain, bringing the peoples of that island more completely into the orbit of Christian romanitas.

Ruling as he did during the period of the Byzantine papacy, Gregory might naturally be expected to have communicated Eastern elements of piety and practice to the West. The style of liturgical chant associated with his name might be an example of this, as Constantinople was in his time the center of the liturgical arts. Gregory is also credited in the East (no record appears in the West) with an undisclosed contribution to the Lenten Liturgy of Presanctified Gifts. This service became the standard weekday liturgy in the East during the annual Great Fast, and in the West a variant of it came to be used for the solemn day of Good Friday.

Though his exact contribution to the Presanctified Liturgy remains unclear, the service itself expresses powerfully the theme of paradise in traditional Christendom. It features, for instance, a hymn sung at the moment when the consecrated Body and Blood of Christ are borne in a procession to the altar table. The hymn is known by the title "Now the Powers of Heaven." It was undoubtedly inspired by another hymn, sung during the equivalent moment in the regular Divine Liturgy, known as the Cherubic Hymn.

Since this earlier prototype was itself of recent origin in Gregory's time, dating perhaps to the middle of the sixth century, it is worth quoting here:

> *Let us who mystically represent the cherubim, and who sing the thrice-holy hymn to the life-creating Trinity, now lay aside all earthly cares; that we may receive the King of all, who comes invisibly upborne by the angelic hosts. Alleluia, alleluia, alleluia.*

Gregory would have become familiar with the Cherubic Hymn during his years in Constantinople. (In fact, it is believed that he lived around the corner from Hagia Sophia, where the Eastern liturgical tradition was reaching its fullest consolidation.)

"Now the Powers of Heaven" bears equal witness to the experience of the kingdom of heaven in Christian worship. Its text reads:

> *Now the powers of heaven with us invisibly do serve. Lo, the King of glory enters; lo, the mystical sacrifice is upborne, fulfilled. Let us draw nigh with faith and love, and become communicants of Life eternal. Alleluia, alleluia, alleluia.*

The statements in these two hymns about the presence of paradise in this world—the capacity of human beings to share "mystically" in the heavenly experience of the cherubim, on the one hand, and the angelic powers of heaven serving "with us" on earth on the other hand—demonstrate clear continuity with the culture of early Christendom. Pope Gregory's encounter with this culture in the East and his subsequent contribution to the development of the liturgy in the West therefore establish a fascinating but elusive impression of early Christendom's cultural unity.

Less elusive was Gregory's contribution to transmitting the ecclesiology of the East to the West. We have noted his predecessor Leo's innovative claims about the papacy's universal preeminence. Gregory does not seem to have shared these claims. In fact, on one significant occasion, he argued strongly against the principle of papal supremacy and any other form of universal ecclesiastical preeminence.

The occasion was a statement made by the patriarch of Constantinople, John the Faster. The latter sent a letter to Rome in 595 in which he assumed the title of Ecumenical Patriarch. This term had already been in use for some time and appears to have meant, due to the patriarch's proximity to the capital, something like "imperial" rather than "universal." Nevertheless, Gregory saw in it a dangerous precedent. He claimed in letters of protest that no single bishop could play with the thought that he exercised jurisdictional preeminence over all others, even in the name of Saint Peter.

What happened next in Gregory's correspondence with the East proved even more significant. He received a letter of sympathy from Patriarch Eulogius of Alexandria, who in sharing a reluctance to address the patriarch of Constantinople as "ecumenical patriarch" addressed Gregory as "universal pope." This title, too, had been used before by the popes. But now Gregory decided, to his own disadvantage, to expose its flaws. The well-meaning Eulogius must have been stunned.

"I beg you never let me hear that word again," Gregory humbly complained,

For I know who you are and who I am. In position you are my brother, in character my father. I gave therefore no commands, but only endeavoured to point out what I thought was desirable . . . I said you ought not to use such a title [that is, "universal bishop"] in writing either to me or to any one else; yet now, in your last letter, notwithstanding my prohibition, you have addressed me by the proud title of Universal Pope. I beg your Holiness, whom I love so well, not to do this again . . . I do not consider that anything is an honour to me, by which my brethren lose the honour that is their due. My honour is the honour of the Universal Church, my honour is the united strength of my brethren. Then and then only am I truly honoured when no one is denied the honour which is justly his. But, if your Holiness calls me Universal Pope, you deny that you are yourself that which you say I am universally. God forbid! Far from us be the titles which inflate men's pride and deal a wound to charity![61]

As forcefully as Cyprian of Carthage, and in striking contrast to Leo the Great, Pope Gregory hereby rejected the very possibility that any one bishop could exercise jurisdictional preeminence over others, even from Rome. A more eloquent expression of the East's conciliar ecclesiology could hardly be found. And in this case it was voiced by the most influential and famous pope of Christendom's first millennium.

But Gregory's witness to the Eastern character of Western Christendom did not end there. He also advocated an anthropology that was remarkably optimistic in that it emphasized the capacity of man to participate in divine grace.

Defending Traditional Christian Anthropology

THE DOCTRINE THAT man possesses a free will and that through the life of the Church he can direct it to participate in the life of God, becoming spiritually transformed in the process, had, as we saw in chapter one, always existed in some form within Christendom. In its fullest expression, it was known as *deification*. The Apostle Peter had spoken of becoming "partakers of the divine nature" (2 Pet. 1:4), and Christ Himself rebuked the unbelieving Jews, saying, "Is it not written in your law, 'I said, "You are gods"'?" (John 10:34). Athanasius, in the fourth century, famously declared (in paraphrase) that "God became man so that man might become God."

While the Greek fathers frequently employed the language of deification

Above: Sunrise from the heights of Villa Jovis, the palace on the island of Capri from which Emperor Tiberius Caesar ruled Roman pagandom at the time of Pentecost.

Below: The ruins of Villa Jovis.
Shutterstock.com

The interior of the Anastasis (known also as the Holy Sepulcher) in Jerusalem, built on the site where Jesus was buried and rose from the dead.
Shutterstock.com

Aerial view of Constantinople (with Hagia Sophia) as the city would have looked in Byzantine times. (antoine-helbert.com)

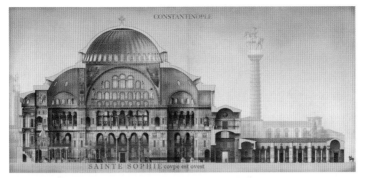

Reconstruction of Hagia Sophia as it would have looked after Justinian's reconstruction. The huge central dome was intended to symbolize heaven on earth to worshipers gathered underneath. The cross on top of the dome was later removed when the church was converted to a mosque following the fifteenth-century Turkish conquest.
Byzantine Renderings of Antoine Helbert, antoine-helbert.com

The "orientation" of the sixth-century basilica of Sant'Apollinare Nuovo in Ravenna directed worshipers' attention eastward toward the altar, which symbolized paradise.
Shutterstock.com

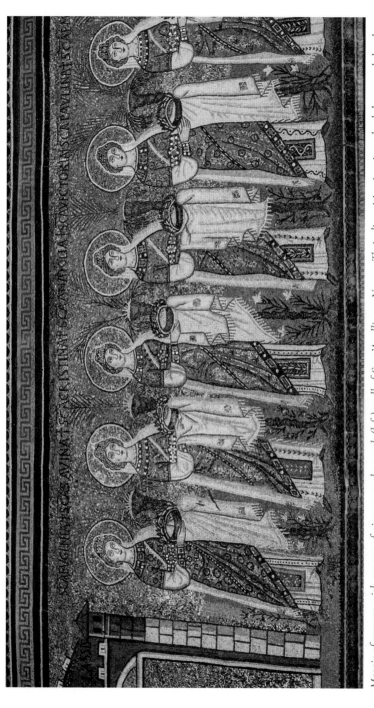

Mosaic of women with crowns of victory on the north (left) wall of Sant'Apollinare Nuovo. Their disposition is oriented subtly toward the altar area, the focal point of the female worshipers who would have gathered below during liturgical services. Opposite the mosaic, on the south (right) wall, a line of men bearing crowns manifested the same disposition to the congregation's male worshipers assembled there. Ravenna, Italy - 01.12.2018: Famous Early Christian mosaics from Basilica Saint Apollinare Nuovo in Ravenna. - Shutterstock

Interior of the church of Sant'Apollinare in Classe in Ravenna. The upper section depicts the Transfiguration of Christ, who is visible at the center of a cross flanked by Moses and Elijah. Below, Saint Apollinaris glorifies Christ at the center of a transfigured cosmos.
(Claudio Giovanni Colombo / Shutterstock.com)

Interior of the eleventh-century monastery of Hosios Loukas, located in modern Greece. A customary Byzantine icon of Christ Pantocrator within the central dome proclaims the ecclesial headship and sacramental presence of Christ to those assembled below.
Shutterstock.com

Reproduction of eighth-century mosaic at Lateran Palace in Rome. At the center Christ commissions the Apostles. On the left, He bestows authority upon Sylvester and Constantine. On the right, Peter bestows authority upon Pope Leo III and Emperor Charlemagne.
Shutterstock.com

The eighth-century Kildalton Cross on the island of Islay in Scotland. Its nimbus (or halo) was characteristic of Celtic high crosses and symbolized the Church's sanctification of the world. (Shutterstock.com)

The westwork of Corvey Abbey in Germany.

Above: The ruins of the monastery of Skellig Michael off the Atlantic coast of Ireland, the westernmost extent of eleventh-century Christendom.

Below: A view of Skellig Michael looking toward the western horizon at sunset.
Shutterstock.com

(*theosis*), Latin fathers were less inclined to speak of it. To be sure, this was not an absolute divide: someone like Hippolytus of Rome in the third century could assure his reader that

> thou shalt receive the kingdom of heaven, thou who, whilst thou didst sojourn in this life, didst know the celestial King. . . . For thou hast become God. . . . whatever it is consistent with God to impart, these God has promised to bestow upon thee, because thou hast been deified.[62]

But beginning with Tertullian there was, in the West's theological heartland of North Africa, an emphasis on legal images of salvation. Tertullian, the earliest of the Latin fathers, spoke of Christ's death as "satisfaction" for man's sins, though he did not develop the idea systematically. What is more, he believed that the individual human soul is generated by the parents at conception along with the body. This doctrine, known as traducianism, had the virtue of countering heretical teachings about the soul's eternal preexistence, a teaching associated with the Greek theologian Origen. But by causally linking the child's soul to the parents, Tertullian suggested that all souls therefore ultimately have their origin in the fallen Adam.

Augustine was in certain ways an heir to Tertullian's thought, and to it he added a far more sophisticated but generally consistent emphasis upon man's inability to will good on his own. This he developed in his famous disputes with Pelagius, a Celtic theologian who naively assigned to man complete autonomy in determining his spiritual fate. Augustine countered Pelagianism by claiming that because of Adam's fall, every human being suffers from a condition called "original sin."

For Augustine, this condition had two grievous effects on the human race, which he considered a "mass of damnation" (*massa damnata*). First, it transmitted the actual personal guilt of Adam, rather as, in the traducianist view, the immaterial soul was traced to its primal source. Second, original sin resulted in the degradation of human nature itself. All desire that is not directed toward God is therefore corrupt, something Augustine called *concupiscence*. Here he emphasized sexual desire in particular. This tendency in his thought may have been influenced by the overwhelming power of lust that had controlled him as a young man, as related in his *Confessions*, the West's first autobiography.

Additionally, alongside or perhaps as a consequence of this very pessimistic anthropology, Augustine claimed that man's free will required "prevenient grace," or the unilateral intervention of God's will, to become active. As he put it, God's grace "predisposes a man before he wills, to prompt his willing."[63] Accordingly, he believed divine will predestines the salvation of believers. Left on its own, the human will is incapable of desiring what is good, let alone pursuing it.

It should be said that in recent years there has been an effort to "rehabilitate" Augustine within a religious climate grown weary of the West's long history of anthropological pessimism. David Vincent Meconi, for instance, has argued that while Augustine used the Latin word for deification (*deificare*) a mere eighteen times in all his writings, he nevertheless used important metaphors such as man's sonship in Christ to reveal the essential experience of deification.[64] There is certainly a very optimistic side to some of Augustine's statements about man and the world. After all, he was a Christian. But his overwhelming emphasis is on the unhappy plight of a humanity saddled with Adam's guilt and incapable of willing good without the prevenient grace of a transcendent God.

In any case, Augustine's was not the only anthropological doctrine in the West. Another, more optimistic one also appeared during the fifth century. It looked not to the soteriological disputes of North Africa but to the monastic life of Egypt for its inspiration. In other words, it was rooted in the East.

Its most effective advocate was John Cassian. A contemporary of Augustine, he spent his formative years in the East—first among the earliest Christian hermits of the Egyptian desert and then later in Constantinople, where he was ordained a deacon by none other than John Chrysostom. Cassian then traveled to southern Gaul and settled in the coastal city of Marseilles, where he established a monastery on the Eastern model. His writings, *Institutes* and *Conferences*, were records of Eastern ascetical practice and piety that became widely influential in the West. They celebrated the hermit's intense efforts to achieve spiritual transformation and his experience of deification.

Cassian helped ignite a movement of Gallic monasticism bearing this Eastern character. The most famous example was centered on the lonely island monastery of Lérins off the coast of modern-day Cannes. It was there that another of Augustine's contemporaries, Vincent of Lérins, composed a work challenging the African bishop's pessimistic anthropology, entitled the *Vincentian Objections.*

Vincent was convinced that traditional Christianity glorified the human condition and that Augustine, despite his great service to the Church, had deviated from this. Most alarming for him, as for other Gallic monks, was the doctrine of predestination. In fact, one of these monks, Prosper of Aquitaine, who had become a disciple of Augustine, took it upon himself to write to the African, warning of a growing consensus that the doctrine represented a "novelty," or, put less delicately, a heresy.[65]

Soon after, Vincent published his most famous work, called the *Commonitorium.* It is a treatise on church tradition, not in terms of its content but in terms of its characteristics. How, Vincent asked, can one identify true catholic doctrine? His famous answer is known as the Vincentian Canon: authentic Christian tradition is that which has been believed "always, everywhere, and by all." Put differently, tradition is attested by its antiquity, its universality, and its reception by a consensus of authority. For many scholars, this statement represented a veiled rebuke of Augustine, whose pessimistic anthropology appeared to deviate from the much more widely attested thought of the Church's Greek fathers.

Nevertheless, the brilliance of Augustine's teaching earned a permanent place for his views in the West. At the fateful Second Council of Orange in 529, his latest advocate, Caesarius of Arles, succeeded in obtaining acceptance of much of his teaching on grace. The council renewed the Church's condemnation of Pelagian autonomy. It also affirmed Augustine's teachings about original sin and prevenient grace. But Orange was not yet a decisive victory for Augustinianism in the West. This same council emphatically rejected one principle suggested by the African theologian's doctrine of predestination, that God condemns some to damnation despite their love for Him and desire to do His will. For the time being, the West was still Eastern.

And with this we can return to Pope Gregory the Great. He largely disagreed with Augustine's assessment of the human condition. It was not because he was unfamiliar with the African bishop's many works. In fact, Gregory's own writings reveal more influence from Augustine than from any other church father. But he did not follow Augustine into the labyrinth of anthropological pessimism as so many in the West would come to do in later centuries.

It may have been Gregory's early commitment to monasticism that prevented this. The legacy of Eastern asceticism, which was for the most part very positive about the human condition, had by now become widely known in the West. John Cassian and the monks of Lérins had assured that. It was also found in the rule of Benedict, who as we have seen provided Gregory with a model of spiritual life. Benedict's rule was influenced strongly by John Cassian, as well as by the monastic rule of the Greek father Basil the Great. In the latter, Basil, a consistent witness to the Eastern principle of deification, wrote about free will in a way that contrasted sharply with that of Augustine: "Good action arising from free choice," he insisted, "is . . . present in us by nature."[66] Under these Eastern influences it is no surprise, then, to find that Gregory adhered to a view of man that was much more optimistic than that indicated by the recent Council of Orange.

The pope's contribution to the culture of Christendom thus represents an alternative, in the words of George Demacopoulos, to the "anthropological pessimism" that was beginning to creep into the West under the posthumous influence of Augustine. Gregory, for instance, generally avoided the phrase "original sin," using it just five times in all of his writings (compared to Augustine's five hundred times). And perhaps most importantly, Gregory fully assimilated the Eastern—and ancient—view that through free will and ascetical struggle man actively participates in the salvation he receives from God, enjoying a life of continuous spiritual transformation.[67]

Orientalizing Rome

THE CULTURAL EXCHANGE from East to West intensified during the two centuries that followed Gregory the Great's tenure as pope. The seventh century was marked by upheavals in Byzantium related to the invasions of first the Persians and then, more consequentially, the Arabs. Bishops and scholars fled to the Occident, and with them they brought the Christian romanitas of the Orient.

One of the most tragic emperors in the history of Byzantium was Heraklios. His reign was marked by a pair of military disasters. The first of these came at the hands of the Persian Empire, which defeated his army near Antioch and advanced deep into Byzantium's southern territories. The greatest blow was the fall of Jerusalem, which resulted in the desecration of the Anastasis and the seizure of the True Cross, which the Persians carried back to their capital of Ctesiphon. Miraculously, Heraklios rallied his army, and in an amazing reversal of fortune, invaded the Persian heartland and dealt a fatal blow to his enemy. Though several more years in the making, his counterattack resulted in the Battle of Nineveh in 627, after which Persia was forced to sue for peace. Heraklios returned to Constantinople in triumph, bringing the True Cross with him and temporarily placing it in Hagia Sophia before returning it to a liberated Jerusalem.

Less than a decade after the recovery of Jerusalem, however, an entirely new military threat arose in the south that would prove far more dangerous. Islam was from the start a militant faith, which, empowered by the forced unification of the Arabs by Muhammad, broke upon the world with brutal and unstoppable energy during the seventh century. One of Islam's core principles was *jihad*, righteous warfare, by which believers were encouraged to wage war in order to extend the influence of the new religion. After Muhammad's death in 632, his successors made much of this principle to motivate their followers in a series of aggressions against the southern flank of Byzantium.

The Christian Empire proved a poor match, partly because of her exhaustion after the recent wars with Persia. Heraklios again took to the field, but this time his armies could do nothing to stop the progressive fall of every significant city from Antioch to Carthage. In 638 Jerusalem fell again. At least this time its Muslim conquerors, influenced by the holy Patriarch Sophronios, who met them at the city gates to negotiate surrender, agreed to leave the Anastasis and its precious relic unmolested. But by the time the miserable Heraklios died in 641, most of Palestine and Syria were lost; the Arabs had already plunged into Egypt and were on the verge of capturing Alexandria. Only Anatolia would be spared the Arab onslaught. Byzantium, an empire that had straddled East and West, was now largely deprived of an East.

This territorial reconfiguration of Christendom had a profound effect on the West. For one, a flood of refugees from eastern territories overrun by Muslim armies began to pour into Italy and settle in Rome. Various calculations of the makeup of the Roman clergy during the seventh and eighth centuries reveal that it was predominantly of eastern provenance, with eastern clerics outnumbering western in some cases by three to one. Notably, the great majority of popes during these centuries were of Greek or Syrian rather than Latin ethnicity. What is more, the infusion of hellenophone clergy reversed the trend toward an exclusively Latin mentality that had marked western theology since the time of Tertullian and Augustine. The Greek fathers were once again on the minds of western fathers.

Eastern immigrants tended to be vigorously Orthodox in their doctrine. They had fled territories populated by large concentrations of monophysites. The latter had been given preferential treatment by the conquering Arabs due to their innate resistance to Byzantine rule. Dislodged from these areas, Orthodox clergy therefore brought to the West a renewed commitment to the doctrine of Christ's two natures.

This doctrine, of course, had been defended by Rome under Pope Leo, whose *Tome* helped establish the definition of Orthodoxy at Chalcedon in 451. Since that time, as we have seen, various impulses toward compromise with monophysitism had come from the Byzantine state, whose emperors had a political interest in accommodating the opponents of Chalcedon. Such an impulse returned under Emperor Heraklios, whose reign witnessed the loss of Asian and African territories in which monophysitism was widespread. The Patriarch of Constantinople at this time was Sergios, a man whose devotion to the emperor was equal to his dependence upon him. Knowing the emperor's political quandary, he proposed a new doctrine by which Christ, while irreversibly recognized as possessing two natures, nevertheless was said to possess only one "energy." This was a concession to the monophysites in that it appeared to assure them of the unitary personhood, or *hypostasis*, of Christ.

The innovation was almost immediately opposed by Sophronios, a Syrian by birth who, as we have seen, later became the patriarch of Jerusalem and negotiated its surrender to the Arabs. He was the author of Eastern Christianity's beautiful rite of the Great Blessing of the Waters. The rite was composed to mark the holiday of Theophany, the commemoration of the Baptism of Christ on January 6, which was the original date for celebrating the Incarnation (it became distinguished from the Nativity of Christ on December 25 only later).

The rite's poetic witness to the Incarnation says much about Christology and by extension cosmology and anthropology. As he stood outdoors over a spring or stream of water (presumably Sophronios himself would have stood over the Jordan River), the priest who administered the rite called down the Holy Spirit upon the most life-sustaining element of creation, asking God to bless and sanctify it. Through this sacrament, earthly, chronological time shifted to eschatological time, and the world entered paradise. "Today," the priest declared,

> *the time of the feast is at hand for us: the choir of saints assembles with us and angels join with men in keeping festival. Today the grace of the Holy Spirit in the form of a dove descended upon the waters. Today the Sun that never sets has risen and the world is filled with splendor by the light of the Lord. Today the moon shines upon the world with the brightness of its rays. Today the glittering stars make the inhabited earth fair with the radiance of their shining. Today the clouds drop down upon mankind the dew of righteousness from on high. Today the Uncreated of His own will accepts the laying on of hands from His own creature. Today the Prophet and Forerunner approaches*

the Master, but stands before Him with trembling, seeing the condescension of God towards us. Today the waters of the Jordan are transformed into healing by the coming of the Lord. Today the whole creation is watered by mystical streams. Today the transgressions of men are washed away by the waters of the Jordan. Today Paradise shines down upon us.[68]

The rite of water blessing reveals in part why Sophronios so vigorously opposed the doctrine of a single energy when he learned of it. Such a doctrine seemed to minimize the humanity of Jesus, suggesting that the nature he took from the Virgin Mary was different from that shared by all men. How could the reality of the "hypostatic union" of two distinct natures in Christ be preserved if one of them, the human, was either negated by the union or made to seem an abstraction? What is more, through the humanity of Jesus the entire material creation received sanctification, as the poetic prayer over the waters indicates.

Sophronios's objections compelled Patriarch Sergios to seek input from Rome. At this time a Greek named Honorius sat upon the papal throne. He responded in a letter to Sergios that the doctrine of one energy might preferably be rendered as a doctrine of one will. "We confess," the pope concluded, "the one will of our Lord Jesus Christ." This fateful statement was the origin of a new though related doctrine, monothelitism.

Honorius's statement was a boon to the beleaguered Heraklios. With the active encouragement of Sergios, he issued in 638 a statement called the *Ekthesis,* which banned any discussion of Christ's energies and instead proclaimed, following Pope Honorius, that Christ possessed only one will. That very year Sophronios died, as did both Honorius and Sergios. As the Church held her breath, a new voice then rose up against Monthelitism that proved even more compelling than that of Sophronios. A monk named Maximos, who knew Sophronios closely and regarded him as "father and master" in the faith, now challenged the doctrinal innovation.

Like Sophronios, Maximos the Confessor was of eastern provenance, and he had even served as an official in Constantinople. And like Sophronios, his resistance to monothelitism grew from insights into the cosmological and anthropological implications of the doctrine. Maximos was one of

St. Maximos the Confessor
Photo by Jim Forest

Christendom's greatest theologians—the "father of Byzantine theology" in the words of John Meyendorff.[69] At the heart of his theological vision was deification, the doctrine that man, as the biblically defined image of God, can experience direct communion with God through the sacramental and ascetical life of the Church. As Maximos put it, man,

the image of God, becomes God by deification. He rejoices to the full in aban-
doning all that is his by nature . . . because the grace of the Spirit triumphs
in him and because manifestly God alone is acting in him. . . . Thus God and
those worthy of God possess in all things one and the same energy, or rather,
this common energy is the energy of God alone, since he communicates himself
wholly to those who are wholly worthy.[70]

On the surface, this might appear to endorse the same "one energy" doctrine
behind monothelitism, as Maximos speaks of "one and the same energy" for
man. But that is exactly the point of difference: Maximos's use of the techni-
cal term "energy" here is to describe deified man, not the incarnate Christ. It
is a fundamentally different point from that of Sergios.

Drawing upon his eastern predecessors, especially Gregory the Theologian, Maximos appropriated the Aristotelean term "energy" to communicate
what can be called its "existential" meaning. It speaks of the real humanity
that is transformed by Christ in His Incarnation and then shared with His
disciples. In this sense, Christ becomes the perfect man, or "second Adam,"
to paraphrase the Apostle Paul. For Maximos, Christ must possess two wills
if He is to offer the way toward man's union with God. In Christ the human
will actively participates with the divine will, not as an abstraction or as a
fantasy, but as an existential reality. Only this can lead to deification. Without two wills, then, Christ could never offer the sacramental means toward
man's voluntary and transformative ascent to paradise.

Unlike his spiritual father Sophronios, Maximos spent the latter part of
his life in the West as a refugee from the Arab conquests. He was in Carthage
before the city finally fell and there successfully debated against a prominent monothelite named Pyrrhus. But Maximos's most important work was
in Rome, where a theological resistance movement against the caesaropapist
doctrine of monothelitism was being mounted.

That movement was launched by Pope Theodore, another of the era's
eastern pontiffs. He was of Palestinian origins and realized that the theological stature of Rome was insufficient to provide a decisive end to the heresy. According to Ekonomou, "the intellectual poverty displayed by Theodore's immediate [papal] predecessors had to be replaced with a revitalized

theological knowledge and skill sufficient to pierce the subtlety of the East and expose [monothelitism's] apparent truth for the heresy it really was."[71] Theodore therefore turned to Maximos, newly arrived in Rome after his debate in North Africa. Theodore settled on a plan to assemble a synod of bishops that would represent, he hoped, an ecumenical council. Significantly, for the first time ever the pope ignored the requirement that the emperor issue the summons to such a council and assumed responsibility for it himself.

This act was the beginning of what might be called the heroic papacy, a self-conscious effort by successive popes to wrest doctrinal authority from caesaropapist emperors and to establish it instead as the prerogative of Rome. The irony, according to Ekonomou, "was that Rome would experience its revitalization not by drawing upon its own pitiable resources, but rather through the collaboration of a Greco-Palestinian pope and a Constantinopolitan monk employing a style of theological discourse whose tradition was purely Eastern."[72] In other words, Theodore, Maximos, and the legacy of eastern patristics now elevated the papacy to a heroic status it had never before occupied in the history of Christendom.

As it turned out, Theodore did not live to see the council he organized. But an even more resolute pope succeeded him and presided over it when it assembled in Rome's Lateran Palace. Pope Martin turned out to be one of the era's rare Italians, but he had spent years in Constantinople as *apokrisiarios*, that office of papal envoy that assured close contact between Rome and the East, and which earlier popes such as Gregory the Great had occupied. While in the East, Martin had imbibed deeply of Christian *romanitas* there. As a result, he was content to follow Theodore's lead and allow Maximos—whose Greek theological credentials were impeccable—full latitude in determining the council's agenda. Nor did Maximos work alone; he was assisted by a large team of Greek monks and theologians who had themselves traveled from the East. When this team was finally ready, the Lateran Synod of 649 opened—and did so, it might be noted, without imperial authorization.

With more than one hundred bishops in attendance, the synod issued a statement unconditionally rejecting monothelitism as a heresy. Its careful citation of patristic theological precedent, prepared in advance by Maximos, drew far more upon the Greek fathers than on the Latin tradition. But its methodology was universally Orthodox. In this it can be seen to have conformed closely to the canon of tradition articulated by the Latin father Vincent of Lérins, who, challenging the one-sidedly radical teaching of Augustine about original sin and prevenient grace, declared that not local or individual doctrinal opinion is to be followed, but that which has been believed "always, everywhere, and by all."

In the long run, the fathers of the Lateran Synod were vindicated when a new emperor, Constantine IV, convened in Constantinople what came to be accepted as the Sixth Ecumenical Council of 680–681. This council's conclusions repeated those of the Lateran bishops and constituted the definitive rejection of Monthelitism. The council also anathematized those who had advanced the heresy, including not only Patriarch Sergios but Pope Honorius as well. For centuries to come, newly elected popes of Rome were required upon taking office to renounce by name the teaching of their heretical papal predecessor, who had been the first to speak of "one will."

In the short term, however, Maximos the Confessor and Martin both paid dearly for their defense of Orthodoxy. In the aftermath of the Lateran Synod they had been excoriated by a more immediate successor to Heraklios, the resentful Emperor Constans II. The latter resolved to have them abducted in Rome by the Byzantine exarch of Ravenna and brought to trial in the East. Both were tortured; Martin was publicly flogged on the streets of Constantinople, and Maximos had his right hand chopped off and his tongue cut out to prevent continued theological influence. Both died in exile, reviled by a caesaropapist state that demanded the final word in defining Christian doctrine.

Rome's defense of Orthodoxy at the Lateran Synod and the heroic ideal of the papacy that went with it were the result of Eastern influence in the West. But it was not only doctrine and church administration that were orientalized during this time. At its very roots, western piety was nourished by a stream of liturgical practices that had their headwaters in the East.

This is true of the veneration of the cross on September 14, known as the feast of the Elevation of the Cross. Prior to the seventh century, no such feast existed in Rome. Under the influence of first Palestinian and then Constantinopolitan practice, however, it became one of the most important celebrations on the western church calendar.

Even more significant was the veneration of the Virgin Mary in connection with various holidays. Following the Council of Ephesus in 431, where Mary was definitively recognized by the title Theotokos ("Birthgiver of God"), devotion grew rapidly in the East. Marian holidays began to define the liturgical calendar. This development found early, fifth-century expression in Empress Pulcheria's construction of the Church of the All-Holy Theotokos in the Blachernae district of Constantinople.

Integrated closely with the calendrical and architectural celebration of Mary was a flowering of hymnography about her. The most famous example is the work of the sixth-century Syrian monk Romanos the Melodist, whose elaborate Akathist hymn became inspiration for innumerable compositions in later centuries.

Byzantium's insuppressible Marian creativity was also exemplified by the eighth-century Syrian bishop Andrew of Crete, who served within the jurisdictional boundaries of Rome. His Great Penitential Canon invented an entirely new form of hymnography and continues to this day to dominate the first week of the Great Fast among Eastern Christians. In addition to this, Andrew composed numerous homilies and hymns commemorating Mary on the occasion of what had become her principal holidays: her Nativity (September 8); her Presentation of Christ in the Temple (February 2); her Annunciation (March 25); and her Dormition (August 15). Under the influence of the Eastern popes, Rome appropriated all four of these holidays from Constantinople and Jerusalem during the course of the seventh century, laying the foundation for a rich Marian piety that would shape Western culture for centuries to come.

The influence of the Byzantine liturgy on Rome during this time went far beyond the introduction of feasts of Mary and the cross. In fact, virtually no area of Western worship was untouched by this orientalizing cross-cultural exchange. The cosmologically rich rite of water blessing composed by Sophronios has been discussed above; a version of it was introduced at this time in the West, along with the eschatological phrase "today" (*hodie* in Latin), which, in the case of Sophronios, indicated that the "now" of chronological, earthly time was transformed through sacramental worship into the "now" of heavenly immanence.

The liturgical rhythm of time in the West came to resemble that in the East. At the Latin Mass during Pentecost, Western Christians became accustomed to the communion hymn "O Taste and See" (*Gustate et videte*), which was borrowed directly from the Presanctified Liturgy of Constantinople (which, as we have seen, was in turn said to be, in an undisclosed way, the work of Pope Gregory the Great). Palm branches came to be used at the celebration of Palm Sunday in Rome in imitation of the ancient practice of Jerusalem. On Good Friday, one of the most characteristically Greek hymns, the Trisagion, was inserted into the service of the adoration of the cross. In fact, what would become one of the most characteristic liturgical expressions of Latin piety, the hymn "Hail Mary" (*Ave Maria*), was itself directly imported from Greek use at this time.

Heaven on Earth

BY THE EIGHTH CENTURY, then, the culture of Christian romanitas—whether in the East or the West—had become thoroughly imbued with the sacramental character of worship. God's presence was very nearly everywhere felt—even, as we saw in the previous chapter, at the imperial court of Constantinople. An experience of the divine had, indeed, been characteristic of pagan romanitas before Pentecost. The temples scattered throughout the empire's towns and cities, the miraculous portents, the seasonal festivals—all of these manifested divine activity on earth. As a result, traditional Christianity was successful during its first centuries among Romans as much for its claims about heavenly immanence as for its sublime theology or compelling morality. Unlike paganism, however, traditional Christianity claimed that there was one true God, and that His only-begotten Son had come to Earth in the Incarnation. It claimed that through the sacramental life of His Church, that very God continued to fill the world He had created with His divine presence.

This cosmological belief had an anthropological corollary. In traditional Christianity, man was seen as a microcosm, or "little world." This had been elaborated most fully by Maximos the Confessor. He brought attention to the biblical doctrine of the Incarnation to emphasize the bodily as well as spiritual presence of God in the Church. He also drew upon earlier fathers such as Irenaeus, who viewed the material world as a good thing, most especially because God's Son entered into it. Irenaeus had claimed that man's material and historical existence is the context in which salvation is achieved. Maximos believed that the entire creation, or macrocosm (literally, "bigger world"), is brought into harmony with God through the agency of man the microcosm. Man therefore played the role of mediator in bringing the world back into communion with God.

This required the heavenly transformation of the world. Since the world had been overcome by sickness and death, by sorrow and uncertainty, by the demonic principalities and powers, it was necessary radically and completely to reconfigure it. Because of sin, nothing in it, whether at a macrocosmic or microcosmic level, could save itself. To be saved, it must enter the kingdom of heaven.

The heavenly transformation of the world was possible through a principle called orientation. This remarkable word, used with such carelessness and ignorance today (in expressions such as "freshman orientation" or "sexual orientation"), was once symbolic in the classical sense of representing a reality that cannot readily be seen or described. It is based on the Latin for "east," oriens. Though coined in the English language only in modern times, it explicitly related to the act of facing east or possessing an eastward disposition. It described the practice in traditional Christianity of worshipping toward the east.

This practice of facing eastward was indeed ancient. It is explicitly noted as early as the fourth century in an aside by Basil the Great, who was speaking of various ancient traditions of the Church that had been handed down in unwritten form. The tradition was undoubtedly inspired by several biblical passages. Jesus Himself had indicated His second coming would occur as "lightning comes from the east" (Matt. 24:27). The Prophet Malachi had used eastward imagery for the Messiah, bringing to mind the sunrise by calling him the "Sun of Righteousness" (Mal. 4:2). And, finally, the Book of Genesis had identified the east as the very location of paradise (Gen. 2:8). All of this led early Christians to pray toward the east and, when they began building public temples, to enter them from the west and stand facing the east during worship. Eventually, the altar would be located in the eastern-most point of the building, and the bishop or priest would stand at the head of the assembly facing eastward along with it.

But liturgical orientation was much more than a formalized approach to worship. It was a symbol of baptism, of the new creation that was born again from the sacramental fountain of life. The old man now dead, the Christian lived his entire life oriented toward communion with Christ, or paradise. This is why the rites of baptism that came to be developed began in the westernmost part of the temple, near the entrance, and culminated in the easternmost part of the temple, near the altar. Most dramatically, in the East there arose a series of exorcism prayers prior to baptism that were prescribed to be spoken at the very doors of the temple. To this day, the candidates for baptism in the Orthodox Church are ordered literally to turn at this moment to the west and spit upon the devil as a total rejection of him and of the spiritually untransformed world over which he presides.

By contrast, living for the fallen world and not for the kingdom of heaven—living in communion with Satan and not the Savior—was revealed by such symbolism as a life of acute *disorientation*. Christendom would in modern times reorient itself thus from paradise to utopia, but for the time being its beliefs and values were to be found in this liturgical symbolism.

Two of the temples built by Justinian expressed the symbolism particularly well. Hagia Sophia was designed with a huge central dome rising over the nave, the area where the people stand in liturgical assembly. Standing was, of course, the normative disposition of a Christian in prayer. Assembled as the body of Christ, the people were in the presence of their Lord, and not even the emperor remained seated in the presence of the King of

Kings. A comfortable or even casual disposition seated on pews would not become common until the decline of sacramental worship and the rise of the extended sermon during the Protestant Reformation many centuries in the future.

Standing beneath the central dome of Hagia Sophia, worshippers gazed upward into its dizzying, voluminous space. There they saw an icon of Christ known as the Pantocrator, or "Almighty." Gazing downward in return, the Savior's image was a visual proclamation that Christ is present as the Head of His body the Church. What is more, the symbolism of a central dome was also a proclamation that Christ is present on Earth in sacramental worship. As one standing in an open field at midnight would look up at the starry dome of heaven, so Christians in Hagia Sophia and the innumerable other churches built throughout Christendom in imitation of it experienced heaven while worshipping on earth.

A second good example of paradisiacal symbolism was the church of Sant'Apollinare Nuovo in Ravenna (not to be confused with its namesake Sant'Apollinare in Classe). Unlike the innovative central-domed Hagia Sophia, this church was a more conventional basilica-style temple. The basilica had been the earliest form of architecture used by Christians when they began to venture out of the catacombs during the third century. Elongated and rectangular in form, the basilica had been used extensively by the Romans as a standard public hall. But it had the virtue of orienting the Christian congregation when the entrance was placed at one end and the altar at the other. In the case of Sant'Apollinare Nuovo, a remarkable pair of mosaics that ran the length of the nave served to direct the attention of the assembled worshippers from the entrance to the altar.

By this time, men customarily stood on the right side of the temple and women on the left. The separation of the sexes was intended to prevent distractions, the sort of disorientation that always threatened spiritual life, even in temples. It was not, however, a statement about one sex being less important than the other. In fact, the practice symbolized just the opposite. The Old Testament temple had placed women behind men, who were the only fully initiated Jews by virtue of their circumcision. Baptism had now replaced circumcision, so that women as well as men were full initiates in the community. With the rise of Christendom, then, men and women truly became "one in Christ Jesus" (Gal. 3:28) when at worship.

Both sexes were on their way into the kingdom of heaven as they stood in a part of the temple called the nave. This architectural term is rooted in the Latin word for ship (*navis*), as the experience of worship in traditional Christianity was of going somewhere—namely, from a broken world into the kingdom of heaven. And Justinian's iconographical mosaics at Sant'Apollinare Nuovo proclaimed so very much to the assembled worshippers. On each side of the nave in which they stood, a row of saints was depicted— male on the right, female on the left. But they did not face the congregation so much as the altar. Both lines of images directed the worshippers' attention toward the east, toward the altar, toward the kingdom of heaven.

Christendom's liturgical transformation of the world did not end with temple architecture. It affected virtually all areas of Byzantine culture, resulting in what one historian aptly called the "liturgification of life."[73] It can be seen in the way the most elemental features of the cosmos, time and space, were spiritually transformed.

Time, for instance, became integrated into the Christian experience of paradise. Roman society had recorded time in relation to natural phenomena, such as the planets, or political events, such as the founding of Rome. Christians changed this, with consequences that are still visible today. Genesis had revealed that time was part of God's creation. And having fallen along with the rest of the world, time was called to be redeemed in the New Covenant.[74] Daily, weekly, and annual cycles of time were therefore reoriented to the liturgical calendar. The setting of the sun became marked by vespers and its rising by matins. Every week was Passion Week in miniature, with fasting on Wednesday (the day Judas betrayed Jesus) and Friday (the day Jesus died on the cross). After a day of rest—Saturday, when the Lord lay in the tomb and martyrs were commemorated—a new week began with the Lord's Day, when the Resurrection was commemorated. Annually, Pascha and the long season of repentance that preceded it regulated and gave new meaning to the experience of spring. The dark winter became a time for contemplating the advent of the Light of the world. Eventually, every day of the calendar was claimed by a saint or a feast.

The conversion to a linear calendar was particularly cosmological, as it related time initially to the creation of the world and then, a little later, to the Incarnation. Pagan Rome had measured the succession of years "from the founding of the city" (*ad urbe condita*), which was believed to have occurred in 753 BC. Later, the reigns of emperors were employed. At first, Christians did not categorically reject these systems, but they gradually showed a preference for more spiritualized reference points. In the East, years came to be marked from the supposed creation of the world. In the West, the system of measuring time from the Incarnation became common. The latter was the work of a sixth-century monk named Dionysius Exiguus, who worked under a commission from the pope. His Anno Domini (AD) system entered broad circulation through the work of Venerable Bede, whose eighth-century *Ecclesiastical History of the English People* made use of it. The designation Before Christ (BC) came to be applied to dates prior to the Incarnation.

Interestingly, the incarnational system of linear dating has been attacked in recent decades by secular-minded academics and publishers in the West. Squeamish about using a system that is explicitly Christian, they have devised an alternate system using the strange term Common Era (CE) instead of Anno Domini, and Before Common Era (BCE) instead of Before Christ. However, it is not clear what is "common" to events since the Incarnation or uncommon before them. Ironically, the system simply

Venerable Bede

reproduces the earlier one under new designations (with BCE even serving to echo BC). An earlier, unsuccessful effort to replace the incarnational system with a secular one had occurred during the French Revolution, when the storming of the Bastille in 1789 was used to reset linear time. At least that failed project had been inspired by a utopian zeal for something, namely the revolution. The CE system, by contrast, is nihilistic in that it lacks any originating ideal at all. Its legitimacy rests exclusively on being "not Christian."

For now, however, Christendom measured time in a spiritually transformative way. It did the same with the other elemental feature of the world, space. The scriptures had themselves revealed the capacity of the Earth and physical creation in general to possess holiness. Moses had been told during his encounter with God on Mount Sinai that he was standing on "holy ground," and the Jewish temple had been made holy by the presence of that holiest of all objects, the Ark of the Covenant. Physical objects had been given a miracle-working power by contact with the physical bodies of the apostles, as the healing cloths distributed by Paul show (Acts 19:12).

Even the relics of departed saints were revealed to possess such powers. For instance, the Old Testament recorded a case in which the bones of Elisha, when touched at his burial site, caused a dead man to spring back to life (4 Kingdoms/2 Kings 13:20–21). The biblical Christianity of the early Church thus revealed heaven's presence within the spatial and physical limitations of creation.

Because the Incarnation had sanctified not only the human spirit, but the human body as well, the remains of saints were treasured by early Christians. We have already noted the statement made in the second-century *Martyrdom of Polycarp*, that after his death the saint's bones were gathered for subsequent veneration, being more precious to believers "than costly jewels." Worship was being arranged in the catacombs and graveyards in the third century, and soon after that time, particles of bones and other relics were being transported to places of enshrinement. The Church of the Apostles in Constantinople was the most celebrated such shrine, but Saint Peter's Basilica in Rome—also built by Constantine—was a close second since it was the site of the first apostle's internment.

The Church of the Resurrection (Holy Sepulcher) in Jerusalem was a particularly good example of the sanctification of space. The first Christians would have known well the site of their Lord's burial and Resurrection. But with the frightful destruction of the city by the pagan Roman army in AD 70 and then the expulsion of the Jews by Emperor Hadrian in 135, very little memory of the site survived. When Helen arrived early in the fourth century, a temple of Venus stood there. This was now demolished and cleared, and a costly and ornate Christian temple was ordered by Constantine. Known as the Anastasis ("resurrection"), it was consecrated in 335 by Bishop Macarius of Jerusalem, with Emperor Constantine in attendance. The temple's architecture was designed to communicate the experience of paradise. A modern historian describes its entrance as a "gate of heaven in the sense that in this holy place earth meets heaven and one may pass between."[75]

Many over the centuries did pass from earth to heaven in its space. One of the earliest to do so was a woman named Egeria. She went on a pilgrimage to the Anastasis from distant Spain during the late fourth century and recorded her impressions in a travel journal. That a woman could do such a thing in the ancient world was remarkable and says much about the elevated status of women that Christendom fostered. Once there, Egeria participated in the weekly celebration of the Lord's Day that began after sunset on Saturday. She described a liturgical rite that came to be known in Eastern Christianity as the Resurrectional Vigil, an all-night service of worship and fasting that culminated after sunrise in the reading of accounts of Christ's Resurrection, followed by eucharistic communion.

With such a sanctification of space, Christendom became a civilization of pilgrimage. Following Egeria's example, its members sought out places that manifested the material presence of divine grace. Where saints' bodies reposed and the sacramental life of the Church was conducted, they believed, God dwelt on earth among men. As Robert Markus put it, pilgrimage represented "a journey towards a place of holiness where power was present: power to transform the pilgrim's inner life, and, perhaps, miraculously, his outer, bodily existence; and, certainly, a power to transform, momentarily, the social constraints which anticipated that community in which the pilgrim would, at the end, share in the full freedom of the life of the saints."[76] Pilgrimage introduced the believer not only to the possibility proclaimed by the Gospel of personal transformation, but to that of the spiritual renewal of society itself.

Another historian of Western Christendom, Peter Brown, noted how the relics of the fourth-century Martin of Tours brought paradise into the world of pilgrims living in Gaul.

> To come to the tomb of a major saint, such as Saint Martin at Tours, was to breathe in a little of the healing air of Paradise. The fragrance of incense and of scented oil filled the sanctuary around Martin's tomb. But that fragrance was only a symbol of the real, healing breezes of Paradise which wafted from the tomb. To be healed at such a place was to experience a sudden flowering of the body. When he described cures performed at the tomb of Saint Martin, Gregory [of Tours] lingered, in gripping details, as much on the physical rhythm of each cure as on its outcome. For the rhythm of the cure itself showed dried and ruined human flesh regaining the first, exuberant good health associated with Paradise and with the Garden of Eden. . . . He had been touched for a moment by the all-healing abundance of Paradise, from which Adam had been cast out and in which Saint Martin now lived.[77]

What Adam had lost in the primordial paradise, then, early Christendom now offered as a partially realized eschatological paradise.

Traditional Christianity's sanctification of the world was a key reason for the successful conversion of the Roman Empire. Its joyful, exuberant cosmology became the heart of Christian romanitas, and this assured that church membership would not be limited to theological rationalists or dour moralists—that is, to an obscure community of intellectual elites. The world Christendom revealed to pagans was beautiful, and few there were who did not want to become a part of it.

Beyond Romanitas

THIS COSMOLOGICAL BUOYANCY was profoundly important for the Christian mission. Christianity had begun in the Mediterranean basin among peoples acculturated by the Roman Empire. Planted in the empire's cities, communicated in Greek, the faith had yet to cross the boundaries of romanitas.

As early as the fourth century, Christianity had indeed broken free of the empire in the East, being planted first in Armenia and then, even more distantly, in Georgia. A century later, a distinct eastern Syrian form of Christianity began to flourish within the pagan Persian Empire. But in the West, Christianity in many ways appropriated Roman civilization even as it transformed it. Even in Ireland, Patrick initially evangelized the Celts using Latin texts (though he himself had learned at least rudimentary Gaelic). In these distant lands, the Church's capacity to engage converts within their own distinct cultures became crucial.

Ulfilas, as we saw, was the first to do so. In the fourth century he evangelized the Goths using their native language. He translated the Bible into Gothic, though notably he elected to exclude the Books of Kings in fear that his militant audience would use these works to justify conquest. The decision had little effect, and the Goths soon after conquered much of southwestern Europe. Wherever they went, they brought Ulfilas's Arian form of the faith with them. However, they ultimately converted to Orthodoxy.

The Goths had always been something of a parasitic presence in the lands they conquered, establishing ruling dynasties that were not integrated into the social, cultural, or religious fabric of their realms. Significantly, the vast majority of their subjects belonged to the catholic faith. The Goths' allegiance to Arianism was really a function of politics and not faith. The Nicene Orthodoxy of the Byzantine Empire, which even after the fall of Rome to Alaric in 410 had continued to loom over the West, was seen as a tool of suppressing barbarian independence. This was especially true after the spectacle of Justinian's sixth-century wars of reunification. In Visigoth Hispania (Spain), for instance, the empire established a fortified presence on much of the southern coast. Arianism was thus a means of keeping the Visigoths' more powerful Byzantine antagonists at bay.

However, after the sixth century, the capacity of Byzantium to reach into western lands declined, and with it the political logic of Arianism. Western rulers came to see more advantage in embracing the faith of their catholic subjects. One by one, they all became Orthodox. One of the most symbolic conversions was that of King Reccared of Hispania. He ended his dynasty's allegiance to Arianism and formally converted to Orthodoxy at the Third Council of Toledo in 589.

To reinforce Orthodoxy against Arianism, the bishops of this synod introduced an addition to the Nicene Creed, which, according to the canons of the Fourth Ecumenical Council, could not be changed without thereby changing the faith. Despite this sacred prohibition, the Spanish bishops believed Arians would come to accept Christ's divinity if the Creed were reworked to claim that the Holy Spirit proceeded not only from God the Father but from His Son as well. Accordingly, to the clause about the Holy Spirit they added the Latin word *filioque* ("and the son"), so that the Creed now read ". . . the Holy Spirit . . . who proceeds from the Father and the Son." The innovation would prove fateful and tragic in the subsequent history of Christendom.

Hispania had long been a part of the civilization of Rome, even if the Visigothic ruling elite had itself remained aloof from romanitas. But in the lands to the north, beyond the Rhine River, much of the West remained untouched by Roman culture and was therefore a greater challenge to Christian missionaries. Some approached this *terra incognita* by concentrating on its ruling elites. They believed that converting the nobility and courts of the barbarian tribes would trigger the mass conversions of their subjects. In many cases they were proven correct.

The result was a form of Christendom distinct from that of the Byzantine East. Some historians have called it the *adelskirche*, or "nobility-church." It was a church culture centered upon the local court and expressing the values of warrior elites. Militancy was its most notable expression. This, obviously, could threaten adherence to the traditional Christian values of mercy and humility. In fact, the theme of militancy would characterize significant developments and episodes in the future of Western Christendom. For the time being, it could certainly lead to incongruity. In one case, a group of warriors submitted to baptism on condition that they be allowed to wage war freely once they were Christians. When the time came for their immersion, they held their right hands up out of the transformative water to prevent the loss, as they saw it, of the power to wield weapons![78]

It was certainly a warrior class that controlled the government of the Germans, most notably the Franks. This tribe had centered itself upon the Rhine throughout the fifth century. In the 480s, King Clovis began what proved to be an enormously successful war of expansion to the West, ultimately joining most of modern France—named after the Franks—to his realm. As this was happening, he decided, under the influence of his catholic wife, to receive baptism. The conversion of Clovis to Orthodox Christianity in 508 established an important foothold for Christendom in what until that time had been a predominantly Arian West.

Then, about a century later, another important western territory was brought into Orthodox Christendom. The Germanic Saxons had invaded England during the fifth century, long after Rome had evacuated that northern island outpost of romanitas. Once established, they came to be known as Anglo-Saxons to distinguish them from their continental cousins, known simply as Saxons. Intermingling with the native Briton population, the Anglo-Saxons forged a distinct culture. They also created a network of political units called, somewhat pretentiously, kingdoms.

It was the king of Kent, Aethelbert, who sometime shortly before 600 converted from paganism to Christianity. In doing this he was influenced by his Christian wife, Bertha. He was also influenced by a missionary named Augustine, who had been sent to England by Pope Gregory. Following his conversion, Aethelbert established the capital city of Canterbury as the center of Augustine's administration of the catholic Church there. Other warlords and petty rulers followed Aethelbert's example in Britain, which, along with Ireland, now placed northwestern Europe firmly within Orthodox Christendom.

The conversion of the West was not limited to the adelskirche, however. Missionaries proved themselves attentive to cultural issues too, though in some cases with condescending results. One important example of this is Boniface. During the eighth century, he obtained Frankish protection to preach the Gospel in the northeastern German borderlands of Saxony and Frisia. He boldly appropriated cultural and religious symbols of the native population to do so.

Boniface held to a policy of what might be called shock evangelism. Arriving at a pagan shrine, he would knock it to the ground, preach a sermon on the powerlessness of its idols, and call on the native population to accept baptism. In his most notorious act, he felled an ancient sacred oak at Geismar and then, having proven the oak's powerlessness in the face of a transcendent God, used its timbers to erect a Christian temple in which to baptize locals. Perhaps many of them viewed the temple the way they had once viewed the tree, as a source of magical power. In any case, Boniface's action is an example of the early Church's appropriation of pagan objects and the transformation of them into a means of Christian worship. But his policy of evangelization through shrine-conversion was confrontational, and the pagans may have been reacting to that when they martyred him in 754.

A more culturally sensitive approach to evangelization was articulated by Pope Gregory the Great. It was he who had sent missionaries to Britain under the leadership of Augustine of Canterbury, the bishop who baptized Aethelbert. In 601 Gregory wrote to Augustine the following letter, admonishing him not only to honor the culture of Anglo-Saxon pagandom but to apply the same buoyant cosmology that had won over the Romans.

The idol temples of that race should by no means be destroyed, but only the idols in them. Take holy water and sprinkle it in these shrines, build altars and place relics in them . . . When this people see that their shrines are not destroyed they will be able to banish error from their hearts and be more ready to come to the places they are familiar with, but now recognizing and worshipping the true God. . . . Thus while outward rejoicings are preserved, they will be able more easily to share in inward rejoicings. It is doubtless impossible to cut out everything at once from their stubborn minds: just as the man who is attempting to climb to the highest place, rises by steps and degrees and not by leaps.[79]

It is interesting to note the tone of pastoral insight here. The author of the psychologically brilliant *Pastoral Rule,* Gregory astutely predicted how pagans could be settled effectively in the new faith. When presented with a form of Christianity that honored cultural precedent while maintaining unswerving fidelity to the true faith, they would be much more inclined to conversion than if their entire cultural order were swept away.

"At the Edge of the World"

ALL OF THIS BRINGS attention to the cosmology of the Great Commission, especially the Marcan version of it, in which Christ sends evangelists to the "whole creation." The conversion of the world was a process that engaged the world in its entirety. Culture was part of the world, and it was called to bear the saving faith wherever the Church planted herself. Culture was therefore as much a means of evangelization as an object of it.

But not just culture. For nature, too, was caught up in the salvation of the world. For the newly converted Christian, the natural world, lately animated by spirits, was none the less holy for being the creation of the transcendent Creator God proclaimed by the Gospel. The best of the early Church's missionaries were scrupulous in honoring the creation even as they directed converts toward the kingdom of heaven. For them, paradise was to be discovered in this world to the extent that it was transfigured by the kingdom of heaven.

Perhaps the best example of their affirmative cosmology was found in neophyte Ireland, located, as one of its earliest evangelists put it, "at the edge of the world." There the Celtic natives flooded into Christendom because it seemed the fulfillment of their former culture, one in which the natural world was charged with spiritual significance.

Patrick was himself not Irish, but a Briton. Abducted as a youth from his homeland to serve as a slave in Ireland, he escaped only to return years later as an evangelist. But before that happened, he travelled to Gaul, where he is believed to have sojourned for a time at the famous monastery of Lérins. There he would have received an education in the faith that was profoundly influenced, as we have seen, by the monastic tradition of Eastern Christendom. With his theological formation complete, he then returned to Ireland. Though a foreigner, he assimilated the Celtic culture perfectly and was therefore able to present the Gospel in a way both recognizable and transformative.

A story about his early contact with the Irish illustrates this. Its facticity is challenged by nearly all modern historians. But whether it happened or not—or perhaps happened in a different way—it provides a good illustration of the way the Christian mission engaged the culture of Irish pagandom. Soon after his arrival on the island, the story claims, Patrick ran into strong resistance from the High King Laeghaire, who kept his court at Tara. The king, surrounded by his druid priests, had given orders that no outdoor fires be allowed during a spring pagan festival since fires were considered holy on that night. That particular year the festival happened to occur on the Christian feast of Pascha, and Patrick boldly set a bonfire on a neighboring hill in view of Tara. His point was to proclaim the Gospel of Christ's Resurrection. But he did so by appropriating a symbol familiar and even magical to the Irish—fire. In this and other ways he successfully laid the foundation for Celtic Christendom.

As an effective Christian missionary—one of the most effective in history—Patrick was able to reconfigure the world without eradicating its perceived holiness. A celebrated book by Thomas Cahill—who, it might be noted, expresses little sympathy for the traditional Christianity of Rome—has put it thus:

> *Patrick could put himself—imaginatively—in the position of the Irish. To him, no less than to them, the world is full of magic. One can invoke the elements—the lights of heaven, the waves of the sea, the birds and the animals. . . . The difference between Patrick's magic and the magic of the druids is that in Patrick's world all beings and events come from the hand of a good God, who loves human beings and wishes them success. And though that success is of an ultimate kind—and, therefore, does not preclude suffering—all nature,*

indeed the whole of the created universe, conspires to mankind's good, teaching, succoring, and saving.[80]

Of particular interest is the famous prayer attributed to Ireland's evangelist known as *Saint Patrick's Breastplate*. It is a work, according to Ian Bradley, "shot through with a sense of the presence of God." Like all things attributed to Patrick, the prayer may have had nothing personally to do with him. This at least is the conclusion of many scholars. Nevertheless, it is accepted as an authentic expression of early Celtic Christendom, being composed no later than the eighth century.

From a doctrinal point of view, the *Breastplate* could not be more Orthodox. It launches itself with praise of the Holy Trinity. It speaks of Christ's Incarnation; of His baptism; of His crucifixion; of His Resurrection; of His ascension; and of His second coming in judgment. The prayer speaks also of a natural world overrun by demons, against whom the Christian desperately needs heavenly assistance. It speaks finally of the evils of heresy, witchcraft, and idolatry. There is no ambiguity in the prayer: the transcendent God of Christianity is utterly different from the animistic spirit of paganism.

And yet this same God descended to the earth and filled it with His presence. He is, according to the prayer, the "Creator of creation." This title for God appears at the beginning and the end and gives the prayer its meaning. All of creation speaks of the transcendent God, points to Him, manifests His presence upon the earth. "I bind unto myself today," one stanza reads,

> *The virtues of the star-lit heaven,*
> *The glorious sun's life-giving ray,*
> *The whiteness of the moon at even,*
> *The flashing of the lightning free,*
> *The whirling wind's tempestuous shocks,*
> *The stable earth, the deep salt sea,*
> *Around the old, eternal rocks.*

The starry skies, the glory of the sun, the moonglow of evening—all of these natural phenomena are caught up in Saint Patrick's ecstatic vision of a world transfigured by paradise. Even the rocks find a place within it. Hard, compressed, "eternal"—their materiality speaks of the transcendent and immaterial glory of God's kingdom.

For Bradley, the *Breastplate* reveals how "the whole stress of Celtic Christianity was on the immanence of God." This he contrasts with Western Christianity in both its later Roman Catholic and Protestant forms, where an "over-transcendent view" of God came to prevail. What is more, this modern scholar locates in the immanent cosmology of the Christian Celts a strong theological affinity with the "Eastern Orthodox churches."[81]

Indeed, one is reminded here of the cosmology expressed in Sophronios's rite of water blessing. One could scarcely get any further west than Ireland, yet the piety there was as radiantly expressive of divine immanence as that found in Christendom's eastern borderlands. For the author of the *Breastplate*, Christ is everywhere present and fills all things.

The penultimate stanza, before the author returns to dogmatic statements about the Trinity in the final one, uses prepositions to emphasize the real presence of God in the world. Christ is "with me," "before me," "behind me," "within me," "beneath me," "above me." He is "at my right hand" and "at my left." He is everywhere. All of creation is filled with Him and has become a means of communion with Him.

Celtic piety was not in most cases pantheistic, however. This, it appears, is the consensus of its most sober-minded and theologically informed historians. In early Celtic culture, according to Esther de Waal,

> there is never any confusion between the Creator and the world of his creating. God is involved in his creation, and is close to everything that he has made in his world, but there is here a vision of creation which yet avoids pantheism. In this, once again, we find distinct echoes of the East. Gregory of Nyssa or Basil the Great see creation as a revelation of the presence of God, but they are careful to preserve the distinction of the two and insist on their separateness.[82]

The emphasis such scholars place on the Celts' Eastern connections is somewhat speculative, as we have very little direct evidence of oriental influence. However, the obvious similarities in cosmology are so strong that they become virtually conclusive when it comes to art. Here, Celtic culture, like romanitas, was the obvious beneficiary of Eastern Christianity.

The art of the Christian Celts is famous. Scarcely had they come to own a distinct cosmology when they began producing some of Christendom's most original compositions. This can be seen in a land that they profoundly influenced, Britain. Some of their earliest monastics had pursued what they called a "green martyrdom," the dying to one's native land in order to practice an asceticism of self-exile in foreign lands. A century after Patrick—in about 563—one of these green martyrs, the missionary Columba, sailed across the Irish Sea to Iona, an island in the Scottish Hebrides. There he established a monastery that became a center of Celtic cultural influence. Moreover, Iona became the mother of another famous influential monastery, Lindisfarne, founded by the missionary Aidan on a tidal island off the coast of Northumberland.

It was there, on what came to be called Holy Island, that the Celtic genius first influenced foreign Christian art in the case of the sarcophagus of an Anglo-Saxon named Cuthbert. This monk was the abbot of Lindisfarne in the period after an important event in 664 known as the Synod of Whitby, when certain Roman church customs were given precedence over native Celtic ones. The holy Cuthbert was dedicated to establishing harmony

St. Columba of Iona
Icon by Aidan Hart - aidanharticons.com

between the estranged adherents of each culture. And when he died in 687, he was almost immediately recognized as a saint.

Remarkably, his coffin included on its side a wooden etching of the Virgin Mary holding Christ in her arms. This composition represents the earliest known icon of the Theotokos in Western Christendom outside of orientalized Rome. As we have seen, the empire's former capital had come to assimilate images and liturgical feasts of Mary during the Byzantine papacy of the seventh and eighth centuries. Cuthbert's coffin was thus an example of that movement's most westward penetration, facilitated, no doubt, by the romanizing Synod of Whitby. For centuries to come, images of the Virgin Mary would dominate the art of the West, and the Celts played an important role in navigating this cultural turning point.

In the meantime, back on Iona, another element of Eastern Christian romanitas had begun to characterize the most famous form of Celtic art, the stone high cross. Its most common pattern featured a nimbus or ring centered on the transepts. The Hebridean region surrounding Columba's monastery produced some of the earliest examples of this unique form of art. The Saint Martin Cross on Iona, for instance, dates to the late eighth century. Another example from the eighth century is the Kildalton Cross on the Island of Islay.

Given the character of Celtic piety, it is no surprise that the nimbus cross had close Eastern affinities. Both the Saint Martin Cross and the Kildalton Cross include, following the precedent of Cuthbert's coffin, iconographical representations of the Theotokos. Nor was the ring itself an invention of the Celts. A nimbus can be seen surrounding the cross in the apse of the famous sixth-century Byzantine Church of Sant'Apollinare in Classe outside Ravenna, discussed above in chapter three. That cross was part of an iconographical representation of the Transfiguration and therefore bore a strong cosmological significance. Interestingly, the Celtic high cross, with its nimbus, was originally placed in outdoor areas that would have produced a strong cosmological impression on believers. What is more, these outdoor areas may have been used for the Western Church's greatest sacramental action, the celebration of the Mass.

It would be hard to imagine a more striking way in which the spiritual transformation of the world might be manifested. The Christians who assembled together on the Lord's Day to participate in sacramental worship in Italy's Byzantine capital of Ravenna would have seen the stars of heaven above them painted within the apse. But the Christians of Celtic Britain would have seen stars actually floating above them in the limitless expanse of heaven itself. From East to West, from the heart of Christendom to its outer limits, the experience of paradise remained utterly vivid.

CHAPTER FIVE

One Culture, Two Empires

BY THE MIDDLE of the eighth century, the southern territories of Christendom had been all but consumed by the conquests of the Umayyad Caliphate, the successor state to the Arab empire forged by Muhammad and his successors. The geopolitical integrity of the Roman Empire had been severely compromised as Syria, Palestine, Egypt, and North Africa were all overrun by voracious Muslim armies.

The Christians of these lands were granted limited toleration for the time being, not only because they constituted the vast majority of the Arabs' subject population but because they were needed for its effective administration. Assigned second-class status as *dhimmis* by Islam, however, they were forbidden to exercise any kind of evangelical witness. If found guilty of converting a Muslim to Christianity, they were subject to beheading (along with the neophyte). Though granted a significant measure of religious autonomy among themselves, Christians were prevented from building new churches and even from properly maintaining existing ones. They were forbidden to display the cross, and bell ringing was silenced. The official law of Islam, *sharia*, required them to pay an onerous tax called the *jizya* for the privilege of remaining Christian.

Ironically, many of the Christian clergy supported the Arab colonization of southern Christendom. Bishops enjoyed a privileged status under the caliphate, being assigned the responsibility of overseeing their fellow dhimmis. A large number of them were monophysites who had, as we have seen, suffered persecution under Byzantine rule. For this reason many initially accepted as a lesser evil the monotheistic Arabs, who were completely indifferent to the question of Jesus' nature.

As a result the native Christian population became, in Bat Yeor's words, "both agents and victims" of their long-term subjugation to Islam.[83] As they endured decades and then centuries of life within the Islamic state, their resistance to the pressures of apostasy dissolved. What was once a vibrant Christian population slowly became an almost exclusively Muslim one. The Syriac and Coptic churches would survive until modern times, but their hold on the faith and culture of the native populations declined precipitously.

In the meantime, these churches tragically took their leave from the historical experience of Christendom in the West. Once a treasury of its liturgical, monastic, and theological culture, the lands of Ephraim the Syrian and Anthony of Egypt disappeared behind the oppressive veil of dhimmitude.

The same fate might have befallen Christian culture in the West but for the military resolve of its two greatest powers. The Umayyad Caliphate was intent on following the way of *jihad* and during the early eighth century continued its march toward universal conquest. Against Christendom it launched a two-pronged assault, one from the east and one from the west. Heroically, first Byzantium and then the kingdom of the Franks resisted these attacks and by doing so saved the remainder of Christendom from Muslim subjugation.

In the east, Byzantine Emperor Leo III held out against the mighty forces of the Umayyad Caliphate during the course of a year's siege of Constantinople. Though the Arabs marshaled more than one hundred thousand attackers, Leo's use of a new military technology known as Greek fire, as well as the city's famous Theodosian land walls, assured Christendom of survival in eastern Europe. Even the Virgin Mary assumed a role in the defense. Her icon was raised above the city walls, and it was on the Feast of her Dormition in 718 that the Arab force finally relented. Muslims would not return to lay siege to Constantinople again until the mantle of jihad had passed to the Turks during the fifteenth century.

Only a few years after the Byzantine defense of the East, the western borders of Christendom were attacked by the Umayyad Caliphate. This time it was the mighty Franks who defended against Islamification. The Arabs had already conquered most of Spain by this time, and they used it as a base for a thrust across the Pyrenees into southern Gaul. But at the Battle of Tours in 732, the Frankish King Charles Martel finally ended Islam's hope of conquering the rest of western Europe.

The military defense of Christendom by the Byzantines and the Franks was momentous. As Syriac and Coptic Christians were mostly driven underground, returning to an earlier catacomb culture, European Christendom had been saved. Nevertheless, the very states that so vigorously defended it at the beginning of the eighth century were about to launch reforms that would serve to estrange East and West from each other, thus forever altering the character of Christian civilization.

The Scandal of Byzantine Statecraft

IT IS AN IRONY that less than a decade after the Muslims withdrew from the walls of Constantinople, one of their principal doctrines suddenly sprang up within those very walls. Islam holds that a monotheistic deity stands over the world, radically transcendent from it, and that he can in no way be represented with visual images. In this it revealed its derivative relationship to Judaism, whose Second Commandment had condemned the fashioning of images. For Muslims, the deity was largely aloof from the world and very often contemptuous of it, a cosmology that resonated with some of the Old Testament's grimmest accounts of sin and judgment. For both Islamic and Jewish monotheism, Christianity's doctrine of the Trinity was incomprehensible. The Christian claim that God actually became incarnate in the person of Jesus Christ was for a Muslim one of the greatest of blasphemies, as it was seen to denigrate God's transcendent majesty.

In the absence of the triune God of Christianity, Islam and Judaism both taught that iconographical representations were illicit and deserved the severest measures of correction. Indeed, as the earliest Muslim armies swept through Egypt and Syria, they often destroyed icons of Christ and the saints that they found in Christian temples there. In 721 the ruler of the Umayyad Empire, Caliph Yazid II, issued an edict that all Christian icons in his lands be destroyed. This, perhaps, was the first act of iconoclastic destruction and persecution in the history of Christendom, albeit one now under the sharia law of an Islamic state. But it was really more like a prelude, for the first act of iconoclasm was a drama set in Christian Byzantium. (The second act, it might be noted, was also a Christian affair and would come during the Protestant Reformation.)

Emperor Leo III—the recent hero of Constantinople's defense—hailed from Syria, a territory recently conquered by the Arabs. This may have made him familiar with Islam's ban on religious imagery and the precedent of Yazid's legal imposition of that ban. Leo was also conscious of the Jewish attitude toward icons, and, remarkably, early in his reign issued orders for the compulsory baptism of all Jews. It may be that he interpreted the breathtaking advance of Islam against Christendom largely in the same way as did Muslims and many Jews—namely, that God had turned against Byzantium because of its impiety. A volcanic eruption that devastated the Aegean in 723 seems to have confirmed this superstition.

In any case, Leo formed the conviction that the widespread use of icons in worship was causing the empire to lose its faith. A reform of the Church was needed, and it would start with a fundamentalist application of the Scriptures. Encouraged to read Exodus 20 through the nomocentric (or law-centered) lens of Jewish scholars, as well as in light of Islam's anti-incarnational ban on images, Leo made the decision in 726 to launch what may be called Christianity's first reformation, the iconoclastic movement.

At the center of Constantinople stood a monument of the Christian state known as the Chalke Gate. It was a structure that connected the imperial palace on one side of a public square to Hagia Sophia on the other. The gate was known to every Constantinopolitan passerby for the enormous golden icon of Christ Pantocrator that stood sternly at the top of it. Leo now decided to have that icon removed and sent a team to perform the work. It might have seemed a modest start to his reformation. But as the team got to work atop the gate, a riot broke out. Christian culture was now so thoroughly imbued with the sanctification of space that it had become unthinkable to live in a city without holy objects such as icons adorning public monuments. So violently did the people of Constantinople resist the removal of the Chalke Pantocrator that they quickly turned on the team and lynched its hapless foreman.

This disturbing outcome does not seem to have dissuaded the zealous Leo. He was convinced that God had turned against Byzantium and that He had done so because icon veneration was a violation of His divine law. Leo was convinced that he was God's anointed ruler over the Christian common-wealth and that his religious convictions deserved to be instituted as law. So he charged ahead with the iconoclastic reformation.

We see in Leo's policy a particularly conspicuous example of that greatest of all Byzantine political vices, caesaropapism. Having made his decision, he issued an edict in 730 requiring the destruction of all—not selective, but all—icons in the empire. The Muslim Yazid would have been impressed. That the tradition of the Church—what Vincent of Lérins had defined as that which was held "always, everywhere, and by all"—regarded icons as a basic part of Christianity mattered little to the palace fundamentalist.

And when certain bishops began to resist his imperial will, he did what a true caesaropapist ruler always did: he persecuted them. Many were deposed. The most notorious case was that of the Patriarch of Constantinople, Ger-manos, who because of his refusal to abandon church tradition was deposed the very year of Leo's iconoclastic edict. His replacement was a careerist named Anastasios, who favored, then opposed, then finally at the end of his miserable tenure once again favored iconoclasm—all in response to the ever-variable political winds coming from the imperial palace.

After Leo died in 740, the scandal of Byzantine iconoclasm only increased as his son and heir Constantine V took control of church policy. He was nicknamed Copronymus, an epithet that causes Greek speakers to cringe, and which he earned when as an infant he fouled the font in which he was baptized. He was as much the reformer as his father and more theologically minded. With the assistance of the iconoclastic bishops that now ruled the East, Constantine composed a treatise against icons entitled *Inquiries*.

This work came to represent the most sophisticated statement of iconoclastic policy. It argued that the only true "image" (Greek, *eikon*) of Christ was the eucharist. What is more, it seized upon the hard-won dogma of Christ's two natures to argue that a physical object such as a painting could not properly represent Christ or His saints since it would be unable to express the spiritual, non-material reality of humanity. Isolating Christ's two natures, Constantine's *Inquiries* furthermore insisted that though an icon might successfully represent the physical element in humanity, it could not represent divinity, which was by nature unrepresentable. Icons were therefore not only innately idolatrous, as Muslims and Jews claimed, they were an expression of heresy.

In 754 Constantine assembled a large number of his bishops in the town of Hiereia to confirm the views of the *Inquiries*. Claiming falsely to be an ecumenical council (the compromised patriarchate of Constantinople was the only one represented), it did as it was told. The gathering was yet another example of caesaropapist conciliar politics, what the adamant Pope Leo I had once called a "robber council."

In the end, Constantine's council failed to win the day among the church leadership. Already in the time of Emperor Leo, the iconoclastic argument had been ably refuted by John of Damascus, an Orthodox scholar living within the Umayyad Empire. He is known for much more than the defense of icons. His liturgical poetry found its way into the heart of the Eastern liturgy, providing both the hymnography of the Paschal Canon and the basic hymnbook regulating the weekly cycle known as the Octoechos. He also composed the Church's first effort at systematically arranging Christian doctrine in a work entitled *An Exact Exposition of the Orthodox Faith*.

But on this occasion, it was John's defense of icons that proved invaluable. He was of course well aware of the Second Commandment but noted that soon after its issuance in Exodus, God had commanded the Israelites to make graven images of cherubim to surmount the Ark of the Covenant.[84]

Other images authorized in the Old Testament included the embroidered angels that adorned the temple veil. Clearly, the Second Commandment was not absolute.

But the heart of John's defense of icons was not contained in the Old Covenant. The new wine of the New Covenant (Matt. 9:17) was the proclamation that God had in the fullness of time become human in the person of Jesus, completing a revelation that had only partially been disclosed in the days of Moses. With the Incarnation, the old wine of the Second Commandment was now seen in the light of Christ, whose humanity was as real as His divinity. The commandment against idolatry was still in effect but had to accommodate the reality that the indescribably transcendent God had entered His creation and assumed human form, which, if real and not a fantasy, must be depicted to be fully honored. To ban icons of Christ was to undermine Orthodox doctrine about His two natures and to drift back into a kind of monophysitism that tends to minimize His humanity.

John's defense of icons provided a theological base against the attacks of the iconoclasts. But its cosmology went further than the eighth-century conflict over images. By asserting God's immanence in the created world through the Incarnation, it reestablished the basis for Christendom's continued experience of paradise.

In 787, a new assembly of bishops gathered in the city of Nicaea to issue a definitive defense of icons. This event came to be known as the Seventh Ecumenical Council. It involved representatives of all five patriarchates. Its declaration was remarkable in its expression of Orthodoxy. "We keep unchanged," its bishops declared,

> all the ecclesiastical traditions handed down to us, whether in writing or verbally, one of which is the making of pictorial representations, agreeable to the history of the preaching of the Gospel, a tradition useful in many respects, but especially in this, that so the incarnation of the Word of God is shewn forth as real and not merely phantastic . . . This is the faith of the Apostles, this is the faith of the orthodox, this is the faith which hath made firm the whole world.[85]

Icon of the Fathers of the Seventh Ecumenical Council
© Theologic Systems

Claiming to follow the apostolic faith, the bishops placed the Incarnation at the center of their defense of icons, indicating that the pedagogical function of images was secondary to that of revealing heavenly immanence.

It is of great significance that the Byzantine ruler who called the council was not an emperor but an empress. Irene had been chosen by Constantine

Copronymus as the bride for his son and heir, Leo IV. When the latter died at an early age, Irene found herself elevated as co-ruler with their only son, a boy named Constantine VI. Ambition ran deep in the family, and within a few years mother and son found themselves enemies across a partisan divide that always existed at the Byzantine court. In this case the two parties were the iconoclasts and the iconophiles (or iconodules as they are often known). The young Constantine came to align himself with the former, while Irene, having recently hosted the council of Nicaea, aligned with the defenders of icons.

In 790 Constantine acted to exclude Irene from power, becoming himself sole ruler. He did so with great cruelty, blinding potential enemies at court, including his own uncle. He also signaled a return to iconoclasm, despite the results of the Seventh Ecumenical Council. But to the leadership of the Church his actions became even more alarming. In 795 he decided to divorce his wife in order to marry a courtesan, a union the iconophile Patriarch Tarasios refused to bless. The result was another act of caesaropapism, in which Constantine simply ordered a local priest to perform the sacrament. This created a new level of tension between the emperor and the bishops known as the moechian controversy (from the Greek word for "adultery"). In fact, it penetrated well beyond the bishops to rank-and-file monastics, especially those under the leadership of an abbot named Theodore in the capital's Monastery of Studios.

But Constantine's iconoclastic tendencies, violent behavior, and blatant violation of canon law were not allowed to aggravate church conservatives very long. In 797, Irene returned to prominence at court and had her son arrested. She then ordered that he be blinded in the very palace room in which she had given birth to him. Soon after, he died of the wounds.

Another Byzantine tyrant had been overthrown, but only through the loathsome act of filicide. And for the first time in history—and to the consternation of Christendom—a woman was proclaimed Emperor of the Romans. It was a fitting, if ominous, end to a century that had witnessed scandal upon scandal from the throne in Constantinople.

The Franco-Papal Alliance

FROM THE WEST, the iconoclastic spectacle was difficult to behold. Old Rome was thoroughly integrated, as we have seen, in the culture of Eastern Christendom. Not only had most of the popes of the past two centuries been Greek, but much of Italy remained an integral part of the Byzantine state. This was symbolized by the city of Ravenna, whose exarch acted as the official representative of the emperor in the West. Its churches, as we have seen, were a visual reminder of the continued influence of the East. But heresy was heresy, and Rome's Orthodox popes could not ignore Constantinople's accursed relapse into it.

The first to react was Pope Gregory II. Even before learning of the iconoclastic edict, he had fallen out with Emperor Leo after the latter unilaterally reassigned tax revenue from the papacy's territories in southern Italy to the needs of the Byzantine state. When he learned of Leo's attack on the icons, he organized a local synod to condemn the action and sent letters to Constantinople demanding an end to it. Needless to say, he defiantly refused to comply with the iconoclastic edict in his own territories. When Constantine removed Germanos, Gregory sided with the beleaguered patriarch and acclaimed him a defender of the true faith.

Leo regarded these actions as treason and dispatched agents from Ravenna to hunt down Gregory in Rome. A century earlier Emperor Constans had abducted Pope Martin and brought him back to the capital for trial. No such respect was to be shown to Gregory. Leo simply ordered his agents to murder the pope. Because of the universal dismay at iconoclasm among the people of Rome, however, Gregory enjoyed protection and managed to evade the assassins. Nevertheless, the relationship between the two most important offices in Christendom was becoming impossible.

When Gregory was succeeded by a namesake in 731, Emperor Leo continued his relentless efforts to subjugate the papacy. Again the emperor sent assassins, but this time their ship foundered in the Adriatic. Unable to lay hands on Gregory III, Leo decided to punish the papacy as an institution by transferring to the patriarchate of Constantinople the papal territories of Calabria (in southern Italy), Sicily, and, for good measure, Illyricum (constituting the eastern coast of the Adriatic). Some historians consider this act to be the definitive turning point in the collapse of relations between Constantinople and the papacy, for by wresting these local churches from Roman jurisdiction, Constantinople demonstrated its intention to assume the final authority over church affairs. The act, committed against the background of the systematic heresy of iconoclasm, severed Roman attachments to the East and contributed to the future division of Christendom.

When Gregory III's successor Pope Zachary was elected in 741, he therefore cancelled the ancient practice of obtaining imperial confirmation. This, the last of the Greek popes, had begun to look to another power as the protector of the Church.

That power was the kingdom of the Franks. They were an attractive alternative to Byzantium because, unlike most other western kingdoms, they were Orthodox. Clovis, their first Christian ruler, had received baptism from Rome, unlike the Arian Ostrogoths and Visigoths. For the same reason the Franks were much preferred to the Arian Lombards, who during the past century and a half had conquered much of northern Italy and threatened Rome itself. What is more, in 751 any hope of Byzantine protection faded when the Lombards captured the empire's administrative center in the West, Ravenna. As the Lombards looked greedily toward a helpless Rome, the popes desperately turned to the most powerful Orthodox power in the West for help.

Gregory III had earlier approached the Frankish strongman Charles Martel, the defender of Western Christendom from the Muslims. But Charles had at that time been unable to oblige. For one, he was not formally the Frankish ruler. The Franks at this time possessed a king who ruled only in name, leaving real power in the hands of an official known as the mayor of the palace. When Charles died, he assured that this office would be inherited by his son Pepin the Short, thereby creating a dynasty known as the Carolingians (after the Latin form of Charles).

Pepin proved more ambitious than his father. Knowing of the papacy's interest in an alliance, he sent a famous query to Gregory's successor Pope Zachary (who, as we have seen, signaled his rejection of Byzantium by refusing to seek imperial confirmation of his election). In this query the mayor of the palace asked if it were appropriate that he, Pepin, should hold real power among the Franks and yet still be denied the legal title of king? The pope replied that no, this situation was abnormal. Favoring power over legitimacy, the pope's response enabled Pepin to overthrow his king and have himself elected in his place in 751.

But the Franco-papal alliance was not yet complete, at least from Rome's vantage point. Zachary died the very year of Pepin's usurpation of the crown. It was for his successor Stephen II to consolidate the new order of things. With its spiritual authority, the papacy may have given a free hand to Pepin to manipulate Frankish politics. But Stephen did not want the papacy to be engulfed by them. This was the lesson learned from Byzantine caesaro-papism, which in recent years had caused so much harm to the Church. For too long political rule had overstepped its boundaries, distorting the ideal of ecclesio-political symphony. Therefore, Stephen imposed upon his new ally a carefully designed principle that later generations would call *papal supremacy*.

It was expressed most symbolically in the fact that it was the pope, not Pepin's military electors, who confirmed the royal title. Zachary had already sent the respected missionary Boniface to anoint the new king. But Stephen knew he could achieve an even greater effect by performing a ceremony of anointing himself. This, after all, was the Eastern precedent; all Byzantine emperors since the time of Leo I in the fifth century had received the crown from the patriarch of Constantinople. So the pope set out across the Alps for the Frankish city of Paris to bestow upon the usurper Pepin III (as he came to be known) the Church's spiritual legitimacy.

The magnificence of the ceremony that took place in 754 was exceeded only by its consequences. Stephen performed the royal anointing—the first ever by a pope—at the Cathedral of Saint Denis. For good measure, he also anointed Pepin's sons Charles and Carloman as his heirs. Years later, the former of these offspring would receive his crown from the pope too. Finally, Pope Stephen bestowed upon all three Frankish leaders the innovative title Patrician of the Romans, which alluded to another goal he had in making his journey to the north.

That goal was to enlist the military support of the Franks against the Lombards back in Italy. As expected, Pepin proved complaisant. Within two years, his war machine had permanently broken the power of Stephen's Lombard enemy, taking Ravenna and surrounding Rome with an unconquerable shield of Frankish warriors. But Pepin's largess did not end there. As the new ruler of Italy, he granted the territories of Ravenna and Rome to Stephen as the core of what would become known as the Papal States.

An integral part of the Byzantine Empire since Justinian had recovered them in the sixth century, these territories had been ruled from Constantinople until only five years previously, when the Lombards seized them. Naturally, the decision not to return them to Emperor Constantine V was considered a betrayal in the East. But it was all part of an emerging new plan for a distinctly Western Christendom. Through this massive land grant of 756, known as the Donation of Pepin, the papacy received geopolitical security against future encroachments by heretics on the Byzantine throne. Henceforth, popes would exercise secular as well as ecclesiastical rule in the West.

So far, the narrative of Franco-papal relations would suggest that Stephen was a junior partner in the alliance with Pepin, since it was his vulnerability in Italy that had given rise to it. On balance, he had certainly gained the most from the arrangement. Yet his erstwhile neediness concealed a deeper abundance of purpose, and one that would eventually alter the course of the papacy.

When he came to Paris to plead for support against the Lombards, Stephen appears to have brought in his baggage train a document never before attested in the long history of the papacy. Indeed, in this case what he possessed was probably only a draft or early version of what would come to be known as the Donation of Constantine. This notorious work was a complete forgery, as later scholarship came universally to realize. However, for some seven hundred years its authenticity would be widely accepted, enabling it to make a permanent mark on Christendom.

The Donation of Constantine claimed to be an edict by Emperor Constantine himself, expressly dated to the years after his relocation of the capital to Constantinople. It addressed the bishop of Rome at that time,

Sylvester. The document declared that in gratitude for healing from leprosy, attributed to the miraculous intercessions of the bishop, Constantine had decided to grant the entire western half of his empire to Sylvester, with the territories passing on to subsequent occupants of his see.

Strangely, the edict did not end there. Constantine supposedly also proclaimed—though he had no right by canon law to do so—that the other patriarchates of the universal Church were subject to the authority of Rome. This meant that Rome enjoyed jurisdictional "supremacy" (a term the document actually uses) over the sees of Constantinople, Alexandria, Antioch, and Jerusalem. This was one of the claims that would expose the document as a forgery among future scholars, as the Church's administrative pentarchy that included those sees had not even been established in Constantine's time.

In the context of Constantinople's iconoclastic heresy and flagrant abuses of authority, it is easy to understand how eighth-century advocates of papal authority could have composed such an astounding document. Sadly, in an age ill-equipped to detect blatant forgeries, the Donation would be used as a weapon against perceived opponents of the papacy for centuries to come. Indeed, its first explicit use by a pope was in Leo IX's infamous letter of excommunication against Patriarch Michael Cerularius in the fateful year of 1054. But the Great Schism was still precisely three centuries in the future and by no means inevitable when Stephen negotiated a new order for Western Christendom at Pepin's court in 754.

So in a way it was Pope Stephen who dominated the Franco-papal alliance at its inception. Using what was probably still an early version of the Donation of Constantine, he established supremacy over his royal defender for the sake of preserving the papacy's freedom of action.

Constantine's alleged gift of papal supremacy was still very much a myth in the making and might not have been developed much further had Constantinople not shown such an obstinate tendency toward caesaropapism. Certainly something had to be done in response to iconoclasm and the Byzantine emperors' almost maniacal policy of sending assassins to silence recalcitrant popes. But Stephen's solution would create its own difficulties as the Franco-papal alliance progressed. This became apparent almost immediately during the reign of Pepin's son Charles, known to history as Charlemagne.

By the end of the eighth century, the relationship remained promising. Italy had enjoyed a generation of relative political stability, and the Lombards had finally, under Frankish pressure, made their peace with Rome. The papacy's former tormentors had even granted additional territory to the Papal States as a pledge of the new accord. This occurred at the same time as a resurgent iconoclasm manifested itself in the East under Emperor Constantine VI. Not only was the Byzantine crown now worn by another heretic. It was sullied by Constantine's decision to divorce his wife and marry a lover in open defiance of canon law, giving rise to the moechian controversy. It was a good time to have the Frankish ruler as protector.

And Charlemagne was a mighty one at that. After his succession in 768, he expanded the borders of Francia in all directions. From Muslim Spain to the broad stretches of pagan Central Europe, he all but owned continental western Europe. In fact, it was at exactly this time that the hitherto obscure word *Europe* was employed to make geographical sense of it all.[86] Most notable was Charlemagne's conquest of Saxony, where the native pagan population was forced on pain of death to accept baptism.

Francia was now the largest state in European history since the fall of the western Roman Empire. And like the empire of Augustus, its focal point was Rome. Charlemagne maintained close relations with the papacy and again played the role of its protector when the Lombards launched a military venture against some of the recently acquired territory of the Papal States. Handily defeating the Lombards, Charlemagne added their northern Italian lands to his ever-expanding realm. Throughout this episode, Pope Stephen's successor Hadrian showed unwavering support and gratitude.

However, the election of Hadrian's successor caused a temporary crisis. Pope Leo III was not a member of Rome's aristocracy, and a faction emerged soon after his election to remove him from power. One afternoon, while he was traveling down one of the city streets, he was accosted by a band of assassins with knives. They nearly gouged out his eyes. He barely survived the assault, and miraculously, after then being abducted, he managed to escape and flee the city. He knew where to go for protection.

Emperor Charlemagne
Wikipedia - Aachen Domschatz Bueste1.jpg

Unfortunately, when he arrived at Charlemagne's court at Paderborn, Leo discovered that his enemies had sent slanderous accusations ahead of him. His protector was embarrassed to report to him that he was said to be involved in financial misdeeds and sexual immorality. It is likely these were completely false charges, but Charlemagne felt he could not let them go unaddressed. He was, after all, Patrician of the Romans and the ruler of northern Italy. So he organized a formal investigation of Leo to be held back in Rome.

Charlemagne arrived in the city toward the end of 800. He and Leo immediately withdrew to the Lateran Palace, which had been the official headquarters of the pope since it was bestowed on the papacy by Constantine in the fourth century. There they no doubt picked up the conversation that had begun the previous year at Paderborn.

Charlemagne was at the height of his influence. Leo was just discovering his. They were the two most powerful men in the West. As they discussed their relationship, they looked up at a new mosaic Leo had commissioned for the adornment of his conference room. At the center stood the apostles; on the left Christ was flanked by Pope Sylvester and Emperor Constantine, an immediate reminder of the emerging myth of the Donation of Constantine. But it was an image on the right hand side of the mosaic that was most interesting on this occasion. At its center was the Apostle Peter, flanked, in this case, by representations of Pope Leo III and King Charlemagne, the latter-day successors to Sylvester and Constantine. Upon Leo, the first of the apostles bestowed the episcopal pallium. And on Charlemagne he bestowed the Roman banner of war.

When the synod called to judge Leo finally assembled, it was over almost before it began. Charlemagne watched calmly as the pope placed his hand on the Gospel and solemnly swore that he was innocent. All charges were dropped, and those who had dared to accuse the successor of Saint Peter were sentenced to death.[87]

It was on this occasion of Charlemagne's visit to Rome that the most famous event in the history of the Franco-papal alliance took place. On Christmas Day, as Charlemagne was lifting himself from a prostration at the head of the Frankish delegation during Mass at Saint Peter's Basilica, Pope Leo stepped forward suddenly and placed a crown on his head, declaring him Emperor of the Romans. The assembly immediately shouted its approval as with one voice, suggesting that the act had been rehearsed or in any case foreseen.

Perhaps Charlemagne had insisted on this as recompense for rescuing the pope from dishonor. Or perhaps—as a Frank with knowledge only of Salic Law, which forbade a woman to rule—he felt the accession of Irene to the throne in the East effectively vacated the throne of the Roman Empire. Perhaps the title of emperor was a necessary part of his plan to rule the West. Nevertheless, it is unclear whether or not he saw the action coming, and his biographer Einhard at a later date would protest strongly that he had not. Perhaps Charlemagne and Leo had mutually agreed to the plan during their conversations at Paderborn or under the new mural at the Lateran Palace. Perhaps it was in the end all Leo's doing. Historians will never know for sure.

Whatever the cause of the crowning at Saint Peter's, the effect was tremendous. For Christians there could only be one Church, and for four centuries there had been only one empire. *Roman* had come to mean *Christian*, and even though there were states and lands beyond the limits of Christian romanitas, everyone agreed that membership in Christendom necessarily entailed some level of participation in the life and fortunes of the Roman Empire. Even at the edge of the world in distant Ireland, Celtic Christians had prayed regularly for the "Empire of the Romans," that is, for Byzantium. From Constantine to Justinian in the East and from Augustine to Gregory the Great in the West, no one had ever thought there could be anything but a single Christian empire. In a single act, Pope Leo's coronation of Charlemagne changed all of that. Christendom still may have possessed only one Church, but now there were two Roman Empires to claim her.

The Invention of the West

AS A RESULT OF THE POPE'S ACTION, the door was now open to a wholesale reconfiguration of Western Christian romanitas. For this was in fact

Charlemagne's central project as emperor. His highest priority was establishing a Christian state defined by a uniform culture that was distinctively Frankish and not, by definition, "Greek."

Historians have long credited Charlemagne with laying the foundation for Western civilization. Indeed, his contemporaries appear to be the first to define Christendom culturally. To do so they used the word *Europa*. Ironically, they were appropriating an earlier convention that had used the word in an exclusively geographical sense. For Christendom had existed for eight centuries as a geographically diverse culture, encompassing territories belonging to Asia, Africa, and Europe. The Muslim invasions, as we have seen, had greatly reduced that geographical diversity. Now it was further reduced in scope. For the Franks, Christendom became a civilization that even excluded the Byzantine East. For them, Christendom simply became "the West."

In recent decades, historians of the modern West have made much of the term *orientalism*. Promoted by Edward Said to characterize the efforts of Europeans and Americans to justify modern third-world colonialism, it emphasizes the necessary construction of an "other," a civilization or culture that is defined as being "not western." This culture is therefore objectified in order to empower the West. Inevitably, the process of objectification has the psychological effect of minimizing the value of a particular oriental culture, claiming it to be, among other things, superstitious and irrational. In many cases, this also made it eminently conquerable. Though designed as a political theory to make sense of the post-colonial world of the twentieth century, the concept of orientalism can be usefully applied to the much earlier cultural project that was the Frankish reconfiguration of Christian romanitas.

As we have seen, the identity of Christian civilization was closely related to romanitas, the identity of "Roman-ness." This identity had been defined in Christian terms after the conversion of Constantine in the fourth century and spanned both East and West. The loss of western territories to the barbarian invasions of the fifth century had not greatly undermined romanitas, despite claims by modern historians since the time of the so-called Enlightenment. The secularist Edward Gibbon, for instance, regarded the fifth century as the onset of the Dark Ages, during which Western culture was largely forgotten, only to be restored by the fifteenth-century Renaissance. In fact, as recent historians such as Peter Brown have noted, the period following the barbarian invasions was nothing of the kind. A thriving culture that integrated East and West continued for centuries beyond Alaric's sack of Rome in 410.

As I have presented it, that culture was "paradisiacal." It was rooted in traditional Christianity's experience of the kingdom of heaven. And Charlemagne's orientalism—his depreciating effort to isolate the East from the Frankish empire—had the effect of uprooting that culture. To be sure, the roots were deep, and no political efforts, even by one of the West's most imperious rulers, could thoroughly sever them. But in the course of a generation, with the tacit support of the papacy, a distinctly Western Christendom began to appear and to define itself against—rather than with—Eastern Christendom.

At the heart of this movement was a principle Charlemagne called "correction" (*correctio*). It grew out of the same political convictions that guided the Byzantine court in the period of iconoclasm. Correction was, after all, an act of reformation. It was premised on the conviction that it was the proper role of a Christian ruler to supervise the religious life of his subjects and to intervene when correction of that life was required. For Emperor Leo III, the perceived idolatry of icon veneration demanded such reform. For Charlemagne, a perception of ignorance and superstition necessitated the same.

In the West, pockets of monastic learning were surrounded by huge swaths of benighted rural territory in which little evangelism had occurred. Missionaries among the Franks had long attested to the need for reform in this situation. Though Celtic missionaries like Columbanus had come from Ireland at the end of the sixth century to establish monastic centers for evangelism, their ability to nurture the faith was limited by the fact that in Francia monasteries were not, as in Ireland, centers of episcopal administration. The result was minimal instruction in the faith. The peasantry remained ignorant of doctrine, and an illiterate parish clergy could do little to help.

The Anglo-Saxon Boniface, when he came to Francia in the early eighth century, lamented the abysmal condition of religion he found. In one case a Christian woman appeared at a parish church with offerings to the pagan god Thor. In another case a Christian priest baptized the children of his flock *in nomine Patria et Filia et Spiritus Sancti*, that is, "in the name of the Fatherland, and of the Daughter, and of the Holy Spirit"! Here the problem was simply one of incorrect Latin grammar, a matter to which the Carolingian reforms would vigorously address themselves. But the universal lack of basic Christian understanding was astonishing.

In yet another case Boniface encountered a charismatic leader named Aldebert who conducted outdoor liturgical services and claimed to know the sins of his flock before they confessed them. But as dangerous as such a figure might seem to be (and at Boniface's insistence he was later condemned by the pope), his collision with Boniface represented a coming transition to a new order in Western Christendom. By insisting on correction, Boniface and the Carolingian court behind him served to usher in a new approach to church life that placed ecclesiastical good order before all other concerns. Boniface urged local bishops to intervene more frequently in the management of parish life and even appealed to the pope himself to facilitate change. In doing so he became the "unwitting architect" of Charlemagne's broader cultural reform.[88]

For the Frankish emperor, such reform ultimately depended on politically directed learning. Charlemagne was acutely sensitive to the conviction that the western Roman Empire had fallen into a state of obscurity and ignorance after the barbarian invasions. As ruler of these lands, he intended to restore them to cultural greatness and make Francia their new intellectual center of gravity. As one of his supporters put it, the Frankish court would become a "new Athens." The pagan allusion was misleading, however. For Charlemagne, Francia would be an explicitly Christian civilization, making use of classical learning only insofar as it facilitated correct theology and spiritual life.

More appropriate, perhaps, was Einhard's nickname for the capital city of Aachen: Future Rome (*ventura Roma*).[89] After all, Old Rome had ceased to be an imperial city and was now little more than a pilgrimage destination and the West's ecclesiastical headquarters. The New Rome of Constantinople had its own problems. From the Carolingian point of view it was thoroughly corrupted by heresy and illegitimately ruled by a woman, the usurper Empress Irene. Charlemagne's Future Rome, on the other hand, would be the center of a corrected and exclusively Latin Christendom.

Charlemagne's nearly half-century reign was a period of ambitious cultural reform. Ironically, for all his fascination with learning, the emperor himself was unable to write. He could read, however, and loved to do so. He also loved to be read to. It was said that at the royal dining hall he ordered the greatest works of theology to be read aloud during his meals. At the top of his list was Augustine's *City of God*. It is noteworthy that he could speak and even better understand numerous languages, including Greek. But for him Latin was the language of culture. By reforming it and using it as the official language of his administration, he hoped to unify and even redefine the West.

Charlemagne knew that to achieve his goals he would need a cultural center that did not yet exist. Learning in eighth-century Christendom was of course centered upon the East, particularly Constantinople after the loss of Alexandria to the Arabs. Provincial Greek cities such as Thessalonica and Nicaea were also significant centers of culture. In the West, by contrast, learning and art were largely confined to monasteries. Celtic houses such as Iona and Lindisfarne, and to a lesser extent the Anglo-Saxon foundation at Jarrow, maintained sizeable libraries and oversaw considerable manuscript production. It was at Jarrow that Bede, one of the period's greatest scholars, wrote some of his famous works on history, science, and biblical commentary. Though missionaries like Columbanus had brought Celtic piety and scholarship to the continent, there was still no central locus of culture comparable to Constantinople.

Charlemagne was convinced he needed this. He therefore established a makeshift academy at his court, which, for most of his reign, moved with him as he traveled back and forth on imperial matters. Only in 796 was something like a permanent capital established at Aachen. It was extremely modest by the standards of the ancient world, and an earthquake in 813 even caused a temporary evacuation. Charlemagne's architect Odo erected the Palatine Chapel there and attached a palace to it. Though impressive by Frankish standards, it in no way resembled the Great Palace of Constantinople with its courtyard leading to Hagia Sophia. Even the much smaller Lateran Palace in Rome was extravagant by comparison.

But this did not prevent Charlemagne from trying. The Palatine Chapel, for instance, imitated the famous Byzantine Church of San Vitale in Ravenna with its octagonal central dome. The interior icons were likewise Byzantine in character, though more pedagogical than liturgical in their purpose. After all, Charlemagne was not content just to mimic the rival empire he was superseding.

The chapel also contained an interesting glimpse into the future of Western Christendom under Carolingian influence. Like all Christian temples, it was oriented, that is, one entered from the west and worshipped toward an altar located at the easternmost part of the building. But in this case a monumental western entrance was introduced. This "westwork" became a characteristic feature of the Romanesque and later Gothic style of Christian architecture. Atop its tower was ultimately placed a spire, whose point drew the believer's attention toward heaven. In this sense, it was a statement of Christendom's orientation toward paradise, but with a significant difference. Unlike the central dome that came to characterize Eastern Christian architecture, and which symbolized heavenly immanence, the spires of Western Christendom would direct attention away from the world to a distantly transcendent heaven.

It was at Aachen that Charlemagne assembled an international team of scholars around him. Very few were Franks. The best known was the Anglo-Saxon Alcuin, who hailed from York. This highly creative and jovial presence at court (he introduced the Celtic custom of assigning playful names to the emperor and his advisors) would in some ways personify what has often been called the Carolingian Renaissance. His sheer love of learning and clever use of verse (he assumed the nickname of Flaccus after the family name of Horace) was immortalized at the monastery of Tours, where

Alcuin of York receiving the Abbey of Tours from the Emperor Charlemagne (British Library, Royal MS 16 G VI, f. 153v)

he eventually retired. There, elegantly inscribed in Latin over the entrance to the scriptorium, a poetic statement declared to all who entered that they, the monks of Western Christendom, were the defenders of Western culture. Alcuin was the product of the Celtic love of learning that had penetrated the Anglo-Saxon territories since the days of Aidan. Not far from his native York was Bede's monastery at Jarrow, which boasted one of the best equipped libraries in the West.

Alcuin proved to be the leading light of Charlemagne's court and the one best known to posterity. But other brilliant minds were drawn there to participate in the great cultural revival. From distant Spain, the emperor recruited Theodulf, probably the most original theologian of the contemporary West and an heir to the encyclopedist Isidore of Seville. From Italy came two more learned clerics, Paul the Deacon from Lombardy and Paulinus from Aquileia.

So, with a team of scholars assembled to support him, Charlemagne undertook a thoroughgoing reform of Western Christendom. The reformation was marked by the publication of his *General Admonition* (*Admonitio generalis*) in 789, which directed local authorities—especially bishops—to begin conforming to the court's directives about correct beliefs and practices. Alcuin's nickname for the emperor was King David, to capture in a flattering way his religiously defined and sanctioned rule over the people of God. But a better nickname, suggested in the *Admonition* itself, would have been the religious reformer King Josiah.

As his biographer Derek Wilson notes, the half-educated Charlemagne was drawn to the example of Israel's most famous royal reformer because of the image of a Christian society that he had seized upon through readings of the *City of God*. After all, Augustine

> had insisted that a true Christian state should model itself on the heavenly city where perfect order and harmony reigned. . . . It was the ruler's

responsibility to pay close attention to the minutiae of all regulations pertaining to the relationship between man and man; man and the state and, above all, man and God. It is Charlemagne's commitment to the Augustinian ideal that explains his constant obsession with regulating the religious and secular life of his people. Though Alcuin saw him as a David, the Old Testament parallel that the emperor preferred was Josiah, the seventh-century B.C. reforming King of Judah, who rediscovered the Deuteronomic law and purified the religion of his people. Education and law had to go together because the heterogeneous traditions represented throughout his empire had to be brought into submission to the perfect laws of God, and the people had to understand what was required of them.[90]

Like many of the Protestant reforms of the sixteenth century, Charlemagne's was to be a magisterial reformation, that is, one directed by the state.

Like those later reforms, the Carolingian reformation was directed against perceived superstition and the abuse of clerical power. Remnants of paganism were to be uprooted, and neglect of religious supervision (through the office of bishop) was to be ended. This reform was no less ambitious than the Protestant Reformation, though due to the limitations of technology (there was as yet no printing press) and education (there was no surplus of university-trained theologians to elaborate divergent doctrines) it never went nor could have gone so far.

Charlemagne's reform was a seismic event in the cultural history of Christendom and expressed in a new way the transformational imperative that had shaped it ever since the apostolic preaching of the Sermon on the Mount. As one scholar notes,

Charlemagne's policy from early in his reign was directed towards the transformation of the entire people of the Frankish realm into a Christian people, the salvation of that people, the formation of the whole of the society in the territories under Frankish rule within a Christian framework, and the integration of the concerns of the faith with those of society as a whole.[91]

But unlike the Protestant Reformation, Charlemagne's correction of Christianity was deliberately and emphatically linked to the papacy. The Roman standard for nearly everything became the standard for the Franks. This began with language. Though he accommodated the use of the vernacular for local affairs, Charlemagne insisted that classical Latin become the only official language of his realm. This more than any other feature of the reform expressed the desire to establish not only religious uniformity but an explicitly Roman imperial identity. It even resulted in the development of a new, more legible script known as Carolingian Minuscule, which was scrupulously employed by later copyists to assure accurate manuscript reproduction. The Minuscule's emphasis on clarity brought an end to the ornate scripts that had decorated earlier manuscripts such as the Irish Book of Kells. Charlemagne also insisted on the adoption of the Roman order of the Mass, which until then had remained distinct in many ways from the liturgies used in and beyond Gaul. The result, ironically, was an importation of Gallican elements into the Roman order. And this too brought greater uniformity.

When it came to certain other elements of Christian culture, however, Charlemagne showed himself ready to ignore the Roman standard. In the case of two burning issues, iconoclasm and the *filioque*, he actually defied the papacy. The apparent paradox of this clash of priorities is explained by his driving ambition to form a Western Christendom distinct from the Byzantine East. On both of these issues, Charlemagne's scholars proved to be more than theologians and church reformers. They became intellectual shock troops.

The Seventh Ecumenical Council of 787 had, as we have seen, affirmed the catholic Church's use of icons. Its resolution had emphasized that though the Second Commandment seemed to ban images, the Incarnation had brought such a ban to an end. Pope Hadrian himself had affirmed the council's resolution, and in 789 he sent a copy of it to Charlemagne's court for review.

Significantly, this copy was in Latin and represented an extremely flawed and therefore misleading record of the Greek original. It stated, in what was almost a complete reversal of that original, that icons are to be given the same "worship" (*adoratio*) as the Holy Trinity. The council's painstaking distinction between forbidden "worship" (Greek *latria*; Latin *adoratio*) and authorized "veneration" (Greek *proskynesis*; Latin *veneratio*) had been completely subverted. Historians have puzzled over this momentous gaffe, unable to understand how the papacy could have overlooked it. Some scholars have suggested that Hadrian may have committed it intentionally in order to provoke the Franks to a scandalized objection so as to balance them against the troublesome Byzantines.

In any case, the theologians of Charlemagne's court seized on the apparent error to fuel an attack on what they denounced as Byzantine idolatry. Their position was documented in a carefully prepared theological treatise entitled the *Caroline Books* (*Libri carolini*). The work is one of the most important expressions of Frankish theology ever produced. It is also something of a cultural manifesto. Composed by Theodulf with substantial contributions by Alcuin, it self-consciously sought to present Charlemagne's case against Byzantium. These cultural activists at court did not limit their scorn to the resolution of the Seventh Ecumenical Council. According to one scholar, the *Caroline Books* were a "polemic of white-hot intensity" that accused the Byzantines as a whole of being, in short, "absurd, childish, delirious, demented, depraved, fatuous, impudent, incautions, laughable, mindless, obtuse, perverse, pointless, rash, reprehensible, ridiculous, risible, silly, stupid, supercilious, and useless."[92]

The Carolingians were already known for a mild tendency toward iconoclasm themselves. But the faulty translation of the council's resolution about icon veneration enabled them to denounce its Orthodox fathers as superstitious idolaters. In fact, in one of the earliest acts of Western "orientalism," they dismissed the Orthodox pejoratively as "the Greeks." They upheld the council's censure of the iconoclasts only because Emperor Leo and Constantine Copronymus had been among them. They also recalled with respect Pope Gregory the Great's approval of iconography as a means of pedagogy for the illiterate. But the council's liturgical defense, which had repeated John of Damascus's views, they scorned. By rejecting both parties of Byzantium, the iconophiles and the iconoclasts, the Franks assumed a position that distanced them from the East altogether. And by nodding toward the moderate though theologically unsophisticated position of Gregory the Great, they secured a claim on the identity of Rome.

The problem was that the current pope categorically rejected the arguments made in the *Caroline Books*. Charlemagne had sent an early draft of the polemical work to Rome, presumably with the expectation of complete approval. Instead, utter consternation greeted it. So grave was the disagreement that Hadrian penned one of the longest letters in papal history to refute the Franks. In it he "reminded" them that he himself had sent legates to Nicaea, and when the council had completed its work there, he had given his approval. In other words, the discussion had been closed. Strangely, however, Hadrian did not demand the formal withdrawal of the *Caroline Books*, and they seem to have been formally confirmed by Charlemagne and the Frankish clergy at a Synod of Frankfurt in 794.

Before moving away from this controversy, so important in tracing the estrangement of the West from Eastern Christendom, it is worth noting one detail about the content of the Carolingian polemic. Theodulf was a highly sophisticated theologian and his arguments against the Byzantine defense of icons, in addition to being rancorous, express a baneful and pernicious new cosmology. As we have seen, traditional Christian cosmology, insofar as it was given expression in the thought of Eastern fathers such as Maximos the Confessor, placed great value on the created world. This was why icons offered more than a means of pedagogy. Because of the Incarnation, they revealed visually the presence of God in the physical human image. Ceila Chazelle has discerned a very different view of the world in the *Caroline Books*. Although they concede that "the material world is good, it exists entirely separately from the spiritual realm, so that the mortal who wants to approach God must finally turn away from material things in order to direct his or her attention completely towards the spiritual."[93] Long before John Calvin, then, the Franks had begun to lay the theological basis for a secularist cosmology.

Frankish contempt for the "Greeks" and disregard for papal Orthodoxy was also exhibited in their dramatic advocacy of filioquism. The Latin word *filioque*, meaning "and the Son," had been inserted into the Nicene Creed to augment its statement about the procession of the Holy Spirit (which itself had been an augmentation of the original version approved by the Second Ecumenical Council). As a result, the original creedal statement "We believe . . . in the Holy Spirit . . . who proceeds from the Father" was altered to conclude as "who proceeds from the Father and the Son." The first time this was done, as we noted in the previous chapter, was at the Third Council of Toledo in 589, when the Visigothic King Recarred was received from Arianism into the catholic Church. The purpose of the altered clause was quite Orthodox; it was intended to assert among Arian-minded Spaniards that Jesus was truly God, insofar as He is equal to God the Father.

And indeed, a widely attested record of doctrinal filioquism was to be found in the West. Augustine helped establish it in his treatise *On the Trinity*. Some Eastern fathers such as Maximos had spoken of the Spirit proceeding "from the Father through the Son." For some this was not really an issue theologically. What was an issue was the alteration of the Church's essential Creed, which was used in many churches as part of the eucharistic liturgy. It was part of the Divine Liturgy of the Byzantine Rite and had become a standard part of the Gallican Rite used in the West outside of Rome (where the Creed was not yet a part of the Mass). Inserting it into the Nicene Creed was in fact a direct violation of Canon 7 of the Third Ecumenical Council. That prohibition was repeated by the Fourth Ecumenical Council, which ordered

> that no one shall be suffered to bring forward a different faith [heteran pistin, the Greek basis for the word "heterodoxy"], nor to write, nor to put together, nor to excogitate, nor to teach it to others. But such as dare either to put together another faith, or to bring forward or to teach or to deliver a different Creed [heteron symbolon] to such as wish to be converted to the knowledge of the truth from the Gentiles, or Jews or any heresy whatever, if they be bishops or clerics let them be deposed . . . but if they be monks or laity, let them be anathematized.[94]

Yet it was precisely this controversial creedal filioquism that Frankish theologians advocated alongside their semi-iconoclasm.

It is easy to understand why they became invested in it. Charlemagne's great empire encompassed many territories, some of which included Arians or their descendants. Creedal filioquism was like much else in the emperor's anti-Byzantine intellectual arsenal—it facilitated the political and cultural unity of an alternative Roman Empire.

Furthermore, many of Charlemagne's court theologians insisted that the filioque had been contained within the original form of the Creed. This was a bizarre conviction, and it is hard for modern historians to understand how so much ignorance could have prevailed among the theologically sophisticated court at Aachen. Paulinus of Aquileia appears to have known better. He made the case for creedal filioquism not by claiming its antiquity, but by arguing that if the Second Ecumenical Council had the authority to alter the original, then surely later councils recognized as Orthodox do as well. This was even more the case in light of the fact that some popes had endorsed the double procession doctrine of filioquism.

The problem, once again, was that the papacy rejected the Frankish argument. In 807, a group of Frankish monks living in Palestine discovered, to their surprise, that the local population did not use the filioque in the Creed. As Franks, they were unaccustomed to this and wrote to Pope Leo III for an explanation. In Rome the papacy neither used the filioque nor placed the Creed in the Mass as the Franks did. Unable to offer an explanation to the monks, Leo forwarded the matter to Charlemagne's court. There the Franks immediately composed an argument justifying their innovation. It was published in the form of another treatise by Theodulf entitled *On the Holy Spirit*. Significantly, the argument drew heavily on Augustine's doctrinal filioquism. Once again, then, a distinctively Western practice was being developed and defended with conscious reference to the great Latin father who had differed so sharply on some points from the Greek fathers.

But the papacy, still maintaining its long-term attachments to the East, continued to resist. In 809 Charlemagne assembled a council of bishops at Aachen itself that declared the Franks' commitment to creedal filioquism irreversible. An argument was even made that brings to mind the famous witticism of Edward Gibbon, whose deism made him supremely insensitive to the question of church tradition and doctrinal integrity. In narrating the decision at the Council of Nicaea to use the term *homoousios,* which clarified that Christ is "of one essence" (or "consubstantial") with the Father, Gibbon brought attention to an alternative term proposed by the Arians, *homoiousios,* meaning "of similar essence." The difference was a single Greek letter, the *iota.* The Christian Church, he sneered, was nearly split in two by the smallest letter of the Greek alphabet. The difference seemed trivial to the secularized Gibbon, but in fact the saving doctrine of church tradition was preserved by using *homoousios* in the Creed.

For the Franks, a comparable lack of respect for the gravity of doctrinal precision was expressed when advocating for the creedal interpolation of the filioque. "The addition of just four syllables," they told the pope in an effort to win him over, "could work wonders" in improving the condition of the Church. Having made their case for creedal filioquism at the Synod of Aachen and through a flurry of writings, they awaited the reaction from Rome.

Disappointment in Hadrian's earlier resistance to their semi-iconoclasm now turned, in the matter of the filioque, to complete discomfiture. Pope Leo III ordered his northern allies and erstwhile protectors to desist immediately from using the filioque in the Creed. The fact that they had been doing so for generations, he observed, was irrelevant insofar as it was a violation of universal church order. Then, to teach the Franks a lesson and make his continued allegiance to the Byzantine East clear, the very pope who had crowned Charlemagne in Saint Peter's Basilica commissioned an elaborate pair of silver shields to be forged. He ordered engraved upon their faces—in Latin and in Greek—the Nicene Creed *without* the filioque. Leo then had these "shields of faith" mounted inside Saint Peter's Basilica, the most prominent church in Rome, on the tomb of the Apostle Peter—the most prominent place in that church, as well as the terminus of thousands of pilgrimages from throughout Western Christendom each year.

It was a symbolic act in the history of an heroic papacy. According to the official papal chronicle of the time, Leo did it "out of the love he bore to the Orthodox Faith and out of his care for its preservation." [95] But if it was designed to express solidarity with the East, events would soon test that solidarity to the breaking point.

The Nicolaitan Schism

IF THE PAPACY under Hadrian and Leo III distinguished itself as a defender of Orthodoxy against the theologically upstart and innovative Franks, it was not out of an abiding attachment to the Byzantines. Scorn for the East may not have been as open in the Lateran Palace as it was in Aachen, but the long and depressing record of iconoclastic policy during the past century had gravely affected Rome's relations with Constantinople.

A major step toward improving them came in 843 when Empress Theodora, following the death of her iconoclastic husband Emperor Theophilus, assembled a council that permanently reestablished icon veneration. The Seventh Ecumenical Council of 787 had definitively legitimized icon veneration, but since that time religious policy had continued to waver under various caesaropapist rulers. Theodora's council was hailed as the "Triumph of Orthodoxy" and was thereafter commemorated annually on the first Sunday of the Great Fast.

Theodora's reign offered little to criticize from the papacy's point of view, but the same could not be said of that of her son, Michael III. He was a lascivious and besotted youth and quickly fell under the influence of an unscrupulous uncle named Bardas. In 856, Bardas talked Michael into murdering his mother's chief minister and seizing power for himself. Bardas remained in the background and continued to dominate policy during the early years of Michael's reign, distinguishing himself especially in wars against the Bulgarians. As for Theodora, she was sent to live out the remainder of her days in a monastery.

For his part, the profligate Emperor Michael spent much of his time in the company of drinking companions and prostitutes, eventually becoming entangled in an affair with the daughter of a mercenary Viking lord named Eudoxia Ingerina. Because of her family's past affiliation with the iconoclasts, marriage was out of the question. But Michael landed on a plan to have her without marrying her.

The first step was to marry a more suitable woman and keep Ingerina as his mistress. This was not so unusual at the Byzantine court. The manner in which it was arranged, however, was definitely unconventional. He decided the best way to maintain access to Ingerina was to place her in the safety of a lawful marriage to one of his subordinates, in this case a loyal courtier named Basil the Macedonian. As compensation to the surrogate husband, Michael offered free pick of any other lady as a mistress. (Ingerina, after all, was naturally off limits.) Perhaps he was a little dismayed when Basil selected Michael's own sister, Thekla, who was at the time living in a monastery. But a deal was a deal, and Michael did not scruple to order his sibling transferred from the cloister to the bedchamber of his court crony. He showed himself completely satisfied with the arrangement as long as Basil promised to keep Ingerina from scandal and to provide Michael free access to her. So satisfied was he that when Basil decided it was time to eliminate his chief rival, Bardas, the emperor's former mastermind, Michael was happy to comply. Another court murder followed.

In the meantime, Ingerina bore a son who was almost certainly Michael's. Intending to cultivate the child for the succession, the emperor elevated Basil to the status of co-emperor. This was a fatal mistake. For on one evening in 867, Basil, having plied the gullible Michael with more than the usual supply of wine and women, arranged to have the lock to his bedchamber disabled. Basil personally accompanied the murderers who entered the emperor's room unopposed in the middle of the night to commit one of Constantinople's most loathsome assassinations. Begging for his life, the drunken and confused Michael was pulled from his bed, and both of his hands were chopped off. Then, as the emperor writhed in agony, the usurper watched as he was run through with a sword. Basil the Macedonian was now in a position to claim for himself not only the throne but the beautiful Ingerina and her son.

It was against this despicable backdrop that a new crisis arose in the relationship between Rome and Constantinople. Though complicated by other matters such as ecclesiastical policy among the Bulgarians, the crisis centered on an action taken by Michael early in his scandal-ridden reign. After deposing his mother, in 858 he had been persuaded by Bardas to depose the patriarch of Constantinople. Ignatios had been a strong supporter of Theodora, and both had worked with the monastic party in the capital to bring a final end to iconoclasm.

Michael had different priorities, and in any case regarded Ignatios as a potential threat. To replace him, he chose a learned diplomat named Photios. It appears the latter was not initially positive about the decision, especially as it came in violation of the normal procedures for replacing the patriarch. But as Ignatios did not immediately resist, Photios submitted to an expedited election, taking him, in the course of a single week, from layman to reader to deacon to priest, and, finally, to bishop. On Christmas Day in 858 he was named patriarch of Constantinople.

Such an irregular elevation of a hierarch from a layman's status was not unknown in church history. Two canonized bishops, Tarasios of Constantinople and, more famously, Ambrose of Milan (whose promotion was initiated while he was still a catechumen), had both experienced something similar. But for some reason, Pope Nicholas (who also had been elected in 858) now decided to intervene. His motivation may simply have been that the procedure followed seemed dubious, since a suspended bishop participated in the consecration. He may also have been reacting to the infernal caesaropapism behind Michael's summary deposition of Ignatios.

Perhaps Nicholas perceived the deposition as the prelude to a new wave of iconoclasm, since Ignatios had been a strong iconophile and supporter of Theodora's council of 843. To be sure, his replacement was no iconoclast. But Photios was considered a moderate by the more rigorist monastic party that began to rally behind Ignatios, and he suffered the fate of all moderates during a state of crisis.

Whatever its broader motivation, Pope Nicholas's decision to act against Photios was precipitated by the arrival of a monk named Theognostos at the Lateran Palace in 863 (that is, a full five years after the deposition of Ignatios). Prior to that, Nicholas had limited his response to Michael's deposition of Ignatios to sending an embassy of legates to investigate the matter. Once in Constantinople, these had actually endorsed Photios. But the story that Theognostos now told made the pope's hair stand on end.

Theognostos described scenes of persecution and torture as gruesome as those in the lives of the early martyrs. Ignatios, the monk claimed, had been repeatedly arrested and beaten in order to obtain a formal abdication of his title. All of this had been orchestrated by an ambition-crazed Photios. In one case Ignatios was taken into the crypt of the Church of the Holy Apostles and placed on a rack made from the sarcophagus of the despised late iconoclastic Emperor Constantine Copronymus. Literally stretched to the breaking point, he finally surrendered and agreed to sign his name to an abdication statement. Throughout the telling of this story, Theognostos did not neglect to emphasize that Ignatios was devoted to the papacy—unlike his supplanter.[96]

It turns out that the story was all a fabrication. The most accomplished modern historian of the controversy, Francis Dvornik, long ago demonstrated that the appeal brought to Rome by Theognostos on behalf of Ignatios was a gross misrepresentation of the situation in Constantinople.[97] In fact, it was driven by the politics of the monastic party there. But it successfully played on fears that Nicholas had about an impending revival of caesaropapism.

The story also stirred memories about past examples of that most Byzantine of all sins. During the early stages of iconoclasm, as we have seen, Emperor Leo III had seized papal territories in southern Italy and Illyricum. By the middle of the ninth century, they had still not been returned despite bitter demands from Rome. In the case of Illyricum, Byzantine as well as Frankish missionaries now found themselves in a tug of war, with the local population playing the two great patriarchates against one another. The pagan Khan Boris of Bulgaria was particularly adept at making the most of this. He went back and forth seeking the best terms under which he might bring his empire into Christendom.

Pope Nicholas decided the time had come to check decisively the influence of Constantinople. Ignoring the decisions of his legates and appearing to accept Theognostos's fraudulent accounts of the mistreatment of Ignatios, he called a synod in 863 and took the drastic step of excommunicating Photios. This act formally separated Rome from Constantinople. The separation would last for four years and is often seen as a kind of rehearsal for the schism of 1054.

The significance of the excommunication was immediately revealed as

Nicholas used the occasion to assert, as no pope (not even Leo I) ever had before, the doctrine of papal supremacy. Not just in the East, but in the Frankish West he declared that the pope is subject to no higher authority on earth and has the power to intervene in ecclesiastical disputes anywhere he sees fit. Nicholas is the first pope on record to make explicit use of the body of documents known as the False Decretals, containing the Donation of Constantine and other claims to papal supremacy. As the title by which they are now known makes clear, these documents were all forgeries. But beginning with Nicholas, they came to be used to advance the claims of papal supremacy over all other powers in Christendom, whether clerical or political. Armed with the False Decretals, Nicholas became for sympathetic contemporaries the "emperor of the whole world."[98]

In its struggle against Byzantine iconoclasm and Frankish creedal filioquism, the papacy until this time had played an heroic role, defending the Church against heterodoxy. Sadly, tragedy often befalls heroes. In the case of Nicholas, a fatal predisposition to see in Photios nothing but the evil of caesaropapism caused him to overreact, and this, coupled with a strident self-confidence in his office, led him into schism.

Historians customarily speak of this event as the "Photian Schism." This term is surely unfitting and misleading. It is the product of an historical bias against the East, advanced by advocates for papal supremacy in later centuries and by their unwitting successors. It also reveals the general ignorance

The interrogation of Patriarch Photios
Unknown, 13th-century author [Public domain]

about Eastern Christianity among historians. In that company, Photios is presented as the archenemy of the papacy, and the slurs against him propagated by Theognostos and his partisans are often accepted at face value. The resulting narrative usually presents Photios as a usurper and enemy of the long-suffering Ignatios.

Nothing could be further from the truth. In 867 Basil the Macedonian, having murdered Michael and seized power for himself, threw out Photios and reappointed Ignatios. Photios does not seem to have made much of a fuss. Then, when Ignatios died in 877 and was replaced—in a dizzying manner—by none other than Photios, the latter began to advocate for his predecessor's canonization as a saint. It is even said that as Ignatios lay dying, Photios, who as one of the period's most learned men possessed medical skills, came to him, comforted him, and even administered treatments. Nor did Photios hang on to the power of the patriarchate until the end. In 886, after another palace coup, he resigned the office of patriarch and lived another seven years in monastic seclusion, doing what he appears to have enjoyed most—researching and writing.

It is the personality of Pope Nicholas, then, that explains the tragedy of the schism that separated Rome from Constantinople from 863 to 867. Acknowledging the Western bias of our faulty historiographical canon, it is time to apply the more appropriate term of "Nicolaitan Schism" to the event.

This is not to ignore the fact that Photios himself contributed to the atmosphere of division. He was certainly a strong personality, as strong as Nicholas. And the collision of these two titanic wills—each driven by a conviction that he was defending Orthodoxy—is just another facet of the tragedy.

In the case of Photios, he did not immediately react to Nicholas's act of excommunication in 863. But when he learned of Frankish missionaries among the Bulgarians who were advancing the use of the filioque, he chose to confront the papacy, under whose authority the missionaries ministered. Photios was also, to be sure, aware of Byzantine interests in drawing the Bulgarians within the jurisdiction of Constantinople. To make his case, in 867 he summoned representatives of the three other Eastern patriarchates—Alexandria, Antioch, and Jerusalem. The action speaks once again of the conciliar rather than papal model of ecclesiology that dated from the earliest record of church tradition and, despite new directions in Nicholas's policies, was still alive and well in the East.

The case brings to mind the Vincentian Canon, which, as we saw, had been issued in the West during the fifth century against the rising influence of Augustinian doctrines not attested "always, everywhere, and by all." While there were numerous statements of papal supremacy dating from the time of Pope Leo I, early ecclesiology and the majority of Eastern (as well as some Western) statements had always emphasized a council-based approach to episcopal authority. According to this approach, all bishops form a mutually accountable brotherhood without a single senior bishop exercising supremacy over the whole. This was the tradition of the catholic Church from earliest times, documented in Acts 15 and declared in the writings of the third-century Latin father Cyprian of Carthage.

In the face of Nicholas's assertions to supremacy in the middle of the ninth century, Photios now chose to call on his fellow patriarchs to address the filioque issue and various liturgical practices that the Frankish missionaries were bringing into the East. So grave were the concerns, and so instrumental was the papacy in causing them, that the synod of 867 made the decision to excommunicate Pope Nicholas.

But no sooner had the condemnation been issued than Nicholas was dead in Rome and Photios expelled from the patriarchate of Constantinople. That was the very year that Basil the Macedonian murdered Emperor Michael III and seized the throne for himself. As a usurper, Basil realized he needed all the political support he could find. So one of his first actions was to depose Photios and reinstate Ignatios, hoping this would secure the backing of the papacy. Politically speaking, it was probably unnecessary. But in any case, with Nicholas now dead and Photios deposed, the Nicolaitan Schism was at an end.

CHAPTER FIVE

Fighting against the Filioque

IN PREPARATION FOR the Eastern synod of 867, Photios had circulated an encyclical that laid out his concerns not just about the interpolation of the filioque in the Creed but about its theological implications. These concerns were primarily logical. First, if the Spirit proceeds from the Son as well as from the Father, then the Father is more remote from the Spirit than from the Son, creating an imbalance in the trinitarian relationship. Second, if there can be a procession from the second person of the Trinity to the third, there must then be the possibility of a procession from the third person to a fourth, and so on.

Finally, if both the Father and the Son (and not just the Father) "spirate" (send forth) the Spirit, then the doctrine of the Trinity degenerates into a form of polytheism in that there are now two "causes" of the Spirit. In other words, the monarchy of the Father is destroyed when His only-begotten Son also becomes a personal source of the Spirit. And this brought Photios to Eastern Christianity's most profound and characteristic conviction about the Trinity: that God is known primarily as a person and not, as advocates for the filioque claimed, as an essence.

Years after the council, when he was in retirement, Photios added to his reflections on the filioque in a work entitled *The Mystagogy of the Holy Spirit*. There he repeated his earlier statements and argued in greater detail why doctrinal filioquism is unacceptable. His presentation of the issue largely followed that made by earlier Greek fathers. Maximos the Confessor, for instance, who had spent a good part of his life in the West among adherents of the filioque, had categorically rejected it, declaring that "the Father alone is the origin of the Son and of the Holy Spirit." Significantly, following the lead of earlier Greek fathers, he could state, however, that "the Spirit proceeds through the Son."[99] But Photios did not so express himself, as he seems to have been concerned primarily with filioquism in an eternal sense rather than a temporal one.

To the Eastern fathers, it was obvious from scripture that Jesus sent the Holy Spirit in time, and in this sense a kind of procession "from the Father through the Son" was conceivable. After the Resurrection, for instance, it was Jesus who, having breathed on the apostles, said "receive the Holy Spirit" (John 20:22). More explicit was John 15:26, where Jesus, assembling His disciples in the upper room before His Passion, promised the coming of the Holy Spirit, "whom I shall send to you from the Father, the Spirit of truth who proceeds from the Father." Here, in a single verse, was the evidence both for a procession in time *from the Son* ("I shall send to you") and for a procession eternally *from the Father* ("who proceeds from the Father"). On this point there was considerable room for agreement with the Latin West.

However, in his *Mystagogy*, Photios chose to focus instead only on Western filioquism's claims about an eternal procession from the Son. Had he sought accommodation with the doctrine of procession "through the Son," he might have helped build a bridge between the East and the West at this critical historical juncture. But in the context of the Nicolaitan Schism, such an irenic approach was not to be. As it turned out, Photios presented a view of the filioque that was consistent and uncompromising, even if it did little to accommodate the tendencies of some within Western Christendom.

One of the most learned theologians of his time, Photios was well aware that advocates of the filioque cited a multitude of Western fathers for support. Interestingly, for the first time in the history of Eastern patristics, he explicitly addressed the views of Augustine of Hippo, who until then apparently had been completely unknown in the East. Though he seems to have known about the latter's work *On the Trinity*—the most venerable source of doctrinal filioquism—Photios does not cite it and seems to have acquired an understanding of its arguments only secondhand. Also interesting is Photios's rather gentle way of disagreeing with Augustine and other Latin fathers. He in no way denies their great contribution to Orthodox theology and regards them as holy men, but he notes that many great fathers— Eastern and Western—have flaws in their thinking, and that in such cases the Church is called to reject those flaws while upholding other points they made correctly.

In the case of Augustine, the greatest flaw was to understand God the Father as primarily "simple essence" rather than as "person" (*hypostasis*). This mistake opened the way for conceiving the procession of the Spirit from the

Father and the Son, since both are, according to the Creed, "of one essence" or "consubstantial" (*homoousios*). As Photios put it, however, "he is consubstantial because he proceeds from the Father, but he does not proceed because he is consubstantial." In other words, the procession of the Holy Spirit is determined by the personhood (*hypostasis*) of the Father, not by his consubstantiality or essence.

For Photios, reducing personhood to a shared essence distorted the Trinity as it had been revealed by the scriptures. The person of the Spirit cannot proceed from an essence but only from a person, namely, God the Father—the "cause" of both the Son and the Spirit. Indeed, so important was the primacy of personhood rather than of essence that true monotheism was at stake. God is one, the Greek fathers claimed, because the particular person of the Father is one. What is more, by conceiving the procession from both the Father and the Son, who share a common essence, Augustine and his Latin heirs necessarily suggested that the Spirit is of a different essence (however much they would in practice deny this). The result of doctrinal filioquism, then, was to confuse God the Father as an essence rather than a person, and to diminish the equal divinity of the Holy Spirit in relation the Son.

Pope Nicholas regarded Photios's challenge to filioquism, in both its creedal and doctrinal forms, as a challenge to the papacy, even though at this time in Rome the Creed was still carefully read without the filioque. Learning of the Eastern synod of 867 and realizing that Photios was shoring up conciliar resistance to the filioque, Nicholas appealed to his own allies, the Franks. In this case they could prove as effective in defending the papacy in doctrinal matters as they had in military matters. He called on their bishops to compose a body of treatises defending filioquism.

The appeal was an important moment in the history of Christendom. Half a century earlier, Pope Leo III had heroically confronted the Franks' use of the filioque and ordered an end to it. They, of course, had ignored the order, provoking Leo to erect his monument to the original form of the Nicene-Constantinopolitan Creed in Saint Peter's Basilica. All of this, by the way, was explicitly hailed by Photios in the *Mystagogy* as an example of Rome's faithful leadership of the Orthodox Church. In a dramatic act, Pope

Nicholas now looked to the Western Empire for support in his confrontation with the Eastern Empire, and by doing so brought the one Church that spanned them both a fatal step closer to disunity.

Nicholas's appeal to the Franks was in fact an ecclesiastical call to arms. It had the effect of dividing Christendom into two hostile theological camps, East and West. In his appeal he provocatively claimed that the "whole Western Church" was under attack from the East. He called upon Western bishops not to permit "the Holy Church of God to be falsely accused," baldly suggesting, no doubt hyperbolically, that those affiliated with the Eastern synod then being organized by Photios were somehow distinct from this "Holy Church of God." The pope clearly felt some vulnerability in his struggle with Photios—due either to the patriarch's formidable intellect or to the weight of Eastern tradition behind him—and so his appeal emphasized the need for a united front in the West. "When [the Greeks] see us advance together in concerted battle, as it were, against them and thus clearly understand that there are also other [that is, non-papal] lovers of Christ and haters of their wickedness, the mouths of those speaking iniquities will be completely stopped."[100]

The warlike Franks proved more than ready to take up theological arms against Eastern Christianity. In doing so they explicitly defined their enemy as "the Greeks." The books they produced during the months that followed Nicholas's appeal often included in their titles the phrase "against the Greeks." This is ironic, of course, as the Byzantines did not regard themselves as Greeks (for them the label was pejorative and meant "pagan"). They were self-consciously "Romans." Even in the ninth century a universal Christian *romanitas* was still alive, though perhaps not quite well.

The Frankish bishops understood well enough what their war against Eastern doctrine was about. Ratramnus of Corbie, for instance, summarized that "we profess that the Holy Spirit proceeds from the Father and the Son, according to the Catholic Faith, while they claim the Spirit proceeds only from the Father." However, in many cases they mistakenly thought that the filioque was originally part of the Nicene-Constantinopolitan Creed, as their predecessors in the time of Charlemagne had believed. Also notable

CHAPTER FIVE

was the fact that Nicholas's appeal for support had been obscurely worded so as to suggest that the filioque was already interpolated into the Creed at Rome, which of course it was not. Ratramnus, who provided the most comprehensive and sophisticated apologetic to the pope, was clearly under this false impression.[101]

The invective on both sides of the ninth-century filioque dispute was fierce, and for understandable reasons. Both sides believed traditional Christianity was being subverted, and both saw themselves as defenders of it. In a certain sense both were. In historical hindsight the "Greeks" clearly had the upper hand, as they held fast to the Symbol of the Faith given at Nicaea, augmented at Constantinople, and scrupulously preserved unchanged since then. For their part, the Franks were convinced that the word *filioque* was a necessary clarification of the Trinity, even if historians now know the interpolation was an innovation of sixth-century Orthodox bishops working in Spain. Clearly, the Creed was no longer just a symbol of the faith. It was also a symbol of Christendom's polarization.

For the time being, Rome still had a unifying ministry to offer the East and the West. It is true that since the coronation of Charlemagne, the papacy had been inclining decisively in a westward direction. The intolerable record of Byzantine caesaropapism had all but assured that. However, as Leo's shields of faith demonstrated, the papal definition of Christian *romanitas* still retained oriental commitments. What is more, the Franks were proving themselves as headstrong as Byzantium's iconoclastic emperors. Neither Hadrian's remonstrance against the Synod of Frankfurt (which had rejected the Seventh Ecumenical Council) nor Leo's order to remove the filioque from the Creed was heeded. If ever there was a time for the heroic papacy to play its role, the ninth century was it. Tragically, Nicholas's reaction to the situation only made things worse.

In the long term, the effect was serious. The Nicolaitan Schism was a crisis. But it was also an opportunity in which the two theological parties of Christendom, the Byzantines and the Franks, might have worked to secure unity, the way they had worked militarily years earlier to secure a defense against the Muslims. They did not. The East, assured it was on the path of the fathers, continued on that trusted path with an almost serene indifference to Latin Christendom. The West faced a more complex situation. The Franks had supplanted the Roman Empire of Byzantium and had obtained papal sanction for the act. Almost immediately, they defined themselves as a civilization set against the East. They were "Europe," and they were now becoming "the West."

And as this distinctive identity took shape, the place of the papacy in it became a burning question. The prestige of that office had always been great in Western Christendom, so much so that at the end of the seventh century, at the Synod of Whitby, long-standing Celtic practices in England could be terminated in favor of Roman ones by a mere reference to Saint Peter.[102] The Franks had obtained papal support for their empire but not for their use of the filioque. Nicholas's appeal for support in defending filioquism had suggested that might change.

And with time it would, leading to an important though elusive feature of Western Christendom that can be called *heavenly transcendence*. It should be emphasized that for the time being this was only a tendency, and that Western Christendom for centuries to come continued to express delight in heavenly immanence. With that of the East, its culture remained intrinsically paradisiacal. But since filioquism, following Augustine's teaching, placed greater emphasis on the divine essence than on the divine personhood of God, His manifestation in the world came to be seen as comparatively circumscribed.

Though causal links are impossible to locate precisely—again, we are speaking only of a tendency—some have associated the later consolidation of papal supremacy with filioquism. Half a century ago, Philip Sherrard claimed as much, noting that the Augustinian concept of divine essence implied God's "absolute transcendence" from the world.[103] The result of this tendency was an understanding of ecclesiology that left the Church without immediate participation in the divine life—something very different, as we saw in chapter one, from the early culture of Christendom.

Because of this absolute transcendence, "Christ cannot be recognized as the actual head and unifying principle of the local churches in His own

Person. Thus, to that extent, this head and unifying principle must be sought for elsewhere, in another head and unifying principle which in a certain sense replaces the absent Person of Christ, and is the visible representation of His invisible, and totally transcendent, unity." In the "real absence of God from the world," the pope became "a visible head who claims [Christ's] titles and powers and unites the visible and multiple local centres of the Church into a single organization under his directing leadership. Once such an understanding of things had become sufficiently general in Western Christendom to have practical effect, it was more or less inevitable that the Bishop of Rome should be regarded as possessing this divine controlling authority."[104] It cannot be denied that by the end of his consequential pontificate, Nicholas had done much to advance papal supremacy alongside filioquism.

Yet as the turbulent ninth century came to an end, Constantinople and Rome enjoyed a restored communion and a common position on the Nicene Creed. In 879, after Igantios's death and the second elevation of Photios as patriarch, a synod assembled in Constantinople to resolve disagreements that had lingered since the end of the Nicolaitan Schism. Along with representatives of the Eastern patriarchates, the synod was attended by legates from Rome. The Pope, John VIII, genuinely wanted to reestablish good relations with Byzantium. The first thing the assembled bishops did was to nullify the decisions of a synod from a decade earlier, which, in Photios's absence, had confirmed the ruling of Nicholas against him.[105] To make their point, the bishops had the acts of that earlier synod burned. Then, with John's approval, the synod formally recognized Photios as the legitimate patriarch of Constantinople.

But the most remarkable outcome of the synod of 879–880 was an anathema issued against advocates of the filioque. John VIII himself set the tone for the Church's defense of the original Creed. In a letter written to Photios, the pope spoke unconditionally. "We assure you concerning this issue," John declared, "which has been such a scandal to the Church, that we [at Rome] not only recite the Creed [in its original form] but also condemn those foolish people who have had the presumption to act otherwise . . ." Was John here alluding to the Franks? Without naming his northern allies, he certainly appeared to be. And since their use of the filioque had been emboldened by the recent appeal of Pope Nicholas, John seemed also to be calling his predecessor's judgment into question. If John was confirming papal precedent in this matter, it was certainly not that of Nicholas. His action was rather to honor Pope Leo III.

The papacy's final word as the ninth century ended was what it had been at the beginning, when Carolingian bishops had defied Leo's order to remove the filioque from the Creed. Aware of the silver shields of the faith mounted resolutely on the tomb of Saint Peter, Pope John again condemned advocates of the filioque "as violators of the divine words and distorters of the teachings of Christ the Lord, and of the fathers who transmitted the holy Creed to us through the councils."[106]

A century and a half had elapsed since that other Leo III, the Emperor of Byzantium, had raised the specter of caesaropapism with his iconoclastic edict in the East. The same interval separated the end of the ninth century from the founding of Pope Stephen II's alliance with the Franks in the West. Both of these earlier decisions had set in motion divisive forces that were becoming increasingly difficult to control. Rome had found herself in the middle of a difficult situation, sometimes ameliorating it and sometimes exacerbating it. It was certain that going forward she would play a crucial role in mediating the unity of East and West. What no one could have foreseen, however, was that Rome was on the verge of a crisis that would take another century and a half to resolve. And when it finally did resolve in the eleventh century, the papacy would be changed forever.

CHAPTER SIX

An Enduring Vision

THE SYNOD OF CONSTANTINOPLE that concluded in 880 was a symbolic event in the history of Christendom. On the one hand, it marked the restoration of ecclesial unity between East and West. The Nicolaitan Schism was over, and Rome again enjoyed sacramental communion with the Church of Constantinople. This bond should not be underestimated. Though difficult to establish empirically, the mystery of shared communion—of participating in the same eucharistic body—was for Christians a matter of capital importance. Christian historians should therefore take it seriously. They might be hard pressed to demonstrate how a shared communion between distant communities produced measurable cultural effects. But the significance of that union is not lessened by a lack of empirical evidence about its impact. For traditional Christianity, communion had always been the basis for community. And now it had been restored.

But there was another, contrary aspect to the synod of 880. That body had gathered under the shadow of a growing cultural rift between East and West. In the person of John VIII, the papacy may have confirmed Rome's long-held unity with the East in the matter of the filioque, but behind the papacy stood the Franks. And they had made it clear during the recent schism that they viewed "the Greeks" as outsiders to Western culture.

Since the middle of the eighth century, the papacy had shown that it could not live without the Franks. It might still mount heroic efforts to mediate unity between the Byzantines and their Germanic nemesis, but as Pope Nicholas had shown, when push came to shove the papacy was inclined to side with the latter. To be sure, this story would not be entirely played out until long after our narrative ends—when, in 1204, western armies descended on Constantinople and through force of arms placed a papal representative on the throne of Hagia Sophia. But the circumstances behind this catastrophe were not too far off. The Great Schism of 1054 was now just a century and a half over the horizon.

The fragility of Christendom was starkly revealed in the fact that the synod of 879–880 represented a reversal of a decision made only a decade earlier. It recognized Photios as the rightful patriarch of Constantinople, while the synod of 869–870 had declared him anathema. What was the universal Church's true conviction? Soon after the Great Schism, Roman Catholics would proclaim the earlier synod universally binding; for them, it became the "Eighth Ecumenical Council." Orthodox, on the other hand, rejected this claim, and some among them actually came to call the synod of 879–880 an eighth ecumenical council. Never had there been in a single historical moment of time such a division of perspectives.

The most powerful source of cultural unity may have been eucharistic communion, and it had been restored by the end of the ninth century. This assured that Christendom's vision of paradise would endure. But time was running out. The century and a half that followed the reconciliation of pope and patriarch would create the conditions for its greatest test ever.

A Universal Liturgy

THE PERSISTENCE OF Christendom's paradisiacal values can be attributed above all to the continued influence, after a thousand years, of sacramental worship. Eucharistic communion preserved a unified cultural community, despite regional variations in its character. From Constantinople to Rome to Aachen—and extending beyond these liturgical centers to new political capitals such as Paris, London, and Kiev—traditional Christian worship oriented an entire civilization toward the kingdom of heaven.

It is true, of course, that the Latin Mass and the Byzantine Divine Liturgy were (and remain) strikingly distinct orders of worship. But this only conceals what they had in common. Both, for instance, shared the same basic structure, which can be traced back to the first centuries of Christian worship and was documented by early fathers such as Justin Martyr. They combined two units of worship: a *synaxis* or "assembly" centered on the proclamation of the Gospel and a Eucharist centered on that assembly's reception of communion. Within this framework they both shared similar content: an introduction; psalmody; scripture reading; homiletic instruction; intercessory prayer; a consecration of the Gifts (known in the East as the *anaphora* and in the West as the *canon*); communion of the faithful; and a dismissal (the Mass actually gets its name from the Latin word for "dismissal"). Today's Roman Catholic and Orthodox would both easily recognize the items on this list, despite the different forms they are given in each rite. And so, in the East and in the West, all members of Christendom reached the first millennium with a common experience of sacramental worship.

By this time the two orders of liturgy had become largely fixed. In the West it was Alcuin who took the Mass bequeathed two centuries earlier by Gregory the Great and reworked it into the form that would endure for the centuries yet to come. For this reason he has been called the "final begetter of the western rite."[107] He and his associates at Aachen augmented the Roman rite to make it more elaborate and, in Joseph Jungmann's characterization, more "oriental."[108] This is ironic, given the Frankish hostility to all things "Greek." But the Roman rite itself had formerly been extremely somber in comparison to the Byzantine—in one scholar's opinion "almost puritanical in its severity and brevity"—and the Franks were eager as always to compensate for their perceived cultural inferiorities.[109]

The effect of Alcuin's reforms was to extend the length of the Mass and to emphasize ceremonial acts such as censing and processions. Alcuin's disciple Amalar helped introduce an interpretation of these ceremonies in which the entire liturgy was assigned allegorical significance. Worship became a kind of participation in the life of Christ. For instance, in Amalar's view, the reading of the Gospel symbolized His Sermon on the Mount and the distribution of the consecrated Eucharist His breaking of bread at Emmaus. Even minor actions were allegorized, such as the deacons' standing behind the priest as an image of the disciples hiding from the authorities after Jesus' arrest. This elaborate approach to the Mass served greatly to enrich the experience of worship for believers, further enhancing the paradisiacal culture of the West. It also served as compensation for the fact that by now most of the laity had ceased to receive communion on a regular basis. Because of this, allegory became a two-edged sword that could ultimately undermine the experience of heavenly immanence by distracting worshippers from actual participation in eucharistic communion.

In the tenth century, these Frankish additions to the Mass were transmitted back to Rome itself by Charlemagne's imperious successors, resulting in the permanent alteration of the Roman rite. In fact, it was another Frankish borrowing from Byzantium that tragically set the context for the division of East and West. The introduction of the Creed, formerly absent from the Western rite, provided the liturgical means through which Frankish influence was again carried to the doors of Saint Peter's Basilica. In 1014, despite the legacy of Leo III's and John VIII's resistance, the filioque would knock down those doors as Pope Benedict VIII finally capitulated to the demands of Emperor Henry II and authorized its use.

In the East, Constantinople had long been the center for the elaboration of the Divine Liturgy, though it borrowed heavily for its ritual from Antioch. Indeed, liturgical scholars have identified a Syrian origin for Christian worship in both East and West. It was from Syria, for example, that much of the Galician and later Frankish inspirations originally came. And it was from there also that the basic pattern of the Divine Liturgy of John Chrysostom came. The saint for whom that liturgy was named had begun his ministry at Antioch and brought its rite with him to Constantinople at the end of the fourth century. He contributed only certain elements to it, such as the anaphora prayers. Other elements, such as the hymn "Only-Begotten Son," a composition of Justinian, were obviously added later. But by the turn of the millennium, the Divine Liturgy of John Chrysostom and the longer order of the Liturgy of Basil the Great had almost completely been brought into their final form.

The anaphora prayers of these liturgies are a good example of traditional Christianity's optimistic anthropology. They bring to mind through the act of *anamnesis* ("recollection") the fact that in Christ, God the Father by the Holy Spirit had "brought us up to heaven and . . . endowed us with Thy kingdom which is to come." The tense of the verbs used here is everything in understanding their meaning: Man has already come to enjoy the experience of heaven even though the ultimate fulfillment of it is yet to come. The anaphora of Basil is also deeply anthropological. It speaks of the deification of man—rendered possible by the Incarnation—thus: the Son of God "emptied Himself . . . being likened to the body of our lowliness, that He might liken us to the image of His glory."

Beyond these anthropological statements in the anaphoras, the content of both liturgies is cosmologically affirmative. The Cherubic Hymn, as we saw in chapter four, speaks of those assembled at the liturgy being united to the highest angels of heaven even while still on earth. But the experience of heavenly immanence is perhaps best expressed in the uniquely Eastern element known as the *epiklesis* ("invocation"). This prayer follows the priest's restatement of Christ's words of institution ("Take, eat . . .") and explicitly calls down the Holy Spirit "upon us and upon these gifts here offered." The effect is to enable the worshiper to relive the experience of Pentecost.

Published commentaries on the Divine Liturgy often reflected the paradisiacal culture of Byzantium. In the seventh century, Maximos the Confessor had written a work called the *Mystagogy*, stressing the eschatological experience of worship. The liturgy, in his symbolic account, represents the unmediated presence of Christ in this world. Maximos even likened the proclamation of the Gospel to the Second Coming of Christ.

Here it might be said that such an experience of worship is evidence that Christendom was not nervously anticipating the end of the world at the millennium. Because of the Liturgy, Christ was already present within it. The "grace of the Holy Spirit . . . is always invisibly present," Maximos wrote, "but in a special way at the time of the holy synaxis."[110] Germanos of

Constantinople, setting the tone for the period after iconoclasm, applied an even more elaborate system of symbolism to the liturgy, seeing in its early elements an allegory on the life of Christ. But unlike his contemporary Amalar, he showed restraint in this, and his account of eucharistic communion emphasized a sacramental reality much more than an allegory of the life of Christ.

Cosmological buoyancy flowed from the liturgy into the very temple in which worship occurred. Once again, Maximos articulated the culture particularly well. The temple for him is an image of a spiritually transformed world. Its purpose is to cause (to use Hugh Wybrew's paraphrase) "man's divinization in union with God."[111] Germanos opens his treatise on the liturgy with a statement about the temple: "The church is an earthly heaven," he writes, "in which the super-celestial God dwells and walks about."[112] This affirmation of heavenly immanence was closely related to the teaching of the Seventh Ecumenical Council, which had defined icons in primarily incarnational terms.

Byzantine temple architecture followed the same thinking, being dominated during the ninth and tenth centuries by a style known as "cross-in-square" (so-called because of the squared walls containing vertical posts that formed a cross). According to this style, liturgical space was arranged so that the temple was experienced as heaven on earth, with the walls relating worshipers spatially to a central dome above them. Within that dome now came to be painted an icon of Christ Pantocrator looking down upon His body, the assembled Church, and presiding at its head in the act of heavenly worship.[113] The tenth-century Monastery of Hosios Loukos is one of the earliest examples of this combination of architecture and iconography to express the cosmological vision of the Divine Liturgy. The central dome with its icon of Christ Pantocrator is, more than any other feature of traditional Christian culture, sure evidence against a tendency toward anti-cosmic millenarianism—that is, toward a fearful expectation that Christ would soon appear in judgment. Christ was already in the cosmos, and rather than threaten it He comforted and upheld it.

Western architecture on the eve of the millennium was also experiencing

dramatic new forms expressive of traditional Christianity. These are generally labeled *Romanesque*, due to their employment of styles from the time of
the ancient Roman Empire. As we have seen, the Palatine Chapel at Aachen
was built in this style during the early ninth century. Unlike it, however,
most Romanesque temples were built according to the basilica form of
Sant'Apollinare Nuovo in Ravenna. They served effectively to orient worshipers' attention toward an altar located at their eastern end.

As we noted in the previous chapter, one of the most interesting features
of Romanesque temples was what came to be known as the *westwork*, the
façade located opposite the altar at the westernmost end of the building.
This westwork became monumental in character, designed to seize the attention of worshipers as they approached the building, filling them with heavenly awe. Passing through the portal at its center was like passing through
the gates of paradise. What is more, the principle of orientation found a
new expression in the use of towers built on either side of the westwork's
entrance portal. These served to direct attention vertically toward heaven,
the ultimate point of orientation for Christendom. Corvey Abbey, built in
Saxony after the Frankish conquest, is a good example of this new architectural feature. However, as noted in the previous chapter, it can also be said
that the heavenly orientation of the westwork towers was something of a
contrast to that of cross-in-square designs, in that towers directed attention
toward a heaven high above this world whereas the central dome of Eastern
architecture proclaimed the coming of heaven into it.

The Ascetical Conditions for Paradise

BUT WHETHER IT EMPHASIZED heavenly immanence or heavenly transcendence, the liturgical architecture of Christendom directed all who
beheld it toward a kingdom that is not of this world. The principle of doctrinal integrity assured that the natural world never became an end in itself.
Those who assembled in the churches of East and West were reminded of the
brokenness of that world and its need of healing.

This was due in no small way to traditional Christianity's teaching about the existence of demons. Christ had come into the world to liberate it from demonic oppression, and much of His ministry was spent driving unclean spirits out of people's lives—or, more precisely, liberating people from demonic influence so that they might experience real life. But He had warned that a complete exorcism of the cosmos would not occur until His second coming.[114] His death itself testified to this paradox. And while after His Ascension He continued to dwell in the world through His Church, the world was not thereby freed from the demonic darkness. Just as divine communion had been severed in the primordial paradise of old, so in Christendom there was a need for constant vigilance and struggle against the sinful passions. Otherwise the experience of eschatological paradise was impossible.

Because of its doctrinal integrity, Christendom cultivated a cosmology that was as sober as it was affirmative. We observed in chapter four how it was "oriented," that is, directed symbolically toward the east. It faced not the spiritually untransformed world but the kingdom of heaven that was beyond it. This heavenward disposition was notable in the liturgical arts, where architecture had literally directed worshipers toward the east. But it was also manifested in cultural institutions such as the incarnational calendar of Dionysius Exiguus, where heaven became the new heading for the world's cultural compass.

The culture of pagandom, by contrast, had from this point of view been directed toward a spiritually untransformed—and in fact demon-riddled—world, one represented by the perversions practiced at Villa Jovis in the first century and, as we shall soon see, the fratricide committed among rulers of neophyte Russia in the eleventh. According to Christendom's evangelical compass, pagandom was profoundly *disoriented*.

To maintain its focus on the kingdom of heaven, Christendom depended above all on the teaching of the cross. Christ's passion was a reminder that nothing in the world—no matter how good or beautiful—could sustain itself or serve as an end in itself. Worldly values must give way to heavenly ones, acquired through death and resurrection. As Christians were baptized into Christ's death in order to participate in His Resurrection, Christian culture developed institutional safeguards against the sheer worldliness that was always a threat to it. The day would come when these safeguards would collapse, and do so spectacularly. But that was still a long time in the future. Centuries before the Renaissance and Enlightenment, Christendom was still firmly supported by a vibrant ascetic tradition.

Ascetic struggle, or *ascesis*, was a basic part of traditional Christian living. Christ had warned that the kingdom of heaven is not approached along a broad and easy path but rather a narrow and difficult one (Matt. 7:13–14). This teaching assured that the vision of paradise remained clear and authentic. Without it, Christian culture threatened to deviate toward two very different outcomes. One was pessimism about the world and man's place within it, a hopeless "sorrow of the world" that Paul had spoken of (2 Cor. 7:10). This was an aberration that would come to envelop Western Christendom after the Great Schism and would eventually lead to the crisis of the Protestant Reformation. The other outcome, reacting against the first, was secular humanism. In an effort to recover Christendom's affirmative cosmology and optimism about the human condition, humanism would look to the spiritually untransformed world as the true home of man, opening the way for Christendom's pagan disorientation during modern times.

For now, asceticism continued to offer a basis for a cosmologically and anthropologically optimistic culture in both the East and the West. It was expressed in the example of the martyrs—saints like Ignatius of Antioch who, as we saw in chapter one, joyfully defied worldly exigencies for the sake of the kingdom of heaven. With the Edict of Milan, however, martyrdom had become almost impossible, and this threatened the ascetical vision of paradise. The "victory of Christianity" under Constantine actually created a crisis for Christendom as a flood of uncommitted and secularly minded converts brought their pagan values into the Church. The rise of hagiography helped address this crisis, as most early saints' lives were accounts of martyrdom. In fact, these martyrologies represent the earliest form of a distinctively Christian literature.

The Sanctification of Society

NEVERTHELESS, CHRISTENDOM NEEDED more than inspirational books to read. Its values had to be lived out in society. One way of compensating for the end of martyrdom was to elaborate the ascetic character of Christian marriage. In pagandom, marriage had been a socially useful institution, providing worldly benefits such as economic security, emotional support, sexual gratification, and offspring. Christianity took these temporal blessings and added to them something truly eternal: sacrificial love. It was *agape* that made a marriage authentic from the Christian point of view. Paul had revealed that the relationship of husband and wife was an image of that between Christ and His Church (Eph. 5:22–33), and the church fathers elaborated this teaching with profoundly countercultural effects.

John Chrysostom, for instance, demanded that husbands honor their wives as their spiritual equals, recognizing their God-given dignity and serving them with tender affection. He also urged both husband and wife to remain faithful to each other even if one should die, assuring them that their union belonged not only to this world but to the kingdom of heaven as well. To a young widow who lost her husband after five short years of marriage he wrote of the transformative power of agape:

> It embraces, and unites, and fastens together not only those who are present, and near, and visible, but also those who are far distant. And neither length of time, nor separation in space, nor anything else of that kind, can break up and divide in pieces the affection of the soul.

Such divine love was possible for Christian spouses, and would unite them in the presence of Christ "for infinite and endless ages."[115]

The Christian liturgy was elaborated to express this tradition. As we noted in chapter four, women now took their place on the opposite side of the temple from men. (The sexes were separated to the left and right to prevent leering at each other, the ultimate act of disorientation during worship.) This was a dramatic and symbolic shift from the physical place of women in Jewish worship, which had been behind that of men. Possessing the image of God in equal measure and being baptized just like them (Jewish women were not as fully initiated as men due to the limitations of circumcision), Christian women were visibly the spiritual equals of men. The liturgy of Christendom prevented men from worshipping with their backs to their wives. And, as they stood facing eastward alongside their equals on the opposite side of the temple, men were called to contemplate holy women—especially the Most-holy Virgin Mary—in hymns and images.

Sacrificial love became the key element of a Christian marriage. But cultivating and preserving this love required an ascetic effort. By the end of the first millennium, Christendom's marriage rituals revealed this. In the West, the relationship was considered indissoluble, and by the eleventh century in England the husband was required to remain faithful to his wife, as the liturgy famously put it, "till death do us part." No such vows emerged in the Eastern order of marriage, since the sacramental actions of the ritual were deemed sufficient without formal pledges from the spouses. The most powerful liturgical action there was the placing of "crowns of martyrdom" on their heads, symbolizing the sacrificial love their marriage requires. In both West and East, then, the liturgy of marriage revealed a sacramental initiation into the divine life of God.

The lifelong union of one man and one woman in marriage became the normative path toward the kingdom of heaven for most living in the society of Christendom. A less traveled but in many ways more celebrated road was monasticism. It might at first seem a totally different way of life from marriage, with its commitment to celibacy and removal from the normal patterns of social interaction. But it was in fact only the opposite side of Christendom's social coin. Also grounded in community rather than individualism, the monastic life led along a path of ascetic effort into the kingdom of heaven.

Monasticism had appeared during the fourth century as a response to the end of martyrdom and the influx of a halfhearted Christianity. Motivated by Christ's call to take up the cross and inspired by His own example of ascetic struggle (such as His forty-day fast in the wilderness), monasticism found its first important expression in the person of Anthony of Egypt. Seeking to live at a distance from society, he established a hermitage in the desert, where he practiced severe forms of fasting and prayer. Because such a way of life produced the spiritually appealing virtues of love and humility, he was soon surrounded by other Christians seeking the kingdom of heaven.

One was Makarios of Egypt, who became a paragon of monastic virtue. Above all, his life was a witness to the extreme, "self-emptying" humility of Christ. One story tells of how he was once falsely accused of impregnating a local girl. Confronted by her kin, he did not protest his innocence but submitted meekly to the demand that he dedicate his livelihood to her—until one day she revealed that he was not the child's father. Another story relates how as a renowned elder he would refuse to speak to those who approached him with reverence, but when someone reminded him of his sins and spoke contemptuously to him, he would open up with eagerness and talk joyfully about the mercy of God. As an ascetic he cultivated an acute sense of sorrow for his sins and in the midst of his work would frequently break down in tears because of them. But this same Makarios was said to radiate heavenly joy to all who knew him. To him was attributed a treatise entitled *Spiritual Homilies* that documents the experience of God's immediate, glorious presence among penitents.

Monastics who followed in the footsteps of Desert Fathers like Anthony and Makarios provided early Christendom with a lived example of paradisiacal asceticism. Their mystical view of repentance always emphasized the joyful, even ecstatic experience of communion with God. It represented a formalized way of living out the parable of the Prodigal Son: Man's sins are great, but God's love is even greater, and repentance assures the sincere ascetic the fullness of the heavenly kingdom. This paradox of glorification through repentance was at the heart of traditional Christian anthropology. It was expressed by the seventh-century abbot John Climacus, who called it the "joy-making sorrow." Repentance, he insisted, properly leads to a joyful experience of paradise. If it does not, it is not authentic.[116]

Monastic fathers insisted that the life of paradise begins in this world, long before death, and continues directly beyond the grave into eternity. It is a process of perpetual deification by which the faithful Christian achieves an ever-increasing communion with God. Basil the Great spoke of this in the fourth century, bringing attention to the biblical statement that men and women were made not only in the image of God, but also in His likeness. "By our creation," he wrote, "we have the first, and by our free choice we build the second."

> And this is what is according to free choice: the power exists in us but we bring it about by our activity. . . . [God] has made us with the power to become like God. And in giving us the power to become like God, he let us be artisans of the likeness to God, so that the reward for the work would be ours. . . . For I have that which is according to the image in being a rational being, but I become according to the likeness in becoming a Christian.[117]

Here the Eastern father was emphasizing a distinction between "being" the image of God and "becoming" His likeness. This distinction between being and becoming would long characterize Western culture and would persist within it to modern times. Its origins are to be found in the uniquely Christian understanding of man and his salvation as a process of becoming godlike. It is a monument to Christendom's core value of spiritual transformation.

Basil's famous Latin contemporary Augustine did not, as we have seen, speak often of deification. In fact, his polemic against Pelagius led him to a much more pessimistic view of the monk's role in acquiring virtue. Nevertheless, he looked on the monastic life fundamentally as Basil did, that is, as an experience in this life of divine love and communion. Like Basil, he promoted what was called coenobitic (or community-based) monasticism, as distinct from the eremitical (or hermit-based) monasticism of the Desert Fathers. The difference lay in gathering monks together in a stable community in which they could practice the apostolic principle of sharing all property in common while supporting one another in love.

This, truly, was a paradisiacal standard of life. For good reason, it inspired the most influential monastic charter in the history of Christendom, the Rule of Saint Benedict. The rule's author was a sixth-century Italian monk familiar with both Eastern and Western monasticism. Benedict was particularly conscious of Augustine's ascetical legacy, but his rule also indicates familiarity with the writings of John Cassian, who, as we saw in chapter four, had been responsible for introducing Eastern monasticism to his Western audience in Gaul.

Benedict's rule established a much more orderly vision of the ascetical life than that of the Desert Fathers or even Augustine. Promoted as an alternative to the relatively unregulated monasticism of the Celts, it spread northward from Benedict's main monastery of Monte Casino in Italy, especially under the influence of Pope Gregory the Great (who as we have seen wrote a celebrated life of Benedict). Augustine of Canterbury, sent by Gregory to evangelize the Anglo-Saxons, brought the rule to Britain, where it soon supplanted the more austere and liberal monasticism of the Celts. Later, under Charlemagne, Benedict's rule actually became obligatory for all Frankish monasteries during the emperor's campaign to "correct" Western Christendom and establish a uniform culture in the West. The monastic father's namesake Benedict of Aniane was instrumental in this development.

Much has been written about the cultural influence of Benedictine monasticism in the West. It provided an alternative to the declining urban culture after the fifth-century barbarian invasions. With their emphasis on stability, scripture reading, and liturgical prayer, monasteries sustained a way of life that was both learned and deeply spiritual. Eventually, their role would be augmented by universities and a renewed commercial urban life, but for centuries they provided a valuable service to Western Christendom. So important have they seemed in sustaining Christian culture that recently Rod Dreher has promoted a "Benedict Option" to guide twenty-first century Christian communities through the nihilistic culture of post-Christian Christendom.[118]

By the end of the tenth century, however, Benedictine monasticism was in trouble. Throughout the West, monasteries had become spiritually degraded under the influence of two very different forces. One was the Viking invasions. Beginning with a sudden attack on Lindisfarne in 793, Norsemen sacked innumerable monasteries along the coasts of western Europe, leaving carnage and material destruction in their wake.

In addition to this assault by Scandinavian pagandom, early Germanic feudalism took a toll on Western monasticism. Under Charlemagne's successors, monastic foundations were often treated as benefices for the powerful. Rulers would distribute them to loyal bishops and, in many cases, even non-ecclesiastical vassals as compensation for service. In some cases monasteries were denuded of their wealth by their worldly abbots, and the ascetic life they were intended to foster all but collapsed. In the tenth century, a new monastic foundation at Cluny in the region of Burgundy marked the beginning of a reform movement that addressed this crisis. Eventually the Cluniac reforms would help rescue Western monasticism from its moribund state, but only through a close alliance with an assertive, reformatory papacy. That, however, is a story that belongs to the history of a later, divided Christendom.

Prior to the Great Schism, monasticism in the East was not so overwhelmed by adversity. With the end of iconoclasm, monasteries took their place in Byzantium as fortresses of ecclesiastical autonomy, guarding against the baneful influence of caesaropapism. The Monastery of Studios in Constantinople was the best example of this, where Abbot Theodore openly challenged the emperor and initiated reforms designed to detach monasticism from imperial policy. He was the leader of the cause against the second marriage of Emperor Constantine VI (known as the moechian controversy and discussed in chapter five), and when the patriarchate itself appeared to be compromised by imperial policy—as alas it had so often been in the past—Theodore was just as principled in defying it. He actually broke communion with Patriarch Tarasios when the latter appeared to turn a blind eye to the marriage. With Theodore the Studite, a new page in the history of Byzantine Christianity is turned, after which the wholesale manipulation of church policy through caesaropapism finally comes to an end.

At a much greater distance from the capital, the monastic republic of Mount Athos was also founded during this period. There especially, the Eastern tendency toward a more intense asceticism inspired by the Desert Fathers developed deep roots. In the middle of the tenth century a hermit named Athanasios arrived on the Holy Mountain and, under the patronage of Emperor Nikephoros Phokas, established the Great Lavra. Completed in

964, this monastery was coenobitic but accommodated eremitical monasticism by placing a limited number of hermitages within close proximity of its central dwelling.

The system set a precedent for subsequent monasticism in the East and even found parallels, as we shall see at the end of this chapter, in the West. It provided those with the most zealous desire to experience the ascetical vision of paradise the opportunity of living within the emotionally stable atmosphere of a community. In building the Great Lavra, Athanasios also managed to keep imperial influence at bay despite his readiness to accept financial donations from Constantinople. A sign of his commitment to a monastic life untroubled by political interference was his decision to adopt the Studite Rule, the fruit of Theodore's struggle against caesaropapism more than a century earlier.

Christendom's Slavic Frontier

AS WE SAW in the previous chapter, the Nicolaitan Schism had brought attention to Patriarch Photios and the filioque. But it took place against the backdrop of a broader dispute between Constantinople and Rome. The issue concerned missions among the pagan Slavs and whether they should be directed from the East or the West.

For centuries, the Slavs had inhabited a large region of eastern Europe stretching from the Black Sea to the Adriatic. From here they radiated northward, eventually reaching the Baltic Sea. They posed a formidable challenge to Christendom, repeatedly attacking Constantinople and devastating territories south of the Danube River. The Slavs were soon joined by another people known as the Bulgars, who settled in their midst and largely assimilated their language and culture.

In the middle of the ninth century, a powerful Slavic state arose in Central Europe called Great Moravia. Its ruler, King Rastislav, resolved to convert his people to Christianity. However, the Frankish missionaries he initially negotiated with made it clear that baptism would require his realm's wholesale Latinization. Latin, after all, had been the linchpin of Christian culture in the West since the time of Charlemagne. Rastislav sent messengers to Rome to request a dispensation from this demand, but when he received no answer from Pope Nicholas, he decided to turn instead to Byzantium. There he found ready support for a Slavic mission. The fact that the Byzantines were proudly Hellenized in their culture did not prevent them from recognizing the value and legitimacy of evangelizing the Slavs in the Slavonic language. In 863, two brothers arrived in Moravia to begin the Slavic conversion. Their names were Cyril and Methodios, and they would go down in history as the "enlighteners of the Slavs."

They came to Moravia prepared. Both brothers already had experience as missionaries to the Khazars, a Caucasian people who had converted a century earlier to Judaism (the only known state in the ancient world to do so). To the north the Khazars bordered eastern Slavic territories, and during the brothers' time among them, they had interactions with the Slavs and learned at least some of their language. In fact, they may even have worked on a rudimentary alphabet for the Slavonic language while living as monks at Mount Olympus in Bithynia. When commissioned by Photios for the Moravian mission in 863, they were able to draw upon a community of monks with scholarly understanding of Slavonic. This was crucial for Cyril, who now composed an alphabet specifically suited to communicate the language. It is known as the Glagolitic alphabet and would soon be replaced by another more effective one named after the missionary. The Cyrillic alphabet would become the one used by most of the southern Slavs and all of the eastern Slavs.

Providing the Slavs with an alphabet specifically designed to communicate their language was a remarkable achievement in itself. But it was only part of a larger "Slavonic project" to equip the Slavs with a formal system of grammar and written usage. This aspect of the Slavic mission established a precedent in the Christian East that would be followed by Orthodox missionaries in later centuries as they worked among peoples as diverse as the Zyrians of Russia and the Aleuts of Alaska. It served the important purpose of acculturating the Christian faith, that is, of integrating it into the world as it was experienced culturally by converts. Because of this, it can be seen

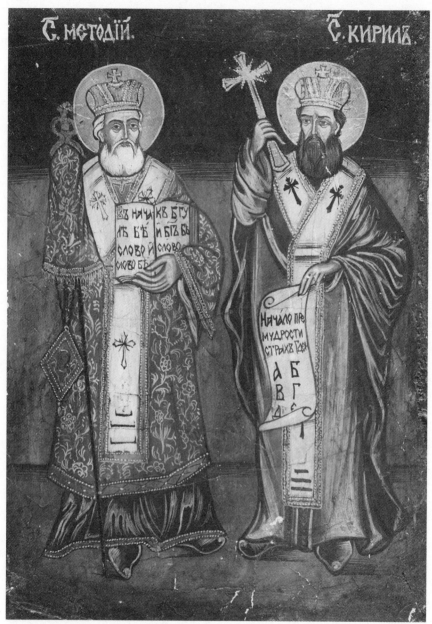

Saints Cyril and Methodios
Shutterstock.com

as an expression of the Church's cosmology. The world with its cultures and languages was to be sanctified by the evangelical transformation of it, in a way comparable to the sanctification of time and space which we explored above in chapter four.

In the West, by contrast, missionaries from Patrick of Ireland to Augustine of Canterbury to Boniface of Germany had all used Latin despite the Gaelic, Anglo-Saxon, and German languages of their respective converts. This resulted in a remarkably uniform church culture that served to integrate diverse peoples into a single ecclesiastical identity, centered upon Rome. More than any other force, the Carolingian program of "correction" consolidated this approach to Christian culture.

For all of Latinization's marvelous uniformity—comparable to the use of Arabic in Islam—the effects were not all beneficial. A distinction inevitably arose between a "sanctified" language of worship and an "unsanctified" vernacular language for everything else. This created an early tendency toward secularization, the process of separating the life of paradise from the life of this world. It also severely undermined the Church's perennial work of evangelization. Not only in the Celtic and Anglo-Saxon north, but even in western lands historically familiar with Latin, such as Gaul, Christians were left in confusion or ignorance about the meaning of the scriptures and prayers at the Mass. Ironically, as we shall see, this comparative deficiency in Latin church culture would result in compensatory efforts at popular enlightenment, reaching truly great proportions during the Protestant Reformation. Such was the legacy of this particularly western dimension of Christendom's transformational imperative.

On the other hand, by affirming the Slavs' native culture through the use of the vernacular Slavonic language Byzantine missionaries ensured that the recipients of the Gospel would have the means of thoroughly assimilating the new faith. This, clearly, is what King Rastislav desired. His letter to the Byzantine emperor requesting missionaries stated quite simply that "since our people rejected idolatry and came under Christian law, we have not had a teacher capable of explaining this faith to us in our own tongue."[119]

Unfortunately, from the start Cyril, Methodios, and their band of missionaries were confounded by the harsh resistance of the neighboring Franks. The Empire of Charlemagne had pushed deep into central Europe, conquering the Saxons in the north and the Bavarians to the south. Everywhere they went, the Franks consolidated their rule by establishing episcopal dioceses that followed, lockstep, Aachen's uniform cultural program. From the newly created diocese of Salzburg, they had already established a mission among the Moravians. Indeed, it was the predatory character of this Latin mission that caused Rastislav to turn to Constantinople. But the appearance of the eminent brothers, confirmed as they were by the emperor of Byzantium himself, did not dissuade the Franks.

Representatives of the Salzburg diocese confronted the missionaries with a novel doctrine that has come to be known as trilingualism. Of recent, Frankish origin, this doctrine claimed that only three languages were legitimate for Christian worship: Hebrew, Greek, and Latin. This claim alluded to the fact that when Jesus was crucified, it was these three languages that were used on the titulus above him, which read "Jesus of Nazareth, King of the Jews." It scarcely needs to be said that there was absolutely no indication in the Gospels that the languages chosen for the titulus by Pontius Pilate, Christ's executioner, should somehow be canonized as languages in which to worship the Lord. But the argument made by the Franks was of course not concerned with scripture or church tradition. It was concerned with administrative uniformity. For the Carolingians, Latin was an instrument of royal authority and ecclesiastical good order.

After about three years, the Byzantine missionaries decided to withdraw from Moravia for a time and return only after obtaining the ordinations of some of their native Slavic converts. It was their long-term goal to equip the Moravians with their own native clergy and not to treat them as an ecclesiastical colony of Byzantium. They decided to take a route through Venice, perhaps because of its Byzantine ties and maritime access to Constantinople. Once there, however, they found themselves assailed by yet more trilingualists, and Cyril was compelled to give an account of why he considered the doctrine a heresy. "Does the rain not fall equally upon all people?" he asked his adversaries.

Does the sun not shine for all, and do we not all breathe the air in equal measure? Wherefore, then, are you not ashamed to recognize but three tongues and command the other nations and races to be blind and deaf? Say, will you have God weak, as though unable to bestow [the Slavonic script], or jealous, that He does not wish to? For we know many peoples who have a script and give glory to God, each in its own tongue.[120]

Here he was alluding to various Eastern Christian peoples who already used their native languages in worship, such as the Armenians and Syrians.

Because of the controversy that engulfed them in the West, Cyril and Methodius decided to continue on to Rome, where they presented their case to Pope Hadrian II. Like his successor John VIII, Hadrian expressed the papacy's continued good will toward the East, and in this case, its missionary policies. He asked for the Gospel book Cyril had translated into Slavonic and solemnly placed it on the altar of Saint Peter's Basilica to bless it. He then gave his blessing for Mass to be served in the Slavonic translation they had prepared.

While in Rome, Cyril fell ill and died, but not before exacting a promise from his brother, who was now ordained a bishop, to return to the missionary field. Methodius left Rome with a group of newly ordained Slavic priests in tow, as well as the blessing of the pope to evangelize in the Slavonic language.

Nevertheless, what the pope blessed in Rome and what the Franks tolerated in Germany were often two different things. No sooner had Methodius returned to Moravia than he was arrested and put on trial by his enemies. This time they had the support of the state, as Rastislav's nephew Sventopulk had seized power with Frankish backing. The new king was intent on reversing the policies of Rastislav, whom he blinded.

Pope John VIII, when he learned that Methodios had been imprisoned, ordered his release. He also confirmed the legitimacy of his mission and the use of Slavonic in it. Methodios thus continued his work of translation and was engaged in it when he died in 885. His funeral was a tribute to a trilingualism of another sort, being served by the clergy in Greek, Latin, and . . . Slavonic.

However, in the years immediately following Methodios's death, the mission was again suspended under renewed Frankish influence, and this time forever. A new pope, Stephen V, warmed to the Frankish case against Slavonic, especially when it was noted that the Slavs were not using the filioque in their liturgy. With Sventopulk and the papacy now both against them, the two hundred missionaries that represented the leadership of an embryonic Slavic church were arrested and expelled from Moravia. Some were actually sold by the Franks into slavery. The Slavic mission in Moravia was finished.

The case of Bulgaria was rather different from that of Moravia in that the Franks never had much of a chance of imposing a Latin church order in the Balkans. Nevertheless, a similar pattern of conflict arose there between Franks and Byzantines during the ninth century, just as events were playing out in Moravia. Since Bulgaria was much closer to the historic sphere of Constantinopolitan influence and the borders of the Frankish empire more distant, this conflict did not have the same outcome.

There was indeed a moment during the middle of the century when Tsar Boris, who had been baptized by the Byzantines in 864, negotiated with Rome. It was this that so alarmed Patriarch Photios, for the filioque was part of the conversion package the Frankish missionaries offered. But given energetic Byzantine overtures coupled with military posturing, Boris finally settled on Constantinople. At the end of his reign, when the Moravian mission had been permanently disbanded, Boris welcomed its Slavic clergy into his realm. This provided scholars like Clement of Ohrid—one of the clergy from the Moravian mission—the opportunity to teach and ordain thousands more Slavic clergy for the mission.

Sadly, a common faith did not prevent the relationship between the mighty empires of Byzantium and Bulgaria from deteriorating in the years following Boris's conversion. Bulgaria was a militant state with a long history of hostilities against Byzantium, dating from the arrival of the pagan Slavs in the sixth century. Boris's conversion greatly improved the situation, but his successors drifted back into an aggressive posture toward their southern neighbor, and Byzantine demands on them only aggravated the situation further. Under Bulgarian Tsar Simeon they invaded Byzantium and even reached Constantinople before being stopped.

Later, under Samuel, the Bulgarians decimated armies sent against them under Byzantine Emperor Basil II. However, at the Battle of Kleidion in 1014, Basil reversed his fortunes and inflicted a devastating defeat on a Bulgarian army of forty-five thousand men. Of this number, only fifteen thousand survived. Their fate was not much better than that of their fallen comrades. The ruthless and vengeful Basil, thereafter known as the "Bulgar Slayer," ordered that of every hundred men, ninety-nine should have their eyes gouged out. Only one percent of the company was left with a single eye intact, in order to provide guidance back to the Bulgarian capital. When the ghastly army arrived, Samuel, who had escaped the battlefield and waited anxiously for news of survivors, fell over dead in shock.

The Conversion of Russia

IN THE MEANTIME, Bulgaria had become the principal operational center for the Slavic mission. Before his death in 916, Clement of Ohrid worked tirelessly on translations from Greek to Slavonic. The clergy he trained spread out into neighboring Serbia and reached as far as Kievan Russia. It was there, on the banks of the Dnieper River, that the process of Slavic conversion reached its high point.

In the early tenth century, the Slavic Russians were ruled by a dynasty that descended from a ruler named Rurik. This enigmatic figure had begun his life as a Varangian warlord and had, remarkably, been invited to come from Scandinavia to rule Russia in 862. His descendants, under the title of grand prince, ruled a very loose confederation of principalities from Kiev. At about the same time, Russia began to receive Christian missionaries from the Byzantine south and Bulgaria. Since most of her rivers flowed southward into the Black Sea, Russia's eastern Slavic population had long enjoyed contact with Constantinople in the form of trade and diplomacy.

In 941, Grand Prince Igor had waged an unsuccessful war against Byzantium, actually reaching the walls of Constantinople. His wife Olga later converted to Christianity, as did many others. Nevertheless, conversions remained limited, and the state maintained a sometimes fierce attachment to Perun, the pagan god of warfare inherited from the Varangians.

In 980, a particularly brutal war of succession broke out among the principalities. The victor, Grand Prince Vladimir, sought to consolidate his rule by reinvigorating the cult of Perun, erecting a large wooden statue of the god on the hillside overlooking the Dnieper. However, after nearly a decade, Vladimir seems to have reached the conclusion that something was wrong and blamed paganism for it. A brutal descendant of Viking warlords who had seized power through murder and rape, he now became a Christian.

The account given in one of only a few sources about Vladimir's conversion reports that the spiritually jaded grand prince dispatched emissaries to surrounding states in which representatives of the world's monotheistic religions could be found. When they returned, these emissaries gave a summary of their findings, dismissing in turn the Judaism of the Khazars, the Islam of the Arabs, and the Latin Christianity of the Franks. But "then we went to Greece," they declared.

> *And the Greeks led us to the edifices where they worship their God, and we knew not whether we were in heaven or on earth. For on earth there is no such splendor or such beauty, and we are at a loss how to describe it. We know only that God dwells there among men, and their service is fairer than the ceremonies of other nations. For we cannot forget that beauty. Every man, after tasting something sweet, is afterward unwilling to accept that which is bitter, and therefore we cannot dwell longer here.*[121]

This famous account, which need not be taken as a literal transcript of the conversation, is notable on a few points. First, it relates impressions of liturgical worship, not doctrinal debate. As we have seen in earlier chapters, traditional Christianity was as much a religion of the temple as a religion of the book. The temple in which Vladimir's emissaries most likely encountered the faith was Hagia Sophia, the most glorious in all of Christendom. Furthermore, the service they most likely attended was the Divine Liturgy, which was at this time comparatively more elaborate and stunning than the

Grand Prince Vladimir
Shutterstock.com

Mass served in the West. They could not "forget that beauty." In this age of paradise, Christendom provided believers and converts alike with an experience, as the emissaries put it, of heaven on earth.

Based on this report, Vladimir chose to be baptized in 988. He then invited Byzantine clergy to come to Kiev to baptize his subjects *en masse* in the Dnieper. While this was happening, he ordered the idol to Perun he had earlier placed in the hills thrown to the ground, and, rather colorfully, beaten with staves as it was dragged to the river and heaved into it, to be washed away from the capital forever. With the exception of the northern city of Novgorod, where pagan priests sparked a riot in protest, the conversion of Russia proceeded peacefully.

For his part, Vladimir was quite a religious personality, and he appears to have embraced the Christian faith with zeal. He dismissed the numerous courtesans he had kept and in exchange took a Christian wife—a Byzantine princess named Anna—to whom he remained faithful for the rest of her life. His new devotion went far beyond personal morality. He instituted regular distributions of bread to Kiev's poor and even opened formerly exclusive court banquets to the common people. Most dramatically, he actually acted to abolish capital punishment throughout the realm, stating that he knew no other way of living out sincerely the precepts in the Sermon on the Mount about loving one's enemies. In this he was ultimately dissuaded by the bishops, who reminded him of his responsibility to institute earthly justice. But the inclination Vladimir expressed was evidence of the way in which Christianity's transformational imperative took hold in the neophyte nation. The kingdom of heaven had become a standard for statecraft alongside the old ways of coercion and violence.

But it was the latter that more often gained the upper hand. After Vladimir's death in 1015, another civil war broke out to determine which of Russia's princes would accede to the grand principality of Kiev. Vladimir had favored his young son Boris, but the surplus of sons from his many pre-baptismal liaisons resulted in multiple claimants. One, named Svyatopolk, raised an army and marched against Boris, finding him well equipped for battle.

However, the younger brother had taken the countercultural values of

Christianity to heart. He gave orders to his men to lay down their arms and even allowed Svyatopolk's agents to approach his tent without resistance. There they found him in sorrow, anticipating his death like Christ in Gethsemane. According to the chronicles, which were written by monks and therefore tended toward pious embellishment, Boris was actually in prayer at the moment of the confrontation, speaking of Christ's passion as he was run through and killed. Soon after, Svyatopolk hunted down another, even younger brother named Gleb and disposed of him in the same way.

Regardless of their historical veracity, accounts of the deaths of Boris and Gleb were soon presented as martyrdoms modeled on the passion of Christ. The effect was remarkable. A recently pagan nation, ruled by the descendants of the Vikings and given to phases of wanton bloodletting, now, through the transformative values of Christianity, elevated a pair of meek and pacifistic children as models of statecraft. Boris and Gleb were the Russian Church's first canonized saints, known by the uniquely Russian title of "passionbearers." Their politically cunning and fratricidal brother, on the other hand, went down in cultural memory as Svyatopolk the Damned.

This revolution in political culture was a sign of how completely the gospel could transform the world. In a way unthinkable in the Roman Empire of Constantine, Vladimir and his two sons had embraced Christianity so completely as to challenge the very basis of pagan realpolitik. Once again, the historical veracity of our sources is really beside the point. Even allowing for exaggeration or pious misrepresentation of the events, the fact that the normative political culture of Russia—enshrined in the written record—now elevated these three as models for subsequent rulers shows how forcefully Christendom could incarnate the values of the kingdom of heaven.

But if Kievan Russia's culture was profoundly altered by Christianity, it was in no way eradicated by it. Here there is a striking distinction to be made between the East and the West, where Latinization had largely resulted in the disappearance of the culture of the Saxons following their conquest and conversion under Charlemagne. The conversion of the Slavs is an example of the Church's tendency toward the acculturation rather than the deracination of peoples.

As we have seen, since the time of the Great Commission the Church was cosmologically affirmative. She looked upon culture as just one part of a cosmos capable of and called to spiritual transformation. Equipped with scriptures and service books in the vernacular Slavonic, Byzantine missionaries baptized converts in a way that enabled them to be both catholic and Russian. While some political and cultural influence was inevitable, they did not impose a particularly Byzantine model of civilization. Centuries later, under different circumstances, Muscovite Russia would embrace elements of the Byzantine state more noticeably, but for now the Kievan state integrated the new faith within a lived national experience that was neither Byzantine nor Roman.

This can be seen in the reign of Yaroslav the Wise, another of Vladimir's many sons who succeeded his brother Svyatopolk as grand prince in 1019. Most famously, he appointed the first native Russian to the newly formed Kievan metropolitanate in 1049. Before Metropolitan Ilarion, Constantinople had required all primates of Russia to be of Greek background. Ilarion proved himself an able administrator. But he is better known for consolidating a strong sense of national identity. In a widely reproduced homily, the learned bishop united Russia in his readers' minds to the catholic Church, demonstrating her Orthodox identity and her love of being distinctively Russian.

As true worship of the Holy Trinity is universal to Christians of all lands, Ilarion claimed, it finds a unique expression within the "Russian nation." His sermon located goodness in the Russian state and her culture, pointing in particular to the revered memory of Vladimir, who, as a recognized saint, intercedes for Russians as they continue to live in this age. "Arise," he declares rhetorically to Vladimir,

> You are not dead. For it is not right that you should die, for you have believed in Christ, the Sustainer of the whole world. . . . You still live upon this earth, unforgotten through your sons. . . . Behold your city radiant with majesty. Behold your blossoming churches, behold Christianity flourishing. Behold your city gleaming, adorned with holy icons and fragrant with thyme [or incense], praising God and filling the air with sacred songs.[122]

The long reign of Yaroslav was also known for the foundation of the Monastery of the Caves in Kiev, located in the hills overlooking the Dnieper. It was here that Russia's first great monastic, Antony, transplanted the asceticism he had learned on Mount Athos to Russian conditions. In addition to the Caves Monastery, Yaroslav built numerous churches. The most famous of these—again expressive of Russia's Byzantine heritage—was Saint Sophia Cathedral, so named in obvious imitation of Constantinopolitan precedent. Finally, Yaroslav passed numerous laws designed to strengthen the place of the Christian clergy in society, and he patronized book copying and scholarship.

By the time Yaroslav the Wise died in 1054, Kiev was the capital of a distinctively Christian state. Russia, baptized by the Byzantines, enjoyed all the cosmologically affirmative features of traditional Christianity. Perhaps the most notable in her case was the emphasis on the tangible, even sensuous manifestation of a sanctified world. Summarizing the consequences of Russia's baptism, Metropolitan Ilarion himself seems to have had this in mind when he declared that

> the darkness of the demonic cult perished and the sun of the Gospel shone over our land. The temples of idols were destroyed, and the churches were built, the idols were broken and the icons of the saints appeared. Demons fled away, the cross sanctified the towns; as shepherds of spiritual lambs, came bishops, priests and deacons, offering the immaculate sacrifice. They adorned all the sanctuary and vested holy churches with beauty. Angel's trumpet and Gospel's thunder sounded through all the towns. The incense rising towards God sanctified the air. Monasteries stood on mountains. Men and women, small and great, all people filled the holy churches.[123]

Russia had come to enjoy the full inheritance of Christendom. For her the world was filled with the manifest presence of God. Icons and temples now marked out the boundaries of the kingdom of heaven as the proclamation of the gospel drove demonic powers away. The very air was sanctified by the fragrant incense of heavenly worship.

A Puppet Papacy

YET IF CHRISTENDOM was flourishing in the Slavic borderlands of the East, it was entering a protracted crisis in the heart of the West. In Rome, the same tenth century that saw the conversion of Vladimir witnessed the total collapse of papal dignity.

The first sign of trouble came in 882 when Pope John VIII was brutally murdered. The most vigorous pontiff since Nicholas I, he had distinguished himself as a defender of papal authority and an advocate for close ties with the East. His assailants, it was said, initially used poison to kill him, but when it failed to take full effect they used a hammer to smash in his skull. This horrid event was the first time since the Edict of Milan that a bishop of Rome had been put to death.

Records of the assassination are scarce, and it is impossible to know exactly what led to it. But John's readiness to recognize Patriarch Photios and condemn the filioque may have played a role. The ninth century had seen the conquest of Sicily by the Arabs, and John had looked to Constantinople as a defense against their latest incursions into Christendom. Byzantium still ruled the southern part of Italy and offered the most immediate means of resistance. Since the Frankish empire of Charlemagne had dissolved by this time into two disunited halves, with internal strife paralyzing each, John reasoned that his predecessors' Frankish policy may have been a failure. Rome was again threatened by the prospect of conquest at the hands of unbelievers. But by turning from the West back toward the East, John had alienated powerful interests in Italy. Some of these were from the region surrounding Rome itself, and some represented the now distant Franks. John's murder brought a sudden and decisive end to what had become a possible road toward cultural reunion with the East.

The imperious days of Pope Nicholas were a fading memory in Rome. As the ninth century came to an end, the papacy entered a crisis of demoralization and irrelevance, struggling to maintain its status as a voice of Orthodoxy and the first among Christendom's great patriarchates. And the more it struggled, the more it slipped helplessly into an abyss. More than a century would be required for its recovery. When, during the pontificate of

Leo IX in the middle of the eleventh century, the papacy attained its former capacity to provide leadership, it did so with an assertiveness so great and so strident that relations with the East became doomed.

If the assassination of John VIII was a sign of what was to come, the pontificate of Formosus a decade later marks the actual beginning of the crisis. Formosus had made his start in papal politics under John as the bishop of Porto just beyond the city limits. He appears to have had a strong ambition to become the pope and was accused by John of conspiring to overthrow him. The consequences were relatively mild by the day's standard: Formosus was compelled to confess his conspiracy before a synod and submit to deposition and perpetual exile. However, after John's death he reappeared on the scene, was restored to the diocese of Porto, and, in 891, obtained the coveted office of pope. However, after his death something unthinkable occurred. His successor Stephen VI ordered his body to be exhumed and, of all things, placed on trial.

The unprecedented spectacle occurred in the Lateran Cathedral in 897. Fully arrayed in papal vestments, flanked by a deacon who served as the defense attorney, Formosus's cadaver was subjected to a fusillade of charges bitterly issued by Pope Stephen. The central offense was rather curious: he was accused of violating canon law by having been elected pope while already bishop of another territorial diocese (Porto). The canons of the First Ecumenical Council had forbidden this in order to protect the Church from disorders caused by episcopal ambition.

The motivation for the charge was clearly not canonical scrupulousness as such, however. As we shall see, the actions of the period's popes were anything but canonical. Rather, the impulse seems to have been the political anxieties of Formosus's successor, for Stephen had also been a duly appointed diocesan bishop (in Agnani) when elected pope. But Stephen saw a way of resolving his anxiety. He had been appointed bishop by Formosus, meaning that if he could discredit his predecessor and have his ordinations retroactively nullified, he would be canonically free to continue as pope because he would not, legally, have been a bishop at the time of his election.

It is hard to imagine such a ploy being used to advance clerical ambition in the East of that time. There, where ecclesiastical intrigue was presumably no less a temptation, the idea that a deceased hierarch's ordinations could be retroactively nullified was inconceivable. But the ruse worked in the comparatively legalistic culture of Rome. Despite the deacon's defense (which was no doubt sincere, as he too had been ordained by the accused), Stephen's tirade convinced the assembled synod that all ordinations performed by Formosus were null and void. The fingers of the dead pope's putrefying blessing hand were then detached as a symbol of posthumous deposition, and his reeking body was hurled into the Tiber River with a curse.

The Cadaver Synod, as this bizarre event came to be known, was a particularly low moment in a century and a half of papal demoralization. While it was motivated most immediately by the ambitions of Stephen VI, it brought to light other, more nefarious forces that threatened Christendom's most revered patriarchate. The question, as it had been two centuries earlier, was largely geopolitical. As we saw in chapter four, Pope Stephen II had sought out an alliance with the Frankish King Pepin in order to secure Rome from

The Cadaver Synod
Painting by Jean Paul Laurens, 1870

the constant threat of the Lombards. That alliance had been strengthened in the time of Pope Leo III and Charlemagne. Now, with the dissolution of the Frankish empire, the papacy again found itself held captive by the variety of powers that craved Italy. The Arabs had recently conquered Sicily. The Byzantines continued to hold the southern part of the peninsula. The Frankish successor states maintained claims over the northern lands once occupied by their ancestors. And now, a new force arose in central Italy itself—the Roman aristocracy.

Present among the bishops at the Cadaver Synod was one of aristocratic origin named Sergius. Like Stephen VI, he had an interest in seeing Formosus's ordinations nullified, as this would benefit his own designs on the papacy. In 898 he obtained the papal office, but he was soon driven out of Rome and deprived of it. In 904 he returned to the city, this time as a co-conspirator of Duke Alberic of Spoleto, who had risen to power through assassination. Alberic reinstated his accomplice as Pope Sergius III.

One of the new pope's first actions was to murder his two predecessors, who had recently been thrown into prison to vacate the papal throne. But Sergius did not long remain dependent on Duke Alberic. Rome now housed an even greater strongman, Duke Theophylact of Tusculum. He and his ambitious wife Theodora, whom the contemporary Liutprand of Cremona called a "shameless strumpet," aspired to be the effective dictators of Rome and saw the vulnerable Sergius as a means toward their objective.

As it turned out, Sergius was the first in a series of popes who could not resist the company of women, and the couple knew exactly how to trap him in their net. Their fourteen-year-old daughter Marozia was by all accounts a girl of stunning potential beauty, and they instructed her to seduce Sergius and establish herself as his mistress. Before long, Marozia was pregnant with the pope's child. The parents then arranged a proper marriage for her to Duke Alberic, assuring that their grandchild would join Spoleto and Tusculum into a kind of provincial superpower. The ploy worked. Theophylact became the papal treasurer and the commander of Rome, thus securing complete financial and military power. Theodora acted behind the scenes to ensure that the clan's interests were always placed first in Roman affairs.

As a result, Theophylact and his Tusculan heirs effectively controlled the papacy for half a century.

This period is known to historians as the "pornocracy," and indeed sexual intrigues often overwhelmed other concerns of the papacy. Indicative of the situation was the pontificate of John X. He was the reputed lover of Theodora, and when as a rank-and-file bishop he found himself transferred to distant Ravenna, the Tusculan matriarch intervened to have him elected pope in order to maintain their affair. The disgusted chronicler Liutprand related how, "with a harlot's wanton naughtiness," she ordered his return because otherwise "she would have few opportunities of going to bed with her sweetling if he were separated from her by the two hundred miles that lie between Ravenna and Rome."[124]

But Theodora was nothing in comparison to her bewitching daughter. At the center of the pornocracy stood the seductive Marozia, the "lover, mother, and grandmother of popes" in John Julius Norwich's phrase. She entrenched herself behind the thick walls of Rome's famous cylindrical Castel Sant' Angelo, and from this vantage effectively ruled Rome for two decades.

Having given birth to Sergius's son, Marozia ensured that he would follow in his father's footsteps. When her mother's lover John X began to show signs of resisting Tusculan influence, Marozia ordered her second husband, Guido, to storm into the Lateran one day and murder John's brother in front of his very eyes. John probably got the message, but not soon enough. Not long after the incident he was deposed and also murdered on Marozia's orders.

But her son was still too young to be pope, having scarcely entered his eighteenth year. So she arranged to have a pair of her most docile political creatures elected in succession and controlled them as puppets during their brief tenures. Finally, when her son had attained the advanced age of twenty-one, he became Pope John XI. For what it was worth, this violated the canonical tradition requiring a man to be of mature age, preferably at least thirty, to be ordained. It is also striking to note that it was precisely the problematic ordination of Patriarch Photios in the previous century (discussed in chapter five) that had so aggravated Pope Nicholas and inclined him toward intervention. But despite the "scrupulous" example of the Cadaver Synod, ecclesiastical canons were decidedly out of fashion in tenth-century Rome.

Yet another example of disregard for canonical precedent was displayed in one of John XI's first papal dignities—or rather indignities. In 932 he was ordered by his mother to preside at her third wedding ceremony, held not in a temple but at her grand residence, the Castel Sant'Angelo. The latest consort was himself as scheming and ambitious as Marozia, and the event might have been the opening of a new phase in her dictatorship. But the marriage alienated her other son, John's half-brother Alberic II. Estranged from his mother, he stormed her citadel and threw her into its notorious dungeon. She would interfere in papal politics no more.

But the puppet papacy was not over yet, nor its tendency toward pornocracy. Alberic II ruled Rome for two decades, thus doubling the reign of the Tusculan dynasty there. He treated the papacy largely as his relatives before him had done; it was merely an extension of his power. Of the four popes who succeeded John XI, Alberic seems to have kept each in his pocket.

But it was the fifth of these popes who stands out in history as the most disgraceful of the age. John XII was Alberic II's own son through an illegitimate liaison with either a concubine or, possibly, his own stepsister (another violation of canon law). More impressive was John's maternal ancestry: he was of course the grandson of the notorious Marozia. In an age accustomed to scandal, he managed to shock everyone. He effectively turned the Lateran Palace into Christendom's greatest brothel. There he organized interminable revelries that drew an endless stream of prostitutes. In some cases, unsuspecting female pilgrims were said to have been raped there by the lecherous pope. Beyond such debauchery and crime, John's most compelling interests centered on hunting and the breeding of horses. For ecclesiastical affairs he showed little inclination.

By the middle of the tenth century, however, the power of the Tusculans was waning. In the north, beyond the Alps, another was rising. A powerful state had risen from the ashes of the Frankish empire and was now centered in Germany. The Saxon Otto the Great had brought order to the chaos of East Francia, one of the two main fragments left over from Charlemagne's achievement. Otto had reduced the power of rebellious duchies, creating an effective feudal military order. With it he had managed to wage a successful war in the east against the pagan Hungarians, defeating them at the Battle of Lechfeld in 955.

On that occasion, Otto's soldiers acclaimed him emperor. But the title meant little without papal confirmation. So when he received envoys from Italy begging him to restore order south of the Alps, the descendent of Charlemagne could not resist. In 961 his massive army crossed the Alps and effortlessly occupied Rome. There he compelled Pope John XII, whose Tusculan power base was now exhausted, to submit to German overlordship. John complied, and in 962 he crowned Otto the Great Emperor of the Romans at Saint Peter's Basilica.

Before returning to Germany, Otto condescended to advise John to reform his ways, but his words fell on deaf ears. History's most profligate pope died in the arms of a married woman, or, according to an alternate account, by the hand of her outraged husband.

Western Caesaropapism

THE FATE OF THE PAPACY had now passed from the hands of the dissolute Tusculans to those of the upstart Germans. But if visionary bishops had hoped Ottonian patronage would free the papacy from secular domination, they were mistaken. Charlemagne's heir now imposed on Rome and her ecclesiastical network in the north a system of control that the Franks had only dreamed about in the days of Carolingian "correction." Otto treated the bishops and abbots of his realm as he did its lords and knights—that is, as vassals. This, perhaps, was the most significant Germanic contribution to Western Christendom prior to the Reformation. Under Otto the Great and his successors—the Ottonians—the culture of German feudalism entered the Church in the West and altered her significantly.

In Germany, bishops were not the charismatic agents of evangelical transformation they had been in the early Church. They were earthly lords, subject to the emperor and dependent on him for their ecclesiastical fiefdoms. When they were appointed to their dioceses through an institution called

Emperor Otto III
By Meister der Reichenauer Schule

investiture, they were obliged to prostrate before Otto or his deputy, pledging solemnly to serve the crown with all their strength. This subjugation was solemnized by a ceremonial rite in which the bishop knelt down and placed the palms of his hands together in a gesture of supplication. With time, this posture became the standard for all Christian prayer in the West and remains a visual expression of its piety to this day. The East, by contrast, retained the ancient posture of raising both hands in the air during prayer, and bishops, while implicitly subjects of the Byzantine emperor, were understood to have a direct allegiance only to the head of the Church, Jesus Christ.

Otto's policy of clerical subordination was not limited to ceremony. Bishops and abbots were required to institute justice and collect taxes. In exchange for their services to the crown, they were given the same freedoms and benefits enjoyed by the highest nobility. More than this, it was from their ranks that the most important advisors and officials of court were often drawn. Otto the Great had faced widespread opposition from the lay nobility early in his reign, and he sought to use the clergy as an alternative cadre of state servitors. This, after all, had been the precedent set by Charlemagne. The system was effective, and under the Ottonians the German clergy became an integrated part of the imperial bureaucracy. As a reward, bishops were promoted, and monasteries received rich endowments of land and serfs.

Needless to say, all of this, while effective in advancing the empire's political fortunes, did not bode well for its spiritual life. Monasteries grew in material wealth but gradually ceased to hold their monks to a high standard of asceticism. Bishops became preoccupied with worldly affairs and lost sight of the universal needs of church administration. Within a century, the spiritual degradation of monasteries and the episcopate would provoke the papal reformation, one of the greatest and most momentous events in the history of Christendom.

Another ominous effect of Ottonian church policy was the requirement of clerical military service. As the emperor's feudal lords, bishops and abbots were expected to raise armies. In fact, they personally bore weapons and often led their warrior serfs into the fray of battle.

This was something new in Christendom. In the past, military service was performed only by the laity and usually entailed a period of penance after it was completed. Apostolic Canon 13, for instance, stated that any member of the clergy who joins in military service is to be deposed, citing Jesus' distinction between the things of Caesar and the things of God. This prohibition was still in place in Byzantium. In fact, a dispute arose when Otto's Eastern contemporary Emperor Nikephoros Phokas proposed that the Church automatically canonize soldiers who fell in battle while defending Christendom against the Muslims. The patriarch of Constantinople rebuked him, reminding him that the Gospel demanded love of one's enemies and adding that any act of taking human life, even if justified for the protection of one's homeland, was necessarily sinful. But in the West, the traditional culture of Christendom was changing.

The German requirement of episcopal military service can be understood in light of the Frankish legacy of conquest. It provides a contrast to the history of Byzantium. Whereas Roman pagandom had been a militantly expansive civilization prior to Constantine, the military history of New Rome after the Edict of Milan was mostly defensive. Armies were maintained and wars were fought, but the overall pattern was of defending or (in the case of Justinian's reconquest) of recovering lost territories. The Gospel's countercultural commandment to love one's enemies was easier to institutionalize under such conditions.

In the West, however, military conquest had not only preceded the conversion of Frankish King Clovis, it had been the dominant political dynamic thereafter, from the Saxons under Charlemagne to the Hungarians under Otto. The latter emperor, a Saxon himself, understood well the way of feudal warfare and saw nothing improper in demanding that his bishops play their appointed role in it. For him Christ was a "god of war," as Tom Holland has noted:

> All his reign, Otto had known it his duty as a Christian king to combat God's enemies on the fields of battle. His subjects—despite the earnest attempts of missionaries and scholars to persuade them otherwise—had known it too. Deep in their souls, the Saxons had understood, as only a people brought to Christ through conquest could possibly have understood, that the God they worshipped was indeed a god of war. . . . No matter that it ran directly contrary to the traditional teaching of the Church.[125]

It was this merger of Christianity and feudal violence in Germany that, more than anything else, prepared the way for the crusades that would come during the next century. All that was needed was a spiritual authority to justify and direct them. This would be provided by a revitalized papacy, reformed in reaction to the Ottonian domination of church life but remarkably consistent in furthering its militancy.

Overall, the domineering ecclesiastical policies of Otto the Great and his successors represented nothing really new in Christendom. They were in fact the same that Byzantine emperors had pioneered and perfected many centuries earlier. It was simply caesaropapism transplanted from the Mediterranean to the forests of the north. In its German form, it assumed a uniquely administrative character by coopting bishops into the feudal system. And it could work to the detriment of doctrine.

Prior to the ninth-century Studite reforms, Byzantine emperors had repeatedly been guilty of imposing doctrinal errors and heresies upon the Church, compelling patriarchs of Constantinople to endorse them or face deposition. We saw in the previous chapter how, in the West, similar doctrinal deviations from church tradition were advanced at Charlemagne's court. The two most significant of these were semi-iconoclasm and creedal filioquism. Carolingian theologians such as Theodulf of Orléans had failed to lay a firm groundwork against the veneration of icons, however. As a result of this and the papacy's consistent opposition to iconoclasm, that heresy eventually disappeared beneath the topsoil of Western culture (though it would resurface later with the eroding effects of the Protestant Reformation).

But creedal filioquism did not disappear. It had been considered essential to the "corrected" good order of the Frankish empire and had, after all, received considerable doctrinal backing among Latin fathers of the Church. Otto was no Charlemagne when it came to intellectual policy, but he and his successors proved equally committed to the cause of creedal filioquism. In fact, it would be the German empire's unique historical achievement to break, finally, centuries of resistance to the filioque by the once-heroic papacy.

To be sure, there was little that was heroic about the papacy as the millennium approached. After the morally grotesque demise of John XII, a pope named Leo VIII was elected with relatively little interference from Rome's

regional powerbrokers. This time he was the puppet of Otto. Leo was soon
forced to flee the city when a mob, enraged by the disgrace of imperial interference, threatened to kill him. In his place the Romans elected Pope Benedict V. But since this was done without consulting Otto, the proud emperor
returned to Rome at the head of his army and, with Leo in tow, ordered the
deposition of Benedict.

In the style of the Cadaver Synod, though not quite as morbidly, Otto
arranged a public confrontation with Benedict at the Lateran Cathedral.
Leo ceremonially smashed the papal staff over Benedict's head and then
kicked him out of Rome. The humiliated and demoralized Benedict spent
the remainder of his days as Otto's prisoner in the north. Like it or not,
the German emperor was drawn into the affairs of Rome. By the end of his
reign, Italian affairs had become important enough that he spent the final
six years of his life in the city, leaving it only months before his death in 973.

Before that, Otto had arranged for the marriage of his son to a Byzantine
princess named Theophano. When this son, Otto II, died in 983 after an
unsuccessful war against the Saracens of Sicily, during which he found it necessary to campaign against the neighboring Byzantines in the south, he left
Theophano alone with their three-year-old son, also named Otto. Because of
the regency that resulted, imperial control of Italy waned, and a new local
clan called the Crescentians came to power. Three successive heads of this
family—each confusingly sharing the same name Crescentius—held the title
of Roman consul and frequently dictated papal elections. Only after Otto
III attained adulthood and resolved to impose his will on the situation did
the papacy again come under the control of the Germans. But when it did,
church life in the West had turned in an even more caesaropapist direction.

The reason for this was the political vision of Otto III. The son of the
Byzantine princess Theophano, he aspired to rule a universal Christendom
in which the most revered patriarchate was even more thoroughly subordi-
nated to his government than ever the patriarchate of Constantinople had
been to Eastern emperors. One of his appointments to the papacy—a fellow
German and the first non-Roman since the end of the Byzantine papacy of
the eighth century—crowned him in 996. Moreover, this pope, Gregory V,

was Otto's cousin and shared with him the dream of a Roman Empire that united East and West.

After nearly a century of Saxon rule, Otto III was poised to bring huge new populations into that empire. He (and before him his father, Otto II) had largely failed to reunite formerly Carolingian lands in the west where in 987 a major rival named Hugh Capet had been crowned King of the Franks, a people subsequently known as the French. But there were other opportunities for expansion. The Germans had been fighting their way deep into eastern Europe since the time of Otto the Great, and their military vanguard—like that of the Franks before them—was followed by equally militant missionaries. They had taken possession of large territories inhabited by the Slavic Wends, forcing these to convert and establishing colonial dioceses to advance Germanization.

The Hungarians also, broken by German arms in 955, had begun to turn to Christianity. Their King Stephen was finally baptized in 1000, taking one of Otto's cousins as his queen. Even earlier in 966 the duke of Poland, Mieszko, had converted under the influence of his Christian wife, Dobrawa. He was succeeded by the first king of Poland, Boleslaw the Brave. Boleslaw had his own ambitions, to be sure, but he was prepared to ally with Otto III in a war against the Wends following a massive uprising—caused largely by aggressive Christianization—in 983. In 1000, he hosted Otto when the emperor made a pilgrimage to the Polish capital of Gniezno to venerate the relics of Adalbert, a missionary to the Wends who, rather like Boniface, had been martyred after alienating the pagan population with harsh methods of cultural assimilation.

As he annexed new territories and converted their populations, Otto began to reconsider the regional character of his empire. The example of Byzantium was often on his mind, cultivated by a Greek named John Philagathos who had educated him. That, with the Byzantine political ideal imported by his mother, led Otto to think of himself as the emperor of a universal Christian state with priestly prerogatives over it. Echoing Justinian, he assumed titles for himself such as "Servant of Jesus Christ" (*servus Jesu Christi*) and "Servant of the Apostles" (*servus apostolorum*). Otto identified strongly with Constantine and even more with Charlemagne, whose tomb he visited in Aachen in order to snatch a relic for himself. At court, he spoke often about the restoration of the Roman Empire, which he believed he had a divine calling to pursue.

The last and perhaps most effective of Otto's hand-chosen popes, Sylvester II, actively encouraged such dreaming. The very pontifical name he chose called the imagery of the Donation of Constantine to mind, as it was the first Pope Sylvester who was said in the spurious document to have benefitted from imperial patronage. Resolving to follow in his father's footsteps, Otto sent an embassy to Constantinople to secure a Greek princess to marry. Negotiations proceeded apace, and the bride was on her way to Italy for a wedding in Rome when suddenly in 1002 the visionary emperor died. With him died the dream to unite the West and the East in a single empire, Byzantine in form but German in content.

But this still left the question of where the papacy fit into the picture of Christendom. Otto III's successor was Henry II. The new emperor was comparatively uninterested in the affairs of Italy, preferring to spend his time in Germany. He was also faced with a war against the Poles, as Boleslaw had reversed his alliance with the empire in order to carve out Wendish territories for himself. Closer to home, Henry advanced the caesaropapist agenda of his Ottonian predecessors, granting more wealth to monasteries and bishoprics in exchange for even greater demands for clerical submission to the crown. When he did set his gaze beyond the Alps, he saw the papacy as a venerable and necessary institution, but one—like his own bishops— that God had placed at the disposal of his anointed earthly rule. For him, Christendom was not universal. It was German.

Back in Rome, things had again slipped into chaos. Henry's Polish distractions enabled the last of Rome's Crescentians to dictate a series of papal elections in the years following the emperor's accession. That situation changed when the clan finally died out after appointing a pope named Gregory VI. However, another candidate was elected at the same time, Benedict VIII, who was another descendant of Alberic II. Benedict decided to flee the city and seek assistance from Henry in the north. This brought the emperor's attention back to Italy, if only temporarily. Benedict was a master at the art of persuasion. For instance, he would soon talk Henry into an invasion of southern Italy to try to drive the Byzantines out. But now he focused on more immediate concerns. In exchange for the expulsion of his rival Gregory, he offered Henry an imperial coronation.

This fateful meeting represented a second Paderborn, the German town where Leo III and Charlemagne had negotiated the first imperial crowning in Western Christendom. A pope on the run for his life, a powerful emperor eager for papal sanction, and the background of a violent and unruly Roman populace: all were a recreation of the circumstances of 800. The significant differences, however, were the demoralized condition of the papacy and the character of the pope. Broken by a century of degradation and shame, the patriarchate of Rome had lost its resolve to stand with the ancient tradition of the Church, defending its autonomous dignity and adherence to universal practice. Benedict, saved from imprisonment and possibly death, was prepared to give his German patron whatever he demanded.

And so, when Henry arrived in Rome in 1014 for the promised coronation, he demanded of the pope what had been denied to his predecessors ever since the days of Charlemagne. The filioque might be a novelty throughout the East, but Henry insisted it was time for Rome to stand with Western Christendom and against "the Greeks." He demanded that for the first time in history the papal Mass be sung in Saint Peter's Basilica with the filioque in the Creed.[126]

And the pope submitted. Forgotten was Pope John VIII's anathema against its use. Ignored was the Fourth Ecumenical Council's ban on alterations to the Creed. But what could not be forgotten or ignored was what stood prominently in the middle of the cathedral where this turning point in history took place. At the very tomb of the First of the Apostles himself, in Western Christendom's most important temple, Pope Leo III's twin "shields of faith" still proclaimed—in Latin and in Greek—that the Holy Spirit "proceeds from the Father." Period.

The Wings of Paradise

BENEDICT'S DECISION was fateful. But its divisive consequences were yet to be felt in all their fullness. For now, a thousand years after Pentecost, Christendom retained its vision of paradise. It remained a unitary civilization with a supporting culture that directed its members toward the heavenly transformation of the world.

This was certainly evident at its geographical extremes. Both the Celts in the far west and the Slavs in the far east participated in the experience of paradise at every liturgy on every Lord's Day in the presence of every nimbus cross or saint's icon. Within the Mediterranean heartland of Christendom this experience likewise continued unabated, despite the gathering clouds of division now hovering over Rome and Constantinople.

In fact, as we reach the end of our narrative, it is in a pair of monastics affiliated with these two historic centers of Christendom that we can find the common root of the Christian culture that had united West and East for a whole millennium. Each embodied in his life and teachings those core values that had been established at Pentecost and which we explored in chapter one. Each contributed to a culture of doctrinal integrity, divine participation, heavenly immanence, and spiritual transformation.

Romuald of Camaldoli and Symeon the New Theologian were both influenced by the early forms of monasticism discussed above. They practiced what was called *prayer of the heart*, a way of life found among the Desert Fathers and concentrated in the writings of Makarios of Egypt, especially his *Spiritual Homilies*. At its center was the anthropologically optimistic doctrine of deification in which man, even in this age, can participate in the life of God.

The son of an aristocrat in Ravenna, Romuald grew up surrounded by the Byzantine legacy of liturgical architecture and piety. As a young man, however, he found himself serving as his father's second during a duel that resulted in the killing of his father's adversary. He repented deeply of his role in this crime and sought consolation at the monastery attached to the Church of Sant'Apollinare in Classe. As we saw in chapter four, this church featured an icon of the Transfiguration steeped in a vision of paradise on

Earth. Romuald must have been moved by its verdant imagery and the cosmic nimbus cross placed at its center. Nevertheless, he found the monastery's Benedictine way of life insufficiently rigorous and decided to travel throughout the West in search of a more transformative asceticism.

After spending time in Spain, Romuald returned to Italy and established a monastery at Camaldoli. From there he established several other habitations during the remainder of his life. Before dying in 1027, he was acknowledged as a great ascetic and actually served as spiritual father to his earthly father when the latter, repenting of the aforementioned murder, came to live at his monastery. Romuald was so well known in his time that he was sought out for advice by emperors Otto III and Henry II. He also visited Rome and there consulted with the pope.

Romuald was a monastic reformer who looked beyond the Rule of Saint Benedict to the example of the Desert Fathers for inspiration. This found expression in the monastic settlement he created, which, like the Great Lavra of contemporary Mount Athos, provided both coenobitic and eremitic dwellings. The spiritual longing he cultivated was perfectly consistent with the most ancient ascetic practices of traditional Christianity and frequently brought him to the "joy-filled sorrow" that John Climacus had described. According to his biographer, Romuald "prayed and wept almost without intermission."

Tears were indeed a regular feature of his piety, and he did not believe human beings could acquire complete union with God without them. Yet he did not inflict upon others undue demands for penance. In fact, he even counseled his disciples not to weep too much for fear of falling into the despair of what Paul had called worldly sorrow. But for Romuald, it was precisely the process of heartfelt repentance that brought him most immediately into the presence of God. On one occasion, his tears even brought to him a vision of the divine light itself.

Romuald wrote virtually nothing about this vision. But to him is attributed a *Short Rule* that provides the background to it. "Sit in your cell as in paradise," it begins,

> *put the whole world behind you and forget it. . . . Above all, realize that you*

are in God's presence. Hold your heart there in wonder as if before your sovereign. Empty yourself completely; sit waiting, content with God's gift, like a little chick tasting and eating nothing but what its mother brings.[127]

This remarkable little statement of the monastic life does much to summarize the thousand-year experience of Christendom. The vision of light Romuald experienced appears to have been the very presence of God, gained through an ascetic effort of self-emptying desire for paradise.

Even more renowned because of his output of spiritual writings was Romuald's Byzantine contemporary Symeon the New Theologian. He was for a time the abbot of the Monastery of Saint Mamas in Constantinople. He died in 1022, only five years earlier than his Western counterpart.

Today Symeon is recognized as one of the greatest ascetics of early Christendom, but in his time he was little known. Those familiar with him were often critical of him. Like Romuald, he believed monasticism had fallen from its high calling through laxity. Like Romuald also, he set himself the goal of the spiritual reform of society, which, in the context of the times, represented a sort of social reform. He brought attention to the need for a completely authentic commitment to Christianity, going so far as to challenge the spiritual leadership of the clergy. He was a priest himself, however, and he never called the legitimacy of the priesthood into question.

Like no other ascetic since the days of Makarios, Symeon had a vision of paradise grounded in a personal experience of deification. His *Fifth Ethical Discourse* was particularly emphatic about this. "True God truly became perfect man," he claimed in it. "For this reason He became man which before He was not, in order to make man a god which he had never been before. Since He is not divisible, He has deified and made us god by his divinity, and not by his flesh alone."

But the paradox of divine participation requires man to live consciously for this alone, as Romuald's rule had indicated. "Now pay attention and answer my questions thoughtfully," Symeon continued. "If the baptized have put on Christ, what is it that they have put on? God. He then who has put on God, will he not recognize with his intellect and see what he has clothed himself with?" The suggestion was that if the experience of spiritual transformation is totally absent from a Christian's life, that Christian is spiritually dead. "Only the dead feel nothing when they are clothed," he concludes.[128]

This was a bold assertion, but the ascetic believed that baptism should be the beginning of a lifetime of spiritual transformation. "Brothers," he urged,

> *this is the new creation in Christ. This is what is accomplished and takes place daily in the true faithful and chosen ones. While yet in the body, as we have often said, they become conscious partakers, in part, of all these things. Nor is this all, but, indeed, after death they hope to inherit these things completely and assuredly. I mean that then they will enter completely into the fullness of those good things in which they even now commune.*[129]

So according to Symeon, while the eternal kingdom of heaven awaits the Christian beyond the grave, "even now" in this world he experiences its glory. This is what it means to be baptized.

In a work entitled *Hymns of Divine Love,* Symeon elaborated this thought further by having Christ state, "I will clearly show you that it is here below that you must receive the Kingdom of Heaven fully, if you want to enter also after your death."[130] It is noteworthy in this passage that Christ speaks of being "here below" with Christians, not in a transcendent heaven beyond.

With Romuald, Symeon prescribed a rigorous discipline of repentance to achieve the experience of paradise. But sorrow must be buoyant, he insisted. It is like the prodigal son's vision of his father's house and the glory that awaits him as he returns to it. "God," Symeon claimed, "has placed the salutary remedy of repentance so clearly visible in the middle of paradise so that those who fall away from eternal life through idleness or negligence return to it again through repentance with a glory that is more brightly visible."[131]

It is with this vision of paradise that we shall leave Christendom as it enters the second millennium of its history. The lives of Symeon and Romuald reveal that while grave concerns about the well-being of Christendom existed—and would probably always exist—solutions were to be found by returning to its original sources, to those values that had nourished it even when it was but a subculture. Doctrinal integrity, divine participation, heavenly immanence, and spiritual transformation all continued to direct this great civilization and its supporting culture toward the transformation of the world.

It was an enduring vision. Even today, it can be found in a prayer attributed to Saint Symeon used by Christians to prepare for holy communion. The prayer is a kind of digest of the great ascetic's *Hymns of Divine Love*. But more than that, it epitomizes the spiritually transformational culture of Christendom during its thousand-year age of paradise.

The prayer speaks poignantly of repentance.

> *From sullied lips, from an abominable heart, from a tongue impure, from a soul defiled, accept my supplication, O Christ. . . . See my lowliness, see my toil, how great it is, and all my sins take from me, O God of all; that with a pure heart, a trembling mind, and a contrite soul I may partake of Thy spotless and most holy Mysteries, by which all that eat and drink in purity of heart are quickened and deified.*

But alongside this contrition there is confidence in God's presence in the world through sacramental communion.

> *For Thou, O my Master, hast said: Everyone that eateth My Flesh and drinketh My Blood abideth in Me and I in him. True is every word of my Master and God; for whosoever partaketh of the divine and deifying grace is no more alone, but with Thee, my Christ, the three-sunned Light that enlighteneth the world.*

Such language of deification fills the prayer with content and brings it to the culminating point of divine communion.

> *With sympathetic mercy, Thou dost purify and illumine them that fervently repent, and makest them partakers of the light, sharers of Thy divinity without stint. And, strange to angels and to the minds of men, Thou conversest with them oftimes, as with Thy true friends.*

Before pouring out his final statement of gratitude to God, who has deigned to share His life—the very life of paradise—with the human race, Symeon likens the experience to a pair of wings. "These things make me bold," he concludes,

> these things give me wings, O Christ. And taking courage from the wealth of Thy benefactions to us, rejoicing and trembling at once, I partake of Fire, I that am grass. And, strange wonder! I am bedewed without being consumed, as the bush of old burned without being consumed. Now with thankful mind, and grateful heart, with thankfulness in my members, my soul and body, I worship and magnify and glorify Thee, my God, for blessed art Thou, both now and unto the ages.[132]

EPILOGUE

On the Eve of the Great Schism

T HUS CHRISTENDOM ARRIVED at the first millennium. In recent decades, historians have been fascinated with the transition from the tenth century to the eleventh century. The millennium has been seen as a moment of crisis, one characterized by an intense spiritual longing, even fear. A burst of research has claimed to discover a widely held belief among contemporaries that Christ would come again in AD 1000, or, alternately, at the millennial anniversary of His death in 1033.

A representative source supporting this view is a comment made by a contemporary French chronicler named Rodulfus Glaber. He often spoke of marvelous and threatening portents, and in one particular case told the story of a French peasant named Leutard who, about the year 1000 (the exact date is not clear), "dreamt that a great swarm of bees entered his body through nature's secret orifices." This unpleasant experience convinced the man that the Apocalypse was imminent. For reasons unknown, he proceeded to smash the crucifix of his parish church at Vertus and then committed suicide.

Recent historians have delighted in this and a handful of other colorful anecdotes about millenarian expectations during the turn to the eleventh century. Some have even centered book-length narratives on them, discerning the emergence of a new form of Western civilization in the shadow of the Apocalypse.[133]

They have not been convincing. In fact, no such wide-ranging apocalypticism seized Christendom at this time.

Nor was it likely to have done so, for Christendom's culture was profoundly anti-millenarian. The vast majority of its members were not seeking the end of history, nor were they terrified by the thought of the imminent appearance of Christ. For them, Christ was already present in the world, for they lived within a culture of heavenly immanence. For ten centuries this culture had fostered the experience of paradise. And with some notable exceptions such as Leutard's bizarre aberration, it continued to do so beyond the otherwise meaningless date of 1000.

It is certainly true, however, that the eleventh century marked the end of one age and the beginning of another. Historians have long been aware that a different culture, manifesting itself in some cases radically, began to appear in the West at this time. It was expressed, for instance, in a new form of piety emphasizing punishment and death. It tended toward a preoccupation with Christ's Crucifixion and allowed for comparatively less interest in His Incarnation and Resurrection.

Its earliest manifestation was the Gero Crucifix, commissioned by the eponymous Archbishop of Cologne in the final decades of the tenth century. Traditional Christian art portrayed the crucified Christ majestically, as the Incarnate Godman who through death would rise again and glorify the human race. The Gero Crucifix portrayed a corpse. Jesus was depicted with a slumped head and a broken body, not only indicating the reality of His death but suggesting defeat in the face of worldly evil. The effect was to fix the viewer's mind on a benighted cosmos and on the experience, not of paradise, but of a diabolical power that the cosmos could never really escape. It was one of the earliest signs of the crucicentric culture that would characterize Western Christendom during the centuries that preceded the Protestant Reformation.

It was not millenarianism that marked the cultural turn of the eleventh century. If there is a moment when the history of Christendom changed course, it was not the year 1000 but the tragedy that followed upon it half a century later. It was the loss of communion between the East and the

West—and the creation thereby of a distinctive West that no longer recognized the East as a participant in its culture and identity. The Great Schism of 1054 marks the sacramental end to a thousand years of a unitary Christian culture. Soon afterward, a defiantly Western Christendom set itself on a course of innovation that would bring it, over the course of many centuries and often against its will, to the decline of Christian culture that is so lamented today.

In the introduction to this book I noted the apprehension felt by many today as the West's Christian culture is systematically uprooted. The quartet of countercultural authors I discussed there provides useful and sometimes brilliant insights into this crisis and how Christians might respond to it. But these authors do not look deeply into the past to find the historical origins of the problems they discuss. Charles Chaput does give consideration to the legacy of the American Revolution, and Rod Dreher offers a brief intellectual history of modern pluralism. But until we acquire a deep historical vision of our culture, our understanding of it will remain epiphenomenal.

Something like the sexual revolution, which deservedly occupies much attention in our contemporary discussions about the cultural crisis, is not so much the cause of that crisis as a consequence of deeper and historically more primary causes. Is not the decline of a belief in the sacramental holiness of the human body, for instance, more fundamental than sexualized popular entertainment in explaining the recent explosion of pornography, promiscuity, and unmarried pregnancies? And if such a decline can be historically linked to doubts about the participation of God in human experience and His presence in this world, then it is necessary to probe deeply into the past to locate those moments when traditional Christian anthropology and cosmology began to falter. Otherwise, our ability to address the culture that surrounds us today will never be more than provisional.

The single most important cause of the collapse of Christian culture is the loss of confidence in a spiritually transformed cosmos and the experience of human salvation within that cosmos. For a millennium, Christendom established and exhibited such confidence. It did so with particular success in the East, where the Byzantine state proclaimed the triumph of Christianity, the

Greek fathers elaborated the theological vision of deification, and the liturgical arts articulated man's communion with the Incarnate God. The West was in no way deficient in traditional Christianity's exalted anthropology and cosmology. In fact, we have seen how fathers such as Gregory the Great and peoples like the Celts contributed to it.

Yet we have also seen how, during the eighth and ninth centuries, advocates for the Frankish and later Germanic Empires took the radical step of defining themselves against an imagined adversary they called "the Greeks." To do so they enlisted Anglo-Saxons, Spaniards, and Italians—in other words, representatives of most of the peoples of Western Christendom. It is significant that the one intellectual outsider among the Franks was a Celt, John Scotus Eriugena, whose love of the Eastern fathers (he alone among the Franks had mastered Greek) led him to ingenious but ultimately dubious neoplatonic affirmations about the created world.

The Franks also sought to draw the papacy itself into their cultural net. Rome, where the Mass had originally been celebrated in Greek and where papal candidates as late as the eighth century were drawn from the East, resisted heroically. But eventually the papacy in the person of Pope Benedict VIII finally adopted the exclusively Western version of that most important symbol of unity, the Nicene Creed. This more than any other act set the stage for the Great Schism and the division of Christendom that followed from it. The civilization that was becoming "the West" and which the Franks simply called "Europe" would not only lose contact with the East. It would lose its affinity for the paradisiacal culture that had always been strongest there.

As for the schism itself, its short-term causes grew out of the century of degradation that began with the Cadaver Synod and terminated with the capitulation of Benedict VIII—great-grandson of the wanton matriarch Marozia—to Emperor Otto III. By the middle of the eleventh century the papacy was set on a policy of "never again." The powerlessness and disgrace of the past, papal advocates declared, must be exactly that: past. Now there arose in Rome a series of pontiffs who, emboldened by a vision of reform cultivated in the autonomous monastery of Cluny, set themselves on a course of change. The first of these was Leo IX. He toured the West demanding submission to the papacy by all, bishops and rulers alike. His ideal was a new principle known as *papal supremacy*. Not only must all ecclesiastical power submit to his office, but all secular authority must do so as well. He even went to war in southern Italy to expand the territories of the Papal States.

While Leo's policies in the West were mostly successful, there remained a frustrating limitation on his efforts to launch the papal reformation. The patriarch of Constantinople continued to hold to the ancient Church's conciliar model of ecclesiology, and he was supported in this by the three remaining patriarchates of the historic pentarchy. Leo, captured on the battlefield during his southern war and subsequently held in captivity, dispatched his principal advisor, a brazen papal idealist named Cardinal Humbert, to New Rome to demand submission. There, an equally haughty Patriarch Michael Cerularius refused even to acknowledge the papal emissary's presence. After waiting in vain for an audience, Humbert entered Hagia Sophia before the Divine Liturgy on July 16, 1054, and slammed a papal bull of excommunication down on the altar.

Leo had in the meantime died, meaning the document was legally invalid. But it mattered not. Now no Pope John VIII came forward to reverse the excommunication. The papal reformation was a force that would not be stopped, and the sacramental division of West and East subsequently became permanent. In the centuries that followed, this division served as both context and cause for changes that would make Western Christendom the cradle of the modern world. For instance, in addition to papal supremacy, Rome would now sponsor the very doctrines and practices—such as purgatory and clerical celibacy—that would provoke the Protestant Reformation.

In the meantime, Western Christendom would depart from its former vision of paradise to embrace a related but radically different model of worldly transformation, utopia. With the Renaissance, Western intellectuals would react against their increasingly pessimistic culture—expressed since the time of the Gero Crucifix by a crucicentric piety—and turn instead to the alternative cosmology and anthropology of secular humanism. Tragically, this was only a counterfeit of the paradise once offered by traditional Christianity, and it would eventually lead to the nihilism that plagues Western culture today. But it was all the West could find in the centuries-long wake of the Great Schism to sustain its integral need to fulfill Christendom's enduring and indomitable transformational imperative. The thought of returning to communion with the Orthodox East never really seems to have occurred to either the humanists or the reformers.

For its part, the East after the eleventh century would continue to hold to the paradisiacal culture of early Christendom. The best example of this was the movement known as hesychasm, which asserted, against fourteenth-century objections from the West, that divine participation for humans was both possible and real. The tradition of iconography, grounded as it was in the sacraments and liturgy of the East, further expressed a belief in heavenly immanence.

This is not to say that the culture of Eastern Christendom was free of trouble. In fact, paradise there was often elusive. The moral standards of Christian statecraft remained as prone to corruption as ever. The history of the Byzantine state was in many ways the history of venality and deceit, epitomized by effeminate court eunuchs and ghastly bedchamber assassinations. And though Vladimir and his saintly sons established a truly heavenly standard for rule, Russia was no less bound by the legacy of pagandom. Violence was everywhere, despite the official honor paid by rulers to the King of Peace. From Basil the Bulgar Slayer to Ivan the Terrible, Eastern Christendom would periodically exchange the kingdom of heaven for the vanity of a spiritually untransformed world. Self-confident in its Orthodoxy, it would eventually drift into isolation and historical irrelevance. Only in recent times would the East begin to offer, once again, a witness to what the West once was during the age of paradise.

And yet the arrival of the millennium found both East and West still united in a common culture that dated back in unbroken continuity to the first century. Doctrinal integrity, divine participation, heavenly immanence, and spiritual transformation all remained integral to its beliefs and values. In the face of troubles and innovations stood the ancient conviction that the world was good and that man, made in the image of God and ennobled by the Incarnation, was also good. Both the cosmology and the anthropology of traditional Christianity continued to nourish the roots of Western culture a thousand years after the Great Commission. And it is by reflecting on this fact that we can bring this book to its conclusion.

Perhaps the best place to do so is on an island similar to that where we began. Skellig Michael is a bleak outcropping of rock situated in the Atlantic Ocean seven miles off the west coast of Ireland. It is virtually uninhabitable, but in the eleventh century it was the westernmost point of Christendom. Like Capri, it is a mountainous place, with cliffs hovering high above a surging sea. But rather than housing the palace of Tiberius, it had as its one habitation a monastery, built by Celtic ascetics seeking the kingdom of heaven at a great distance from society. And whereas the inhabitants of Villa Jovis spent their days in luxury and pleasure, the monks of Skellig Michael passed theirs in toil. Cramped huts provided them a minimum of shelter, and a meager garden yielded just enough food to survive.

The towering cliffs of Skellig Michael afforded vistas no less stirring than those seen from Capri. The grandeur of God's creation was, after all, a powerful draw upon the Celtic soul. But these monks did not spend their evenings staring restlessly into sunsets over the western horizon. Their hearts were set rather on a spiritually transformed world. Standing in vigil like all the monks in Christendom—whether at Lérins, Athos, Kiev, or Sinai—they would have turned their backs on the west. A Christian's life, after all, is oriented. The most western of all of Christendom's children, their lives were fullest when facing east, toward paradise.

Endnotes

1   James Davison Hunter, *Culture Wars: The Struggle to Define America* (New York: Basic Books, 1991).

2   Rod Dreher, *The Benedict Option* (New York: Sentinel, 2018), 3.

3   Anthony Esolen, *Out of the Ashes: Rebuilding American Culture* (Washington, D.C.: Regnery, 2017), 188.

4   Charles Chaput, *Strangers in a Strange Land: Living the Catholic Faith in a Post-Christian World* (New York: Henry Holt, 2017), 3.

5   R. R. Reno, *Resurrecting the Idea of a Christian Society* (Washington, D.C.: Regnery, 2016), 168.

6   Christopher Dawson, *The Formation of Christendom* (San Francisco: Ignatius, 2008), 27.

7   Oswald Spengler, *The Decline of the West*, vol. 1, trans. Charles Francis Atkinson (New York: Knopf, 1926), 31.

8   George Weigel, *The Cube and the Cathedral: Europe, America, and Politics without God* (New York: Basic, 2005).

9   Chaput, 3.

10 Dreher, xvii.

11 Reno, 181.

12 Esolen, 191.

13 C. S. Lewis, *Mere Christianity* (New York: Harper Collins, 2001), 28.

14 Georges Florovsky, *Ways of Russian Theology*, part 1, trans. Robert L. Nichols (Belmont: Nordland, 1979), xvii.

15 Col. 4:14 speaks of "Luke the beloved physician," and biblical scholars have long believed this is likely a reference to the author of Acts.

16 Epistle to the Romans, in *Early Christian Writings: The Apostolic Fathers*, trans. Maxwell Staniforth and Andrew Louth (London: Penguin Books, 1987).

17 That is why the New Testament contains twenty-seven and not twenty-six or twenty-eight books; and the spurious "Gospel of Thomas," for instance, is not among them. Lacking any internal table of contents, the canonical New Testament required an authority that only the apostolic tradition could provide. Thus the canon of apostolic tradition preceded the canon of scripture.

18 Augustine, *Confessions*, translated by F. J. Sheed (Indianapolis: Hackett, 1970), 132.

19 The classic presentation of this topic is C. S. Lewis, *The Four Loves* (New York: HarperCollins, 1960).

20 It is surely not "reason," as early Christianity attests. Only after many centuries and relatively modern developments did rationality come to be considered the most irreducible characteristic of humanity.

21 Christians "ran a miniature welfare state in an empire which for the most part

lacked social services." Paul Johnson, *A History of Christianity* (New York: Atheneum, 1976), 75.

22 Quoted in Rodney Stark, *The Rise of Christianity* (Princeton: Princeton University Press, 1996), 87.

23 *The Ante-Nicene Fathers*, ed. Alexander Roberts and James Donaldson, vol. 2 (Grand Rapids: Eerdman's, 1985), 146.

24 *The Ante-Nicene Fathers*, vol. 1, 185.

25 *Early Christian Writings*, 102.

26 *Ante-Nicene Fathers*, vol. 1, 486.

27 *Early Christian Writings*, 195.

28 *Ante-Nicene Fathers*, 185.

29 See, for instance, 1 Cor. 5:7–8.

30 *Ante-Nicene Fathers*, vol. 3, 670.

31 Quoted in Irenee Henri Dalmais, Pierre Jounel, and Aime Georges Martimort, *The Church at Prayer*, Vol. 4: *The Liturgy and Time*, trans. Matthew J. O'Connell (Collegeville: Liturgical Press, 1986), 14.

32 *The Liturgy and Time*, 19.

33 *The Liturgy and Time*, 15.

34 *The Liturgy and Time*, 168.

35 Warren H. Carroll, *The Founding of Christendom* (Front Royal: Christendom, 1985), 525.

36 Rodney Stark, *The Rise of Christianity*. See also *Cities of God: The Real Story of How Christianity Became an Urban Movement and Conquered Rome* (New York: Harper Collins, 2006).

37 The Stoics were a partial exception to this and have been viewed as a movement compatible in some points with Christianity.

38 Quoted in Stark, *The Rise of Christianity*, 82.

39 This is still the practice of civilizations largely untouched by Christendom, such as modern India and China.

40 Christian bioethicist Wesley J. Smith has brought attention to recent trends in the Netherlands toward normalizing the killing of newborn children by lethal injection and other means. See *Forced Exit: The Slippery Slope from Assisted Suicide to Legalized Murder* (New York: Times Books, 1997).

41 Quoted in Stark, 97–98.

42 Stark, *Rise*, 113.

43 See 1 Peter 3:1–2 and 1 Cor. 7:13–14.

44 See especially 1 Cor. 15.

45 *The Ante-Nicene Fathers*, vol. 1, edited by Alexander Robert and James Donaldson (Grand Rapids: Eerdmans, 1985), 26–27.

46 Eusebius, *The History of the Church from Christ to Constantine*, translated by G.A. Williamson (New York: Penguin, 1965), 328.

47 This is Stark's interpretation. See *The Rise of Christianity*, 10. It is shared by

certain other historians as well. See, for instance, Paul Stephenson, *Constantine: Roman Emperor, Christian Victor* (New York: Overlook, 2009), 5.

48   Peter J. Leithart, *Defending Constantine: The Twilight of an Empire and the Dawn of Christendom* (Downer's Grove: Intervarsity, 2010).

49   Leithart, *Defending Constantine*, 327–333.

50   J.N.D. Kelly, *Golden Mouth: The Story of John Chrysostom: Ascetic, Preacher, Bishop* (Grand Rapids: Baker, 1995), 240.

51   Timothy Barnes, *Constantine and Eusebius* (Cambridge, Massachusetts: Harvard, 1981), 266.

52   Eusebius, *Life of Constantine*, in *Nicene and Post-Nicene Fathers*, vol. 1, 524.

53   Eusebius, *Oration in Praise of Constantine*, in *Nicene and Post-Nicene Fathers*, vol. 1, 581–610.

54   Augustine, *City of God*, translated by Henry Bettenson (London: Penguin, 1972), 881.

55   Augustine, *City of God*, 892.

56   Augustine, *City of God*, 761.

57   Quoted in John Meyendorff, *The Byzantine Legacy in the Orthodox Church* (Crestwood: Saint Vladimir's Seminary Press), 48.

58   Peter Brown, *The Rise of Western Christendom*, 2nd ed. (Oxford: Blackwell, 2003), 98–99.

59   George E. Demacopoulos, *Gregory the Great: Ascetic, Pastor, and First Man of Rome* (Notre Dame: Notre Dame, 2015), 51.

60   Andrew J. Ekonomou, *Byzantine Rome and the Greek Popes: Eastern Influences on Rome and the Papacy from Gregory the Great to Zacharias, A.D. 590–752* (Lanham: Lexington, 2007), 21.

61   Quoted in Meyendorff, *Imperial Unity*, 305–306.

62   Alexander Roberts and James Donaldson, eds., *The Ante-Nicene Fathers*, vol. 5 (Grand Rapids, MI: Eerdmans, 1981), 152–153.

63   Augustine, *Enchiridion* 32.

64   David Vincent Meconi, *The One Christ: St. Augustine's Theology of Deification* (Washington, D.C.: Catholic University, 2016), xv–xvi.

65   Thomas G. Guarino, *Vincent of Lerins and the Development of Christian Doctrine* (Grand Rapids: Baker, 2013), xxiii.

66   Basil the Great, *On the Human Condition* (Crestwood, NY: Saint Vladimir's Seminary, 2005), 114.

67   Demacopoulos, 32–33.

68   *The Festal Menaion*, trans. by Mother Mary and Kallistos Ware (South Caanan, PA: Saint Tikhon's Seminary, 1998), 354.

69   John Meyendorff, *Byzantine Theology* (New York: Fordham, 1979), 37.

70   Quoted in John Meyendorff, *St. Gregory Palamas and Orthodox Spirituality* (Crestwood: Saint Vladimir's, 1974), 40.

71   Ekonomou, 115.

72 Ekonomou, 116.

73 Robert Browning, *The Byzantine Empire* (Washington, D.C.: Catholic University of America, 1992), 37.

74 Paul, for instance, calls upon Christians to redeem the time in Ephesians 5:16.

75 Gregory T. Armstrong, "Constantine's Churches: Symbol and Structure," *Journal of the Society of Architectural Historians* 33:1 (1974), 16. Quoted by Leithart, *Defending Constantine*, 138.

76 Robert Markus, *The End of Ancient Christianity* (Cambridge: Cambridge University, 1990), 151.

77 Peter Brown, *The Rise of Western Christendom*, 2nd ed. (Oxford: Blackwell, 2003), 163.

78 The story comes from the conversion of Clovis's retainers.

79 Quoted in Richard Fletcher, *The Barbarian Conversion: From Paganism to Christianity* (Berkeley: University of California Press, 1997), 254.

80 Thomas Cahill, *How the Irish Saved Civilization* (New York: Doubleday, 1995), 131.

81 Ian Bradley, *The Celtic Way* (London: Darton, Longman, and Todd, 2003), 32.

82 Esther de Waal, *Every Earthly Blessing: Rediscovering the Celtic Tradition* (Harrisburg: Morehouse, 1991), 67.

83 Bat Yeor, *The Decline of Eastern Christianity under Islam: From Jihad to Dhimmitude*, trans. by Miriam Kochan and David Littman (Madison: Farleigh Dickinson University, 1996), 65.

84 Compare Ex. 20:4 with Ex. 25:18–20.

85 Philp Schaff and Henry Wace, *Nicene and Post-Nicene Fathers*, vol. 14 (Grand Rapids: Eerdmans, 1997), 550.

86 Judith Herrin, *The Formation of Christendom* (Princeton: Princeton University, 1987), 295.

87 The sentence was subsequently commuted at Leo's request.

88 Richard Fletcher, *Barbarian Conversion*, 209.

89 Einhard also called Aachen "Second Rome," a name that even more explicitly rejected the legitimacy of Byzantine romanitas and Constantinople's status as New Rome.

90 Derek Wilson, *Charlemagne* (New York: Vintage, 2005), 87.

91 Rosamond McKitterick, *Charlemagne: The Formation of a European Identity* (Cambridge: Cambridge University, 2008), 309.

92 Thomas F.X. Noble, *Images, Iconoclasm, and the Carolingians* (Philadelphia: University of Pennsylvania, 2009), 180–181.

93 Quoted in Noble, 212.

94 *Nicene and Post-Nicene Fathers*, vol. 14, 265.

95 Quoted in Richard Hough, *Photius and the Carolingians: The Trinitarian Controversy* (Belmont: Nordland, 1975), 89.

96 Theognotos's account is retold colorfully by John Julius Norwich, *Byzantium:*

The Apogee (New York: Knopf, 1994), 70–71.

97 Francis Dvornik, *The Photian Controversy: History and Legend* (Cambridge: Cambridge University, 1948), 99.

98 Andrew Louth, *Greek East and Latin West* (Crestwood: Saint Vladimir's Seminary, 2007)

99 Quoted in Meyendorff, *Byzantine Theology*, 93.

100 Quoted in Richard Haugh, *Photius and the Carolingians: The Trinitarian Controversy* (Belmont: Nordland, 1975), 102.

101 Ibid., 119.

102 Bede relates in his account of the event how Colman, after a long defense of Celtic traditions in York, fell into complete silence when the advocate for Roman custom, Wilfrid, spoke of Saint Peter's primacy. Bede, *A History of the English Church and People*, translated by Leo Shirley-Price (New York: Penguin, 1968), 192.

103 Philip Sherrard, *The Greek East and the Latin West: A Study in the Christian Tradition* (Oxford: Oxford University, 1959), 84.

104 Ibid., 85–86.

105 Despite Pope John VIII's rejection of it, this synod of 869–870 came, much later, to be numbered by the Roman Catholic Church as her Eighth Ecumenical Council.

106 Quoted in Aidan Nichols, *Rome and the Eastern Churches* (San Francisco: Ignatius, 2010), 246.

107 Dom Gregory Dix, *The Shape of the Liturgy* (London: Bloomsbury, 2005), 584.

108 Joseph A. Jungmann, *The Mass of the Roman Rite: Its Origins and Development*, vol. 1, translated by Francis A. Brunner (Notre Dame: Christian Classics, 1951), 77.

109 Theodor Klauser, *A Short History of the Western Liturgy* (Oxford: Oxford University, 1979), 82.

110 Hugh Wybrew, *The Orthodox Liturgy* (London: Society for Promoting Christian Knowledge, 1989), 100.

111 Op. cit., 97.

112 Germanus, *On the Divine Liturgy*, translated by Paul Meyendorff (Crestwood: Saint Vladimir's Seminary, 1984), 57.

113 Other subjects sometimes used for the central dome's iconography were Pentecost and the Ascension, but they soon lost out to the image of Christ in glory.

114 The demons themselves recognized this. In Matt. 8:29 they actually ask Jesus why He has come to torment them "before the time."

115 Quoted in David Ford and Mary Ford, *Marriage as a Path to Holiness* (South Canaan: Saint Tikhon's, 1995), xxxiv.

116 John's famous treatise on the monastic life is in fact sometimes called *The Ladder of Paradise*. Its more common title is *The Ladder of Divine Ascent*.

117 Basil the Great, *On the Human Condition*, ed. by Nonna Verna Harrison (Crest-

wood: Saint Vladimir's Seminary, 2005), 43–44.

118 Rod Dreher, *The Benedict Option: A Strategy for Christians in a Post-Christian Nation* (New York: Sentinel, 2018).

119 Anthony-Emil N. Tachiaos, *Cyril and Methodius of Thessalonica: The Acculturation of the Slavs* (Crestwood: Saint Vladimir's, 2001), 57.

120 Quoted in op. cit., 83.

121 Serge A. Zenkovsky, ed., *Medieval Russia's Epics, Chronicles, and Tales* (New York: Meridian, 1974), 67–68.

122 Op. cit., 88–90.

123 Georges P. Fedotov, *The Russian Religious Mind: Kievan Christianity* (Belmont: Nordland, 1975), 411.

124 Paul Collins, *The Birth of the West: Rome, Germany, France, and the Creation of Europe in the Tenth Century* (New York: Public Affairs, 2013), 63.

125 Tom Holland, *The Forge of Christendom: The End of Days and the Epic Rise of the West* (New York: Doubleday, 2008), 69–70.

126 The Creed had until then not actually been part of the Roman rite of the Mass, so that the innovation was twofold: Rome received from Henry both a new element of the Mass, the Creed, and the Germanic form of it with the filioque.

127 Philip Sheldrake, *The New Westminster Dictionary of Christian Spirituality* (Louisville: Westminster John Knox, 2005), 165.

128 Symeon the New Theologian, *On the Mystical Life: The Ethical Discourses*, vol. 2, translated by Alexander Golitsyn (Crestwood: Saint Vladimir's Seminary), 45–46. This passage is from the author's Fifth Ethical Discourse.

129 Op. cit., 60.

130 Saint Symeon the New Theologian, ed. & trans. by George A. Maloney (Bangalore: IJA Publications, 2011), 240. The quote is from Hymn 17.

131 Quoted in Basil Krivocheine, *In the Light of Christ: Saint Symeon the New Theologian*, translated by Anthony P. Gythiel (Crestwood: Saint Vladimir's Seminary), 71.

132 *Prayer Book* (Jordanville: Holy Trinity Monastery, 2011), 362–367.

133 Leutard's story is told by several recent historians belonging to the apocalyptic school. See especially, for instance: Holland, 244; Collins, 417–418; and the more specialized but influential study by Rachel Fulton, *From Judgment to Passion: Devotion to Christ and the Virgin Mary, 800–1200* (New York: Columbia University, 2002), 81–83.

Index

Illustrations indicated by page numbers in italics

About the Author

JOHN STRICKLAND is an Orthodox priest and former college professor. His first book, *The Making of Holy Russia*, is a study of the resilience of Christianity in the modern world. An active blogger and podcaster, he brings to the present work a lifetime of reflection on the religious background of the West. He lives in western Puget Sound with his wife and five children.